THE PROBLEM

OF

HISTORICAL KNOWLEDGE

The Problem of
HISTORICAL
KNOWLEDGE

An Answer to Relativism

By

MAURICE MANDELBAUM

 BOOKS FOR LIBRARIES PRESS
FREEPORT, NEW YORK

INTERNATIONAL STANDARD BOOK NUMBER:
0-8369-5745-8

LIBRARY OF CONGRESS CATALOG CARD NUMBER:
74-152993

PRINTED IN THE UNITED STATES OF AMERICA

TO

WILBUR MARSHALL URBAN

PREFACE

THE present work seeks to serve a dual purpose. Its primary aim lies in the attempt to overcome the widely current scepticism with which historical knowledge is regarded. Its secondary aim is to serve as a critical summary of several important views concerning this problem. For the reader who is primarily interested in the problem of historical truth, and who is less concerned with the theories which have arisen regarding it, it will be possible to omit the critical summaries presented in Chapters II and IV.

The present book arose out of studies originally undertaken in connection with a doctoral dissertation. I wish to thank the authorities of Yale University for their permission to publish the results of that dissertation in this form. I wish also to thank Professor Hajo Holborn of the Department of History at Yale for his friendly aid and advice.

M. M.

Swarthmore College, 1938.

CONTENTS

ix

CONTENTS

THE PROBLEM
OF
HISTORICAL KNOWLEDGE

INTRODUCTION

THE FIELD OF HISTORY

IT HAS often been said that the modern world is characterized by its historical sense; it has almost as frequently been said that our intellectual world is history-ridden. However we choose to estimate the contribution which a historical orientation can bring to the solution of any intellectual problem, it must be admitted that historical studies occupy a prominent place in the thought of our times. And since in the field of philosophy it has come to be a mark of modernity to inquire with what right we lay claim to knowledge, it is not surprising that philosophers and historians have recently been much concerned with the problem of the validity of the historical enterprise.

An examination of the validity of any intellectual discipline properly belongs to that field of philosophy which has often been termed methodology. Methodological investigations are to be distinguished from general epistemology, since they do not concern themselves with problems of perception nor with general formulations of the relation between the knower and the known. They examine the materials and methods of particular sciences with a view to

1

estimating in how far those methods enable the investigator to comprehend the material with which he seeks to deal. Thus it may be said the methodological discussions represent philosophy's attempt to render explicit the working assumptions of the empirical sciences, and to determine whether these assumptions contain any fundamental contradictions which render them suspect.

Such being the purpose of any methodological analysis, it should be clear that in our present concern with historical knowledge we are not seeking to establish a specific epistemological position, nor do we wish to set up a rule of thumb by which any particular historical work may be measured. We assume at the outset that no matter what general epistemological position one adopts, it is still meaningful to inquire into the specific problems of each of the empirical sciences. It becomes our task, therefore, to investigate the actual working assumptions of the historical enterprise without raising questions as to the ultimate validity of human knowledge. On the other hand, we do not wish to set up criteria by means of which particular historical works are to be estimated; we accept these criteria from actual historical criticism as part of the data upon which we build. In short, we presuppose actual historical procedures rather than attempt to define them. Thus, our province of investigation falls between that of general epistemology and that of the handbooks of historical method: we wish merely to establish whether or not it may be said that the historian's task holds forth a promise of fulfilment.

A methodological investigation, seeking to determine the measure of knowledge which a given empirical science affords, might adopt as its point of departure a survey of the method employed in that science. Since the method of any science, however, is shaped by the nature of the material which it seeks to comprehend, a methodological inquiry may equally well approach its analysis through a consideration of the material with which the science in question is concerned. In dealing with the problem of historical knowledge we shall find it advisable first to isolate the material with which the historian deals. This the present introductory chapter of our study will attempt to do.

If one compares a historical work with the results of investigation in the physical sciences, a singular difference immediately appears. The historian deals with specific events which once occurred in a certain place, and he seeks to delineate the nature of those events. The natural scientist, on the other hand, formulates judgments regarding "typical" occurrences, establishing the relation which those occurrences bear to certain of the conditions under which they appear. The chemist, for example, is concerned with describing what happened in his laboratory only in so far as he thinks that his description can be paralleled by the descriptions of other chemists concerning similar events in other laboratories. He is looking for the uniform conditions under which a phenomenon can be observed. The historian, however, appears not to be interested in the typical, the uniform, the readily repeatable; he seeks to portray the particular. While the chemist's mode of procedure is experimental, depending upon controlled observation of the recurrent, the historian's method is descriptive, attempting to portray the given, the uncontrolled, the actual: in Ranke's words, "how it actually happened."

To this difference between historical science and physical science, Windelband, Simmel, and Rickert, among others, have repeatedly called attention. One need not agree with the neo-Kantian epistemology to which they hold to recognize and prize this distinction; the insight is significant, and will stand of its own strength. But, as Rickert has pointed out, the complete separation of the historical method and the method of the physical sciences is impossible. They are opposed to each other only in ideal cases; indeed, in the practice of the physical sciences they often blend. One can see this, in particular, in geology, where historical and systematic geology are inseparable: the past history of the earth could not be known without an understanding of the laws of geologic structures, and these laws could not have been apprehended without a simultaneous advance in knowledge concerning the earth's history.

This blending of the historical method into the method of the physical sciences is inevitable, although not in every case is it so pervasive as in geology. It is inevitable because any formulation of the recurrent and typical depends upon observations of the particular, of that which in one case at least has actually happened. Thus the physical scientist must, in a sense, be a "historian," a person interested in the full description of what has occurred. From this he passes on, however, to the formulation of laws of the phenomenon, that is, to the selection of those aspects of its occurrence which are sufficient, under similar circumstances, to reproduce a like phenomenon. Thus the physical scientist passes from description to generalization. This the historian, as the term is usually understood, does not do. On the basis of his historical knowledge the historian may, to be sure, turn sociologist, seeking to formulate the laws of "typical" historical occurrences; the economic historian may turn theoretical economist; but the historian's whole purpose as historian is to describe, to narrate.

A historical account is a narrative, for that with which the historian concerns himself is always seen in the light of an actual process of change. The historian of philosophy, for example, does not merely give an exposition of the nature of specific systems; he treats each system with relation to other systems, finding in it a continuation or interruption of a given process of change. Even in dealing with one particular philosophical work the historian does not contemplate it in isolation, but attempts to discover the past and contemporary influences which came to bear upon it. This is merely to say that in history every object of investigation is seen in the light of a temporal framework. It is in this that the much-vaunted "historical sense" consists.

But it must not be imagined that the historian deals merely with matters of chronology. The temporal framework of an event is always far richer than mere chronological sequence. Not time alone, but the actual pattern of events in time is that which determines the historical context of phenomena. One can see this even with respect to those historical accounts which depict a cross-section of the life of a community at a given moment in time. Such a historical account is not temporal in character simply because the conditions of life are described and dated. The historian must discern the stresses and strains which are at that moment present in the community, and these have meaning only in relation to the past and the future. Thus the historian never treats an event as a momentary happening in time; he views every event as a product and producer of change.[1]

The concrete nature of the historical context of events accounts for the fact that every historical narrative deals both with one event and with a series of events.[2] For the narrative consists in bringing to light the formative influence exercised by a series of events

[1] Any other view demands that the historian should be concerned with ideal essences which do not change, but merely manifest themselves in time. Such a view we shall not here discuss; we shall meet it again in Scheler and other phenomenologists.
[2] An analysis of the concept of "an event" is to be found in Chapter VII.

6

upon the actual nature of the occurrence with which the historian is primarily concerned. A political biography, for example, seeks to depict the life, the character, and the influence of its hero; for this it must take into account the series of events which determined the scope of his activity and shaped his destiny. The historian does not view his hero as an isolated phenomenon, but seeks to understand him in relation to his background and his times. Thus, even though the overwhelming presence of the hero may tend to focus our attention upon the unity implicit in the historical account, the historian himself must see and describe this unity in relation to that series of events which formed it.

In other cases the formative series of events, as a series, so occupies our attention that we tend to forget that the historian is also concerned with one enduring event. This is often the case in histories of art. The fascination of particular works of art so absorbs our attention that we readily overlook the fact that the historian is dealing not merely with a series of separate art objects, but also with an artistic event which has a reality and duration beyond that which any one of its manifestations possesses.[3] If there were not some such enduring event whose nature the historian sought to depict, there would be no possibility of explaining why these particular works of art

[3] Only a dogmatic and untenable form of materialism would attempt to hold that the life of Caesar constituted an event, while the rise of Gothic architecture, or the spread of the Industrial Revolution, did not.

were selected by him for discussion. Thus we see that every historical work possesses both a continuous unity and a variety. This fact is demanded by the historian's concern with the process of change.

The historian's attempt to depict the formative influence exercised by a series of events upon the character of some one enduring event throws light upon his method of procedure. An invidious distinction has sometimes been drawn between historical research and historical synthesis, between "mere fact-finders" in history and the "great" (or "synthetic") historians. Such a distinction is as false as it is invidious. We have seen that the historical enterprise consists in understanding every event in the light of its actual historical context. "Mere fact-finding" represents this enterprise no less than does the most sweeping and magnificent concern with the rise and fall of empires, with epochs and with eras. In every case the historian must proceed in a manner which is both selective and synthetic. He deals neither with atomic "facts" nor with the fullness and detail of the historical process as a whole. In tracing the determinate interconnection of events he cannot fail to "synthesize" any more than he can fail to be concerned with "fact-finding." Historical synthesis does not refer to a vague and generalizing frame of mind under whose spell the historian brings together discoveries previously made; it consists in the ability to see the actual manner in which events are related to one another. While it has become a commonplace to hold that "the great

8

historian" must possess "tact," "imagination," and "insight" it is too often assumed that this distinguishes him from all other historians. Yet it should be clear that every historical synthesis demands these same qualifications. However full or meager may be the documentary evidence which the historian has at his disposal, and however broad or narrow the scope of his enterprise may be, it is essential that he bring together those events which are relevant to each other so that they can be seen to form that history which it is his purpose to apprehend. Even the cub reporter in his story of the latest and most gruesome crime attempts to fulfil the terms of the historical enterprise, since he too seeks to establish and delineate those events which, taken together, uniquely determine what has taken place.

But it will be objected, and rightly, that the historian is not concerned with any and every type of event. The field of reality which the historian takes as his province is limited to the field of human events which possess significance for societal life. The series of events described by a chemist writing a report of an experiment might be said to form a "history," but with such events the historian does not deal. As Rickert has claimed, history is "Kulturwissenschaft"; or, as we might say, the field of the historian is the study of human activities in their societal context and with their societal implications.

Against such a delimitation Berr, among others, has already raised objection. In *La synthèse en his-*

toire, commenting upon a definition put forward by Bernheim, Berr claimed that any such definition of the historian's task contains a regrettable sociological bias.[4] This, however, is not here the case, as will become clear in our discussion of historical narration and sociological law.[5] Berr's own definition of the field of history is too broad, since it includes all human facts. Only those facts which are seen in the light of their consequences for the social structure in which human beings exist are "historical." An examination of the subject matter of actual histories (which is the sole basis on which we have here a right to generalize) discloses that the historian is always interested in human activities as they form or are formed by this structure. It is this which is intended in speaking of their societal implications and context.

Bernheim's definition, to which Berr took objection, runs as follows: "History is the knowledge (Wissenschaft) of the development of human beings in their activities as social beings."[6] To this we have already assented, in so far as it stresses the human, societal aspect of the province of history. However, the introduction of the concept of development in this and many other definitions is unfortunate. Development, in ordinary parlance, means an advance or growth through successive changes. Thus every development is a specific sort of change taking place

4 Page 1.
5 *Cf.,* below, p. 264 f.
6 *Lehrbuch der historischen Methode,* p. 4.

within an event or series of events, a change in which
what comes earlier in the series is enhanced by what
comes later. In this, a developmental series possesses a
directional sense (i.e., is transitive) not merely with
respect to time, but also with respect to some quality
possessed by all members of the series.[7] Many series
of events, to be sure, are developmental in this sense,
development being, perhaps, the most common non-
temporal order to be found among series of events.
But if development were an essential characteristic of
all series of events the works of our historians would
read like success-stories or moralizing admonitions.
The histories of such enterprises as the National Re-
covery Administration would never be written, and
the final insanity of Kant would not in any way belong to his history. It is for this reason that one is
compelled to omit the conception of development
from a definition of the province of the historian.

Berr, and many others, however, redress this error
only to introduce another one. Berr insists upon the
inclusion of the concept of the past in his definition
of the province of history. Pastness, however, although
a characteristic of many objects of historical description, does not of necessity pertain to such objects.
The example of Thucydides' narrative should, in itself, have been sufficient to dispel this error. That
event which Thucydides sought to describe, as shown
by his introductory words, was the armed struggle
which was, he believed, to determine the hegemony

[7] Cf., Hegel: *Philosophy of History*, p. 54.

of Hellas.[8] He says: "Thucydides, an Athenian, wrote the history of the war in which the Peloponnesians and the Athenians fought against one another. He began to write when they first took up arms, believ-ing that it would be great and memorable above any previous war. For he argued that both states were then at the full height of their military power, and he saw the rest of the Hellenes either siding or in-tending to side with one or the other of them. No movement ever stirred Hellas more deeply than this . . . " (Jowett translation.) This standpoint, this manner of envisaging what he took as material for his work, might have been worthless had future events taken a different turn. Such a risk is run by every historian of the contemporary; his is a wager against fortune. But if the historian, like Thucydides, is will-ing to take his stand in the midst of the flux of affairs, confident of the depth of his awareness of the con-temporary, he can accept this wager. And sometimes he will be rewarded. Thucydides himself found that his original standpoint was justified, for when he came to render an account of the Sicilian adventure, which, as he saw, furnished the climax of the war, he was able in all truth to write: "But worse than all was the cruel necessity of maintaining two wars at once, and they carried on both with a determination which no one would have believed unless he had actually seen it . . . that in the seventeenth year from

---

[8] *Cf.*, Bury: *The Ancient Greek Historians*, on Thucydides. Also Creuzer's old-fashioned but excellent *Die Historische Kunst der Griechen* (particularly p. 207.)

the first invasion, after so exhausting a struggle, the Athenians should have been strong enough and bold enough to go to Sicily at all, and to plunge into a fresh war as great as that in which they were already engaged—how contrary was all this to the expectation of mankind." And at the close of his account of the expedition, Thucydides says: "Of all Hellenic actions which are on record, this was the greatest—the most glorious to the victors, the most ruinous to the vanquished; for they were utterly and at all points defeated, and their sufferings were prodigious. Fleet and army perished from the face of the earth; nothing was saved, and of the many who went forth few returned home. Thus ended the Sicilian expedition."

Whatever other difficulties arise in the way of the historian of the contemporary, this remains the most formidable, that subsequent events may prove his original envisagement of his material to have been mistaken or trivial. But the fact that this obstacle can, in some cases, be overcome, shows that the field of the historian's activity cannot be limited to facts of the past.

We have now before us, in brief, the main outlines of what any analysis of the field of historical inquiry might reveal. We have seen that a history is differentiated from knowledge in the physical sciences in being a descriptive narration of a particular series of events which has taken place; in consisting not in the formulation of laws of which the particular case is an instance, but in the description of the events in their actual determining relationships to each other; in seeing events as the products and producers of change. We have seen, furthermore, that the field of historical inquiry deals with human events of societal significance, treated with respect to their societal context and implications. Finally, we have attempted to show that it is an error to introduce either the concept of development or of pastness into the delimitation of the historical field of inquiry. With this preliminary analysis behind us we may turn to a consideration of the widespread contemporary scepticism in regard to historical knowledge.

Part I

HISTORICAL RELATIVISM

> "De plus, il s'en faut bien que les faits décrits dans l'histoire ne soient la peinture exacte des mêmes faits tel qu'ils sont arrivés: ils changent de forme dans la tête de l'historian, ils se moulent sur ces intérêts, ils prennent la teint de ses préjugés."
>
> J.-J. Rousseau.

CHAPTER I

HISTORICAL RELATIVISM: A STATEMENT

IT IS a well known fact that not only philosophers but practicing historians have become sceptical of the claims that history yields objective knowledge of the past. Most recently both Carl Becker and Charles Beard have enunciated theoretical positions which leave no doubt as to their espousal of what we shall call historical relativism. Becker says: "It must then be obvious that living history, the ideal series of events that we affirm and hold in memory, since it is so intimately associated with what we are doing and with what we hope to do, cannot be precisely the same for all at any given time, or the same from one generation to another." [1] "In the history of history a myth is a once valid but now discarded version of the human story, as our now valid versions will in due course be relegated to the category of discarded myths." [2] "The form and significance of remembered events, like the extension and velocity of physical objects will vary with the time and place of the observer." [3] History is written, says Becker, "in the serv-

[1] Carl Becker: *Everyman His Own Historian*, p. 242.
[2] *Ibid.*, p. 247.
[3] *Ibid.*, p. 252.

ice of Mr. Everyman's emotional needs."[4] And, he adds, that "it should be a relief to us to renounce omniscience, to recognize that every generation, our own included, will, must inevitably, understand the past and anticipate the future in the light of its own restricted experience, must inevitably play on the dead whatever tricks it finds necessary for its own peace of mind."[5] Beard speaks in the same vein when he says: "Every student of history knows that his colleagues have been influenced in their selection and ordering of materials by their biases, prejudices, beliefs, affections, general upbringing and experience, particularly social and economic; and if he has a sense of propriety, to say nothing of humor, he applies the canon to himself, leaving no exception to the rule."[6]

This point of view, as expressed by Beard, received criticism at the hands of T. C. Smith in an article which contended that historical writing could and should be objective.[7] To this article Beard replied with a more comprehensive statement of the reasons for historical relativism.[8] Thus within the American Historical Association the issue has been joined, relativism having at last found a place awaiting it in

[4] *Ibid.*, p. 252.
[5] *Ibid.*, p. 253.
[6] Charles Beard: *Written History as an Act of Faith (American Historical Review*, Vol. 39, p. 220.)
[7] *The Writing of American History, 1884-1934 (American Historical Review*, Vol. 40, pp. 439 ff.)
[8] *That Noble Dream (American Historical Review*, Vol. 41, pp. 74 ff.) *Cf.* Beard and Vagts: *Currents in Historiography (American Historical Review*, Vol. 42, pp. 460 ff.)

the minds of some of our outstanding historians.

When we search out the meaning of what Beard, Becker and others of the relativists have written, and when we reduce this meaning to its least common denominator, we find historical relativism to be the view that no historical work grasps the nature of the past (or present) immediately, that whatever "truth" a historical work contains is relative to the conditioning processes under which it arose and can only be understood with reference to those processes. To use an example taken from Beard, the works of Ranke do not contain objective truth: whatever "truth" they contain is limited by the psychological, sociological, and other, conditions under which Ranke wrote. *And,* according to Beard, the "truth" contained in Ranke's works can only be understood if we take into account the personality of Ranke, the politics of his class and country, and what, in Whitehead's phrase, could be called the mental climate of his times.

Now the fact that every historical work, like any intellectual endeavor, is limited by psychological and sociological conditions (to mention only two) is indisputable. The radical novelty in historical relativism lies in the fact that it claims that the truth of the work, its meaning and validity, can only be grasped by referring its content to these conditions. In short, the relativist believes that to understand a history we must not only understand what is said in it but also why this is said. This would appear to be an example of what philosophers are pleased to call "the genetic fallacy." Karl Mannheim, one of the most acute and philosophical of the relativists, has attempted, as we shall see, to show that in this particular case "the genetic fallacy" is no fallacy, being both philosophically sound and indispensable as a method.[9]

The line of reasoning which leads the historical relativist to this position must now be traced back to its source. Whatever important differences between relativists emerge in the course of their arguments, the fountain-head of relativism is to be found in interpretations placed upon the indisputable fact that the historian selects and synthesizes his material. If relativism is a mistaken view of historical knowledge it is so because the relativist has based his argument on a false view of historical synthesis. Let us turn, therefore, to an examination of what the relativist assumes regarding selection and synthesis.

The clue to the relativist's view on this point lies in the fact that no relativist (with the exception of Croce, a metaphysical idealist) denies that "the facts" of history are objectively ascertainable. He does, however, draw a distinction between these facts as given and the historical account which the historian builds out of them. Beard, for example, quotes Andrew D. White with approval when the latter says: "While acknowledging the great value of special investigations ... to historical knowledge in individual nations, it is not too much to say that the highest effort and noblest result toward which these special histori-

9 *Cf.*, below, pp. 76 ff.

cal investigations lead is the philosophical syntheses of all special results." And Beard, in this connection, himself refers to "both sides of the problem of historiography: the special, the detailed, the verified, the documented—and the philosophical." [10] The intimation here is, of course, that the "research historian" merely quarries stone, while the other, the "philosophical" (the great) historian raises the edifice.

On the assumption that the materials for a historical work are objectively given in the form of manifold signs as to what actually occurred, the historian must collect, compare, and assort these if he is to construct an account of the happening. But the relativist holds that in giving such an account the actual occurrence becomes lost to the historian through his manipulation of the objective traces which those events left. Far from holding up a perfect mirror to events, it is claimed that the historian's account of necessity distorts what he seeks to have it reflect. It will be worth considerable pains to make clear just what the relativist holds to be the nature of the distorting elements in historical writing.

Most obvious of the conditions which make a historical account differ from the occurrences which it seeks to depict is the fact that every occurrence described by the historian is demonstrably richer in content than is his account. This is the case for several reasons.

[10] *That Noble Dream (American Historical Review,* Vol. 41, p. 79 f.)

The first is that much of the actual content of the occurrence cannot have been directly grasped by the historian. Let us suppose that the occurrence in question is a contemporary one, for example a battle which the historian witnessed. He cannot have seen the battle from every point of view simultaneously. He may have been caught in the thick of it, and so be in a position to describe one aspect of it fully; but then he would be obliged to rely on the testimony of others concerning that which he had not himself seen. Or he may have been at some vantage point and have observed the ebb and flow of the whole; but then he would have lost the details in the welter of confusion. If this is characteristic of the historian's position in regard to contemporary events (an exception is of course to be found in historical autobiography), it can readily be seen that when the historian deals with the past he is at even more of a disadvantage: he must see that past through preserved documents which may be in the form of fragmentary, unjoined records, or in the form of contemporary accounts, where the contemporary historian was beset by difficulties identical in kind with those just mentioned. What is true of a historian describing a battle, whether he witnessed it himself, or whether he received information concerning it from other sources, is true of the historian in every case: his contact with the object which he seeks to describe is limited, he can not have experienced it directly in its entirety. How then can any historian hope to render an account which will do justice to the original?

Secondly, the relativist is prone to argue, the historian does not even include in his account all the material with which he is either directly or indirectly acquainted. He selects certain aspects of the event which he describes, ignoring other aspects. No historian, for example, would trace the fate of every common soldier through the course of a battle, even if the necessary documents for such a procedure were at his disposal. Does not this show that a historical description is inadequate to the actuality with which it supposedly deals, giving us but one arbitrarily selected perspective on the material in question? And does not this mean that the description reflects the historian's personal interests and bias as clearly as it reflects the mere facts on which he bases it?

Thirdly, the relativist can argue that the historian's account is inadequate to the object which he seeks to describe, since the whole sense of immediacy and impact which one would have in experiencing a battle is assuredly not accurately portrayed in a historical work. All of the emotion and the sense of immediate presence which is felt by the participants in an event, and which therefore in some sense belong to that event, come dimly if at all through the fine legible pages of print from which we gain our supposed knowledge of history. How then can a historical account be held to be adequate to its object?

It will be seen that the first and third of these arguments refer chiefly to practical difficulties which beset the historian: the incompleteness of his acquaintance with the facts, and his inability to recapture and portray their full emotional impact upon the persons who originally experienced them. But the relativist is not prone to lay much weight upon these practical difficulties; his chief concern, as we have stated, is always with the selective, synthetic aspect of the historian's work. Consequently the major force of this first general argument is felt to reside in the contention that the historian selects—even from among the limited number of facts which are ascertainable—only those which seem of "historical" importance to him. On this ground alone it would (to the relativist) be clear that every historical work falsifies its purported object, never containing the full amount of actual content which that occurrence possessed. This, however, forms but one of the arguments by means of which the relativist attempts to gain support for his view.

A second argument for relativism is drawn from the fact that every historical account reveals its object as possessing a structure, a continuity, a pattern, which, according to the relativist, the original occurrence did not in itself possess. For example, an account of the development of a style of architecture, or of the changes in an institution, follows a single thread of narrative through successive stages, giving the reader a sense of order and continuity. But the relativist argues that our own immediate experience of events such as these yields no clear sense of order. When we, in the midst of changes, seek to say just how architecture, or the pattern of labor organization, is changing, we may seek to prophesy what the future will bring, but we have no feeling that a single, simple strand of continuity runs through the changes which we witness. Yet in turning to a historical account of changes such as these the interconnection of the facts is so apparent that it seems as if there must have existed in the very events some such interconnectedness—precisely what our immediate experience of those events failed to show.

Put in another way, the relativist's claim may be understood if we ask ourselves the question: Why is it that in order to gain any sense of certainty (whether real or illusory) regarding a historical event, we (as historians) must be placed at a distance from the object which we seek to describe? To this question the relativist finds an answer in his contention that selection implies falsification, a rendering simple of what is in itself complex. It is only when we have simplified (falsified) events that we become "certain" as to what has actually occurred. So long as we stand in the midst of change, the future impends, and warns against certainty; only if we should possess the faith of an Augustine or a Bossuet in a divine (or an economic) necessity, could we dare to be wholly convinced by our own simplifications. Only a remote and broken past can be simplified without avenging itself by upsetting our simplifications. Herein lies the relativist's explanation of why historians feel that some events are "too close" to be historically treated.

The full import of the relativist's contention that historical events are in themselves discontinuous and structureless can only be grasped when we take note of the fact that every historical account necessarily bears the mark of continuity and structure. That this is so can readily be seen if we but recall what was said concerning the manner in which the historian views an event or series of events. We found that the historian's task lies in understanding the concrete nature of some event with reference to a series of events which determined its character. This task itself guarantees that every historical work should manifest both structure and continuity. For in viewing each of a series of events as determining the character of some one given event, a historical work necessarily possesses a structure: each of many events is seen as a contributing factor in the change which is manifested through the one event as a whole. And likewise a certain continuity is present, for the historian has singled out of the whole historical process this one event whose nature he seeks to understand and account for; that which does not serve to account for this event is omitted. In this we see that the nature of the historian's task in understanding the concrete processes of change makes it inevitable that every historical work should manifest structure and continuity. Bearing this in mind it becomes obvious that a view which holds that in themselves historical events are unstructured and discontinuous is necessarily a relativistic view of historical knowledge.

The relativist's denial that historical events in themselves possess continuity and structure must, of course, rest on metaphysical grounds. The type of relativist with whom we have been dealing does not attempt to make his metaphysics explicit: for him it is sufficient to claim that his immediate "experience" reveals no such continuity and structure as is portrayed in a historical work. But quite explicit metaphysical considerations—and these of a wholly different sort—may also lead to relativism.

On certain metaphysical grounds it may be claimed that the historian, far from attributing too much continuity and structure to events, is really guilty of vicious abstractionism. Here events themselves possess an ultimate interconnectedness which the historian's merely partial record distorts. Bradley, for example, using the metaphysics of absolute idealism, would claim that every historical work represents an abstraction from a more real and ultimate continuity. In his essay *What is the Real Julius Caesar?* Bradley says: "How far then, we ask, is the reality of the individual to extend? It extends, I reply, in a word, just so far as it works. As far as any man has knowledge, so far, I insist, the man himself really is there in what is known. And it seems even obvious that his reality goes out as far as what we call his influence extends. ... And, if it is objected that the limits have now become too indefinite to be fixed, I reply that I both recognize and accept this consequence. It is a consequence which conflicts, so far as I see, with nothing better than prejudice." [11] Accepting such a conclusion, it will be apparent that the continuity which a historical account possesses does not deal adequately with the material which it seeks to describe, for the continuity of that material will extend far beyond the continuity depicted in the account in question. This view Beard himself appears to accept, when, in defending relativism, he speaks of the historian as "cutting off connection with the universal," and of the historian's view of events as "arbitrarily established." [12]

On metaphysical grounds other than those adopted by Bradley, such diverse thinkers as William Stern and Bergson have come to conclusions quite like those which Bradley reached. For both Bergson and Stern the past is plastic, being formed by the future. For Stern the objects of historical knowledge are actually constituted by the shafts of memory which reach back toward them: their intrinsic nature is but a limiting concept.[13] Thus every historical object changes with changes in its description; every historian alters what he seeks to find. On this view, therefore, it is meaningless to think that the continuity inherent in the historian's account is also characteristic of the historical object which he seeks

[11] *Essays on Truth and Reality*, p. 423; *Cf.*, pp. 425, 427.
[12] *Written History as an Act of Faith (American Historical Review*, Vol. 39, p. 228.)
[13] *Person und Sache*, Vol. III (*Wertphilosophie*), pp. 290 ff.

to depict, for the object changes its nature as often as it is recalled, it develops long after it is "gone." In a similar manner Bergson holds that the past is plastic, being formed by the future. He says: "Nothing hinders us today from linking the romanticism of the nineteenth century to that which was already romantic in the classicists. But the romantic aspect of classicism only became separate through the retroactive effect of romanticism once it appeared. If there had not been a Rousseau, a Chateaubriand, a Vigny, a Victor Hugo, not only would one never have perceived it, but *there would not really have been* any romanticism among those classicists; this romanticism of the classicists only results from the isolation of a certain aspect in their works, and that which is isolated did not exist in its particular form in classic literature before the appearance of romanticism, any more than a pleasing design which an artist perceives in a passing cloud exists in that cloud before its amorphous mass is organized at the pleasure of his fantasy." [14]

In all of these views, the continuity which the historian's account possesses is an inaccurate reflection of the continuity which the object of the accounts possessed.[15] For, according to these views, the past actually changes after it is "past," and, since the historian is caught in the present, the continuity which he

[14] *La Pensée et le Mouvant*, p. 23.
[15] Because of other metaphysical views which Bergson holds it may not be strictly accurate to include him here. But it is obvious that some thinkers might use Bergson's argument for their own relativistic purposes.

ascribes to his object will be relative to the time at which he writes. For example, if the "real" Caesar changes with every influence which Caesar exerted, a historian writing before the Fascist March on Rome could not mirror the continuity and structure of certain events in the history of ancient Rome as adequately as could a historian writing some few years later. And further, unless memory fails, the history of ancient Rome will always go on changing, and no accurate account of it will ever be written.

We have now seen (in its two basic forms) the second major argument for relativism: the contention that the continuity and structure which a historical account contains do not accurately reflect the real nature of the events with which the historian is supposedly dealing. On the one hand this view may be based on our immediate experience of the contemporary, in which case the continuity of the historical account will be a mere reflection of the historian's mental processes: an imposition of order upon chaos. Such is the view of Simkhovitch: "Every time that we appeal to factual relationships of the past all we get is the mentality of the historian or an assorted variety of such mentalities." [16] On the other hand, this view may be based on a metaphysics which holds that the continuity and structure to be found in historical works are different from the continuity and structure which the events themselves possess. As

[16] *Approaches to History,* II (*Political Science Quarterly,* Vol. 45, p. 486.)

we have seen, such appears to be the view of Beard. Regardless of which side is taken in this argument, whether it be the urgency of experience or the compulsion of a metaphysics that is heeded, it is a relativistic position to claim that the continuity and structure which is inevitably present in a historical synthesis is false to the nature of historical events.

The third, and perhaps most characteristic, argument for relativism attempts to show that far from being objective, all historical knowledge is value-charged. By "value-charged" is here meant that every historical judgment carries a positive or negative charge, an aspect of affinity for or repulsion from its object. This value element, this aspect of being for or against the material depicted in the account, is furthermore held to determine the synthetic phase of the historian's activity. According to the relativist, the historian, with a manifold of objectively given facts at his disposal, unwittingly and necessarily constructs his account under the dominance of the particular values which are his. The whole account therefore, being a product of his synthetic vision, is through and through valuational: if one were to try to separate out the implicit valuations which the finished work contains, it would, according to the relativist, disintegrate into a compilation of disconnected, meaningless facts, and cease to be a history.

The grounds for this contention must be admitted to have the virtue of being based on a careful examination of the conditions under which historical works arise. If one asks the question, for example, how it happened that Polybius wrote just such a historical account as he did, one can find at least the rudiments of an explanation in considering the conditions of his personal life. In spite of the objectivity for which he strove, an objectivity which he claimed could alone make historical study fulfil its proper function as an educative force, there are signs throughout his work of a personal evaluation of events. For example, in spite of his claim that patriotism should not influence the historian, his account of Achaean politics is colored by his own Achaean bias, and he is, in Bury's words, "disposed to make their attitude to the Achaean League the measure for judging other Greek States." [17] Likewise, his complete personal reconciliation to the extension of the Roman Empire sets the tone for the second, and major, portion of his work; for, when he says that he is describing the administration of the empire after its military triumph in order that "the present generation will learn from this whether they should shun or seek the rule of Rome; and future generations will be taught whether to praise and imitate, or to decry it," [18] there is some foundation for the contention that he is really justifying Roman dominion and seeking to show his fellow-Greeks the wisdom of acquiescence.[19]

Thus in Polybius, as in others, it is clear that a historian's life is at least partially reflected in his work.

[17] *Ancient Greek Historians*, p. 217; *Cf.*, p. 215 f.
[18] Book III, Sec. 4 (Shuckburgh translation).
[19] Bury, *op. cit.*, p. 217.

Could we really understand certain aspects of the writings of Grote without the background of Benthamism, or interpret some of what J. R. Green has said without his Gladstonian Liberalism? [20] But the relativist, not content with holding to this simple observation, goes on to insist that the values which determine the historian's personality completely determine the nature of his work as a whole. These values, according to the relativist's analysis, reveal themselves in a dual guise in every historical work; like a two-faced Janus the valuational standpoint of the historian looks backward and forward at once. It is the relativist's contention that the values which determine the historian's personality automatically, and perhaps against his will, determine his reactions to various aspects of the past, since that past, being comprised of events having societal significance, is itself value-laden. Thus the past and its values are refracted through the personality of the historian, through the values which he himself accepts; the past as it was in itself cannot be discovered in any historian's work. On the other hand the historian's valuational standpoint is also forward-looking. The historian, living in an age which possesses its own problems, can not be wholly submerged in the past: the future beckons and threatens. Thus there is also a prospective side to the historian's set of values, and through it the future, with its demands and its conflicts, enters into the historian's mind and that prod-

[20] *Cf.*, Ernest Scott: *History and Historical Problems*, p. 32 f.

uct of his mind's synthetic activity, his work. Both of these aspects can be seen in Polybius' work: in his patriotism that colors his account of the past, and in his forward-looking "advice" to the Greek people to subscribe to Roman dominion.

The "new kind of historian" for whom James Harvey Robinson was seeking, the historian "who will utilize the information painfully amassed by the older ones in order to bring it to bear on the quandaries of our life today," [21] is, according to Troeltsch and to Teggart, no different from the older historians. For Troeltsch (although he strives to escape relativism) insists on the close relation between the evaluation of the past and the demands of the future,[22] and Teggart says: "A Mommsen, Ferrero or Eduard Meyer may present the picture of a distant past, but he speaks always with the voice of his own generation, and gives utterance to the ideas and aspirations of his own community." [23]

But this is not all. The relativist is not content to hold that the valuational factors which determine the nature of a historical work are personal sympathies or antipathies for certain aspects of the past and personal hopes for the future. With this he blends the

[21] *Apud* T. C. Smith: *The Writing of American History, 1884-1934 (American Historical Review*, Vol. 40, p. 448.)

[22] *Der Historismus und seine Probleme*, p. 117 (*Cf.*, pp. 113, 116, 119, 169, 200).

[23] *Prologomena to History*, p. 208. *Cf.*, Ernest Scott: *History and Historical Problems*, p. 190 f.; Th. Lessing: *Geschichte als Sinngebung des Sinnlosen*, sec. 15; and, A. v. Harnacwk: *Die Sicherheit und die Grenzen geschichtlicher Erkenntnis*. For an attack on this point of view, *cf.*, Butterfield's excellent little book: *The Whig Interpretation of History*.

view that the categories which determine the basic structure of any specific historical work are but reflections of societal conditions and therefore will change from age to age. In substantiation of this broader argument the relativist can point to the fact that history is constantly being rewritten in terms which each succeeding era best understands. He argues that if historical writing were objective, that is, if it were a faithful description of what actually occurred, the history of a given event would be as unchanging from age to age as is the multiplication table.[24] But the fact of the matter is, according to the relativist, that history must constantly be revised in terms which have meaning for the generation or civilization to which the historian belongs. When new values come to the forefront, as a result of changes in societal conditions, old histories must be discarded, or at least rewritten from the new point of view. It is thus that the relativist explains such phenomena as the changes in interpretation of Ancient Greek history and life: the change, for example, which took place between the "classicism" of Winckelmann and Goethe, and the "romanticism" of Hölderlin and Nietzsche. Croce, expressing this in his own terms, holds, as we shall see, that the spirit of man must always respond to the demands of his age, and that a perpetual rewriting of history is a direct consequence of this necessity.[25]

[24] Beard: *That Noble Dream (American Historical Review,* Vol. 41, p. 76).
[25] *Primi Saggi,* p. viii; *History,* p. 25.

In regard to this third relativistic contention it is important to note that the values which are held to determine the historian's selection and synthesis of his materials are in turn held to be determined by the personality of the historian and by the age in which he lives. According to this analysis, they are determined by the present or future, and the very idea that they can give an accurate objective account of the past is thereby rendered absurd. An insistence on the conditioned (non-transcendent) character of values and an insistence on knowledge as value-charged can have only one resultant: relativism. It is for this reason that we have called this the most characteristic argument for relativism. It is also one of the only two points on which such diverse thinkers as Croce, Dilthey, and Mannheim agree.

In conclusion let us summarize our brief sketch of the arguments on which contemporary historical relativism rests. We may say that the doctrine of relativism holds that no historical account can faithfully depict the past since, first, the actual occurrences of history are richer in content than any account of them can possibly be; second, because the continuity and structure which historical works necessarily possess do not afford a true parallel to the continuity and structure which characterize the events of history; and, third, because the historian of necessity passes value-judgments, and these are relevant to the present but not to the past. All three arguments, it will be seen, are directed against the historian's selective synthetic procedure. Therefore, a full answer to relativism is not to be attained, as most have sought to attain it, by insisting that the values of the present are also relevant to the past; such an answer can only be reached through a patient examination of the nature of historical synthesis.

CHAPTER II

Three Historical Relativists

Turning from a generalized statement of the nature of historical relativism we must examine some of the specific formulations of that position. We have chosen to deal with the doctrines of Croce, Dilthey, and Mannheim as affording a representative survey of the relativistic position. Taken singly, these three men afford three variant interpretations of the nature of historical knowledge, each interpretation forming an integral part of a more general philosophic system. Taken together, however, their work illustrates the basis on which historical relativism is established within any system whatsoever.

In the present chapter our procedure will be confined to the analytical exposition and criticism of each of the positions taken singly. Only after this has been done shall we be in a position to show the common basis which historical relativism has within each of these systems. The great disadvantage of this method of exposition is obvious: it may be difficult for the reader who is unacquainted with the literature of our problem to find any unifying strand in our discussion. On the other hand the advantages of the procedure far outweigh this literary disadvantage which attaches to it. For, in the first place, it is manifestly unfair to rip specific views of the nature of historical knowledge out of their original context and to treat them merely as representative of that which we are attempting to prove. In the second place, if we are to refute the views of Croce, Dilthey, and Mannheim we can only do so by examining those views as they stand. To attack merely the common element in their thought would be, at this point in our exposition, to attack a man of straw. Finally, since there exists in English no adequate summary exposition of the views of historical knowledge held by these men it may be of service to present those views in their entirety.

Following this somewhat ungainly procedure, we shall in the present chapter consider the views of Croce, Dilthey, and Mannheim as unrelated insular phenomena. In Chapter III we shall attempt, among other things, to show the more basic structure upon which these apparently isolated phenomena are reared.

CROCE (1866-   )

In dealing with the doctrine of historical knowledge which Croce expounds we face the problem of rendering explicit views which are not in general acceptable to the majority of philosophers and which demand a thorough knowledge of the system in which they have their being. This system is not without its ambiguities and internal inconsistencies, a fact which makes it difficult to sift out the essential teachings of

Croce in regard to historical knowledge. Added to this systematic difficulty, and closely associated with it, is the fact that Croce's views have developed gradually, so that one may not take any single work as definitive of the Crocean point of view. For this reason we shall approach the theory which is formulated in *History, Its Theory and Practice* (a comparatively late work) through a discussion of some of the key concepts of the Crocean system, showing just how those concepts led Croce to the relativistic position which he finally adopts.

The starting point of Croce's philosophy is its absolute rejection of materialism; as is well known, the volumes which most completely present Croce's thought are collectively known as "Philosophy of the Spirit." The province of the Spirit is then divided into two: that occupied by the theoretic activity and that of the practical activity, the first being the sphere of knowledge, the second of will. It is with the sphere of knowledge that we are here concerned. Now this sphere has within it two forms of activity, the intuitional and the conceptual. The science of pure intuition is Aesthetic, the science of the pure concept is Logic. With Croce's views of these sciences we are not concerned, except in so far as we must understand what Croce means by intuition and by the concept. Our field, the field of historical knowledge, is neither the field of pure intuition, nor of the pure concept. For Croce, as we shall see, the historical judgment contains both intuitional and conceptual elements. Let us now examine Croce's characterization of it.

In his first work on the subject, his lectures to the Accademia Pontaniana (now most accessible in his *Primi Saggi*), Croce examines the problem of whether history is a science or an art. In opposition to Bernheim and others he insists that history can not be classed among the sciences, for the latter deal with concepts: "where there is not a formation of concepts there is not science." [1] According to him science constructs categories and concepts under which it is able to subsume experience and deal with it practically: "If natural *sciences* be spoken of, apart from philosophy, we must observe that these are not perfect sciences: they are aggregate of cognitions, arbitrarily abstracted and fixed"; [2] and, "those sciences ... develop representative concepts, which are not intuitions, but spiritual formations of a practical nature"; [3] "the natural sciences are not directed to action, but *are*, themselves, actions: their practical nature is not extrinsic but *constitutive*." [4] Thus Croce says that what is "true" (theoretic rather than practical) in the natural sciences "is either philosophy or historical fact." [5] This subsumption of experience under concepts is then the characteristic of science. But the historian is not interested in any such procedure, being interested in narration: "the ideal of history has not

[1] *Primi Saggi,* p. 16.
[2] *Aesthetic,* p. 30.
[3] *Logic,* p. 330 f.
[4] *Logic,* p. 332.
[5] *Aesthetic,* p. 30.

changed, because it cannot change. History narrates." [6] But if history is not science, a question remains: is it art? In his first essay, Croce's answer holds that it must be, since there are only two possible cognitive operations: understanding *(intendere)* and beholding *(contemplare)*, the first of which is science, the second art. It is here beside the point to inquire whether or not he is right in drawing such a conclusion, and in saying: "Whenever one subsumes the particular under the general one is being a scientist, whenever one represents the particular as such one is being an artist." [7] Our only purpose is to show that in these essays he subsumes history under the general concepts of art. As we shall soon see, this early view receives later modifications.

Croce, having subsumed history under the concept of art, was then forced to distinguish between historical narration and aesthetic beholding in the narrower sense. This he did in limiting history to the beholding of that which had actually happened. While the sphere of aesthetic activity was free of all questions in regard to the existential status of its contemplated object, historical narration had to separate the actual from the possible, and confine itself to the realm of the actual.

To this difference between art and history Croce in a sense still holds, [8] although he no longer believes that history is to be subsumed under the concept of

6 *Primi Saggi,* p. 19.
7 *Primi Saggi,* p. 23; *cf., ibid.,* p. 56.
8 *Cf., Practical,* p. 265 f.

aesthetic knowledge. This modification in his doctrine took place when he turned his attention to the nature of the concept.[9] Thereupon it became clear to him that the presence of an assertion concerning the actual occurrence of events, which is the distinguishing mark of history, involves a conceptual element. Thus history is not aesthetic (non-conceptual). In the *Aesthetic* he still held that while the content of history is different from that of the aesthetic, its form is the same.[10] But in the *Logic* and in other later works he holds that history is to be equated with the individual judgment, in which the subject is an intuition, the predicate a concept.[11] From this it would appear, then, that history is a third form of the theoretic, to be subsumed neither under the pure intuition nor the pure concept. But this Croce rejects, identifying Philosophy and History in his attempted proof of the identity of the pure concept, or definition, and the individual judgment.[12]

We shall not inquire with what right Croce holds that the definition, or pure concept, is historically determined and thus identical with the individual judgment, but shall confine ourselves to the problem in hand: the nature of a historical judgment.

The Crocean doctrine of the historical, or individual, judgment rests on the foundation that all judgment of fact (perception) demands both a presen-

9 Cf., *Primi Saggi*, p. xi f.; *Logic*, pp. 327 ff.
10 *Aesthetic*, p. 26 f.
11 Cf., *Logic*, Pt. II, Ch. 3; *Problemi*, p. 14; *Practical*, p. 27 f.
12 *Logic*, Pt. I, Sec. III, Ch. 1 and 2; Part II, Ch. 4.

tational and a conceptual element. The doctrine is, however, somewhat complicated on the side of the conceptual element involved, and we can summarize it in only the most cursory fashion.[13] Let us state it as follows: The individual judgment predicates a *true concept* of an *intuition* (which we shall presently examine). A true concept is both ultrarepresentative (not given by a single representation, nor by a group of representations) and omnirepresentative (having a representable content).[14] An example of a true concept would be "quality," "development," "beauty," or the like; examples of pseudoconcepts being "house" (not ultrarepresentative) and "triangle" (not omni-representative). When the predicate assigned to an intuited content is a pseudoconcept, an individual pseudojudgment rather than a true individual judgment is the result.[15] A mark of such individual pseudojudgments is the fact that in them is to be found "only the mechanical application of a predicate to a subject," whereas the true individual judgment evidences a "penetration" of the predicate into the subject.[16] While Croce does not deny the practical importance of individual pseudojudgments, he does deny their cognitive value. He seeks to show that the true individual judgment is presupposed in pseudo-judgments; [17] to use his own example, that the judgment "The Transfiguration is a sacred picture," pre-

---

[13] *Cf.*, *Logic*, Pt. I, Sec. II, Ch. 4-6.
[14] *Logic*, pp. 20 ff.
[15] *Ibid.*, p. 179.
[16] *Ibid.*, p. 181, 287.
[17] *Ibid.*, p. 184 f.

supposes the judgment that "The Transfiguration is an aesthetic work." Without questioning the accuracy of this illustration, or the validity of his general point, we may call attention to the position in which his rejection of the cognitive value of the individual pseudojudgment involves him. He is forced to say that these judgments must be abandoned when one seeks a historical knowledge of facts, although, as he admits, they are indispensable to the communication of the results of this historical knowledge (the latter being, of course, a practical activity for Croce). To use his own illustration: "If I pass mentally in review the material that must go to form the history of Italian painting or literature, I must of necessity arrange it in works of greater or lesser importance, in plays and novels, in sacred pictures and landscapes, and so on; save when I wish to understand those facts historically, and then I must abandon those divisions. I must abandon them during that act of comprehension: but I must immediately resume them, if I wish to give the result of my historical research." [18] This does indeed lead us to doubt whether Croce's analysis is correct, and whether the pure concept (as he understands it) is in reality the predicate of the historical judgment. For it would seem to us that the historian *is* concerned with predicating specific empirical qualities of the subject, and of attributing specific works and deeds to a given series, and all

[18] *Ibid.,* p. 182.

these are surely pseudoconcepts of the non-ultrarep-
resentative type.

But to this general caveat against the Crocean doctrine two rejoinders might be made: the first, that the
historical judgment must place the intuited fact
against the background of "the Whole" [19] in order to
lay claim to validity; the second, that in the historical
judgment only the existential predicate (that the
intuited fact did occur) is demanded.

Now while it is true that the predication of a
pseudoconcept will not place the intuited fact against
the background of the Whole, it is at least question-
able whether this is the purpose, or at least the sole
purpose, of the historical judgment. That must, however, be left an open question for the present. But the
second rejoinder carries no weight whatsoever. It
would aim to say that the whole content of a historical
judgment is given in intuition, and that the historian
need only apply the existential predicate to that content in his judgment. Croce himself emphatically rejects this alternative, insisting that the existential
predicate is not sufficient for the true individual historical judgment, for within the subject are contained
predicates beyond mere existence, and these can and
must be expressed.[20] But there is a reason even more
cogent than Croce's own words which makes us reject
this alternative rejoinder. If it were sufficient for the
historical judgment to apply the pure concept of

[19] *Logic,* p. 180.
[20] *Ibid.,* pp. 175 ff.

existence to that which the mind intuits of the past, all possibility of denying the validity of any historical judgment would cease: whatever had been intuited would *ipso facto* be true, or, at least, could not be held to be false. But this is much farther than Croce wishes to have his relativism lead him: he still speaks in the realistic terms by means of which he had differentiated history from art.[21]

Thus it may be said to be fairly well established that there is a reasonable ground on which to doubt Croce's analysis of the conceptual element in the historical judgment. Much more important, however, is the intuitive element, for in intuition history has its source. Let us now analyze what Croce says concerning it.

By the pure intuition Croce means the expressive aspect of spirit which is productive of images rather than of concepts. This expressive aspect is prior both to the concept and to the practical activity, for it is independent of them, while they are not independent of it. It is thus the basic form of the activity of spirit, and since nothing can be said to exist external to spirit, it is also the basis of existence. This point is of importance to remember, since it implies that intuition, while a form of knowing, is more than mere knowing: that it is creative of the object known. This object, which intuition apprehends in creating, is the image. The image, however, must not be taken as something akin to sensation, considered as "brute

[21] *Cf., Logic,* p. 156.

47

matter," for the image already has form. Sensation, in the sense of formless matter, is a mere limit which we can postulate, but whose presence we can never apprehend.[22] This formless matter is "what the spirit of man suffers, but does not produce,"[23] yet without it spiritual activity could never be concrete. What is this formless matter which the spirit forms? In his later works Croce never again speaks, in the unguarded terms of the *Aesthetic*, of sensations as formless, nor of impressions as the equivalent of these. In the *Logic* he specifically holds that sensation must be considered as "something active and cognitive, or as a cognitive act; and not as something formless and passive or only active with the activity of life, and not with that of contemplation."[24] And in other later works he identifies that which is the "matter" of pure intuition with the "states of the soul." Aside from concepts, he says, there is no spiritual content other than what is called appetite, tendency, feeling, will. These are all that make up the practical form of the spirit; intuition must therefore represent these.[25] The "matter" of intuition thus no longer lies outside of the sphere of the spirit, but is the concrete content of individual volitional experience. Croce therefore denies that the "matter" of intuition, in the sense of a non-spiritual given, exists at all. What exists is concrete form; to speak of the matter is to speak of a

[22] *Aesthetic*, p. 5 f.
[23] *Ibid.*, p. 6.
[24] *Logic*, p. 1.
[25] *Problemi*, p. 23.

48

specific form.[26] With this he has rendered his philosophy of the Spirit consistent; pure intuition no longer demands an Unknown-X or sensibility (to use Kantian terms), for it has its content in the individual psychic experience, and its content is concrete and changing form.

Let us restate what we have found concerning Croce's doctrine of pure intuition. The pure intuition is the basic form of the activity of spirit; in intuition the spirit gives form to the ever-changing volitional states of the soul. Intuition is direct awareness; it is the immediate expression of these states of the soul. Further, it is independent of concepts; if concepts are present they are so fused as to lose their conceptual quality, and it is this that Croce means by "pure" intuition, an intuition to which the predicate of existence (a concept) is not even tacitly applied.

Croce utilizes this doctrine of intuition with respect to the historical judgment by insisting that the subject of such a judgement—e.g., a battle or a political intrigue—must be intuited by the historian.[27]

But we may inquire whether this is really meaningful on Croce's view of intuition. If intuition means the expression of states of the soul in the knower, how is the historian ever to come into "direct contact with the thing that happened?"[28] How are we to "live again" the reality of the fact as it was lived, and as it "vibrates in the spirit of him who took part in

26 *Problemi*, p. 481.
27 *Logic*, pp. 280 ff.; *Practical*, p. 27 f.
28 *Logic*, p. 280; *Cf.*, *La Critica*, v. III, p. 252.

49

it?" [29] Only on one metaphysical assumption would this seem to be possible; that the states of the soul of individuals are parts of the Absolute; that the Idea unrolls, in Hegelian fashion, through each of us. This doctrine Croce, with his teaching concerning the universal Spirit, embraces. He says: "This historical web, which is and is not the work of individuals, constitutes, as has been said, the work of the universal Spirit, of which individuals are manifestations and instruments." [30] And yet our problem is not solved, for it would be necessary for the universal Spirit to manifest itself identically in two different instrumentalities if the historian is to "live again" the occurrence of the past. But it seems evident from Croce's repeated insistence on eternal change that he would not consider this as a serious possibility.[31] Yet even if Croce held to the possibility of a recurrence of at least a "fragment" (so to speak) of the universal Spirit, he would not thereby render the historical judgment possible. For it would not be enough for an occurrence to be relived by an individual; that individual must recognize that he is reliving that occurrence. And for this he must transcend his individual point of view. But how is he to do this if intuition, the basis of all knowledge, "says nothing but what we as individuals experience, suffer and desire?" [32] Here Croce brings forward his doctrine of

29 *Logic*, p. 280.
30 *Practical*, p. 257; *Cf., Logic*, p. 254, *Practical*, p. 249.
31 *Logic*, pp. 315, 317, 319; *Historical Materialism*, p. 102, n. 1; *Practical*, p. 247.
32 *Logic*, p. 293 f.

the memory of the past: that the spirit of humanity remembers what has occurred.[33] Yet if this be not a mere metaphor based on the preservation of "sources as external things" [34] (and thus not yet true history, which is a spiritual act), it must mean that the universal Spirit remembers, for certainly no Leopold von Ranke ever remembered the Diet of Worms. But any memory possessed by the universal Spirit lies beyond the range of our knowledge, as we have seen.

Thus Croce's doctrine of the necessary presence of intuition in historical knowledge makes all such knowledge impossible. It breaks down in the attempt to reconcile two irreconcilable doctrines: that history is the knowledge of what has actually happened in the past, and that "true history is that of which an interior verification is possible." [35] It is impossible that all history should be "contemporary history," as Croce claims,[36] and yet tell what actually happened. And the source of this duality in Croce's conception of history is a confusion in his use of the word "intuition." If intuition is the fundamental expressive activity of spirit which is productive of the image, then intuition is *not* entering into a past fact. Historical knowledge, if intuitive, is productive of fact, but this fact is then present and not past. Thus on Croce's doctrine of the intuitive element in historical knowl-

[33] *Aesthetic*, p. 30; *Logic*, p. 280; *History*, p. 25; *La Critica*, v. X, p. 287.
[34] *History*, p. 28.
[35] *History*, p. 136.
[36] *History*, p. 12, *et pass.*

edge it is impossible to hold to any usual view of historical truth.

Croce recognizes this fact, and in his later works he attempts to build his theory of historical knowledge accordingly: he comes to insist that all history is contemporary history. The meaning of this paradoxical statement is to be found in Croce's view that nothing exists which is external to spirit; that facts, whether present or past, are posited by spirit and are only to be understood as spiritual acts.[37] On such a metaphysical idealism the past can have no real being: each fact posited by the spirit has its being in a perpetually changing Now. It is in this sense that Croce can and must say that all history is contemporary history.

In order to support this view Croce is forced to draw a distinction between history and chronicle. History is a spiritual act; chronicle is the external husk of such an act. The recorded "fact"—the mere fact as it appears in chronicle—is not the foundation stone of a history, it is but a mnemonic device used by the spirit to preserve that which it once posited and which it may someday again bring to life.[38] For it is the life of the spirit, and not any set of "external" things, that gives us history— "It is simply impossible to compose a history with external things, whatever efforts may be made and whatever trouble be taken. Chronicles that have been weeded, chopped up into

[37] Cf., *History*, p. 73, 75, 108.
[38] *History*, Pt. I, Ch. I; App. I.

fragments, recombined, rearranged, always remain
nevertheless chronicles—that is to say, empty nar-
ratives; and documents that have been restored, reproduced, described, brought into line, remain
documents—that is to say, silent things." [39] Thus Croce
relegates the whole sphere of the uncomprehended
past to the limbo of that which is not now present
to spirit, attributing reality only to that which the
spirit, at any given moment of its everchanging Now,
comprehends. In this manner Croce is able to explain
away what is apparently a fact: that a comprehension
of the real past, now represented only by chronicles
and documents, is the goal which the historian seeks.
The belief in such a past, according to Croce, is due
to the misinterpretation of the true nature of chronicles and documents. These are not sources of historical knowledge, but reminders of its death. All
historical knowledge is creative of its own object; the
"facts" recorded in documents are not objects to be
explained, for they themselves were created by spiritual acts and appear now as "facts" only because the
spirit has left them. To overlook the rôle of the spirit
in their formation, to believe in them as having a
reality of their own, is to mistake a corpse for a living
being.[40] This very error is what has led people to deny
that all history is contemporary history; the correction
of this error, that is, the true delineation of the relation between history and chronicle, will enable all

[39] *Ibid.*, p. 27.
[40] *History*, p. 20.

people to see "that contemporaneity is not the characteristic of a class of histories...but an intrinsic characteristic of every history." [41]

In this it will be seen that Croce is a radical relativist in regard to historical knowledge, for historical relativism is the doctrine that a historical work can never adequately represent the past, but must be understood in terms of the situation out of which it arises. Croce himself explicitly recognizes this consequence of his doctrine; he says: "Thus if contemporary history springs straight from life, so too does that history which is called non-contemporary, for it is evident that only an interest in the life of the present can move one to investigate past fact. Therefore this past fact does not answer to a past interest, but to a present interest, in so far as it is unified with an interest of the present life." [42] Again: "Thus it may be said that we know at every moment all the history that we need to know." [43] And Croce does not fail to draw the full consequences of this doctrine. He holds not merely that a historical work is always a function of the present, but that change is perpetual; thus no present situation ever recurs. Speaking of the historically conditioned character of all problems he says: "The doubt of the child is not that of the adult, the doubt of the uncultured man is not that of the man of culture, or the doubt of the novice that of the learned. Further, the doubt of an Italian is not that

[41] *Ibid.*, p. 14.
[42] *History*, p. 12.
[43] *History*, p. 55.

of a German, and the doubt of a German of the year 1800 is not that of a German of the year 1900. Indeed the doubt formulated by an individual in a given moment, is not that formulated by the same individual a moment after." [44] This can only mean that every historical work is a new creation of spirit and contains a new unfolding of that spirit. This being the case, it becomes necessary to establish a criterion of historical truth and error different from the usual criterion of the adequacy of the historical account in dealing with past facts. Such a criterion Croce tries to establish.

According to him there is, strictly speaking, no such thing as error: "Error . . . is not a fact; it does not possess empirical existence; it is nothing but the negative or dialectical moment of the spirit, necessary for the concreteness of the positive moment, for the reality of the spirit." [45] Again he says: "I have contended in that theory, and shown in that history, that man never thinks the false, but from instance to instance responds to the demands which arise, and that the false is simply that which does not respond to effective demands." [46] Error, then, is merely partiality.[47] Put concretely, every historical work is in a sense true, for it represents one stage in the self-manifestation of the spirit; but every historical work will also necessarily be superseded by other works differing

[44] *Logic*, p. 209.
[45] *History*, p. 48.
[46] *Primi Saggi*, p. viii.
[47] *Task of Logic*, p. 213 f.

from it, for the spirit is ever-enlarging. What then is historical truth?

Croce attempts to answer this question by bringing his relativism within a larger philosophical framework which would enable us to transcend doubt and attain an ideal, although changing, objectivity. This framework consists in the metaphysical faith which affirms that all moments of the self-revelation of spirit are inherently compatible. Such a faith is, however, absolutely undemonstrable from any finite point of view. The contradictions inherent in two conflicting standpoints cannot be adequately judged by any third person, since this person himself has a standpoint. Thus Croce's advice to read partisan history, but to make allowances for its partisanship,[48] is unfeasible: we ourselves are partisans. And further, on his own grounds, Croce has no right to criticize the current practice of historical writing in Germany [49] so long as this writing answers to a true need. If it be held that Croce's need is a deeper and more effective one than that of a National Socialist ideologue, a point has been raised which only the Absolute, and not Mr. Croce, can answer. To say that a neutral party can determine the truth in this case is to beg the question, for on the Crocean assumptions there can be no neutral party. Thus we see again that the doctrine of the absolute spirit cannot save Croce from the wholly relativistic implications of his own premises. If his-

[48] *Logic,* p. 290 f.
[49] *Cf. La Critica,* v. XXXII, p. 397 f.; also, p. 473 f.

tory, due to its intuitive content, is always contemporary history; if contemporary history arises always out of the present needs of the spirit; if every historical judgment is necessarily true, then it follows that there is no criterion of truth which any finite individual can apply to a historical work. Only an ultimately expanded judgment, a final judgment of the Absolute, would be absolutely true, embracing all partialities. But we have no evidence that Croce believes in any such finality. For that reason the last will always be the best, if it can be gathered up into a larger concept sometime in the future. As between two sets of judgments not we but only the infinite future can determine which is the more true.

We have now seen that in its earlier stages Croce's theory contained an essential inconsistency due to his attempt to hold that historical knowledge revealed what had actually happened and yet that it was intuitive. This inconsistency he overcame only by relinquishing the ideal of historical objectivity. The relativism which then took possession of his teaching he sought to mitigate by an appeal to the absolute nature of spirit. But his appeal, as we have seen, fails to solve the concrete problem of discriminating between more and less accurate historical judgments. Therefore, any philosopher who seeks to render intelligible the fact that historians do possess applicable criteria of historical truth must relinquish Croce's theory to seek a more adequate one.

DILTHEY (1833-1911)

In attempting to trace historical relativism in the works of Dilthey we are confronted with the problem of dealing with a long series of fragments, few of which (and these the most fragmentary of all) deal explicitly with our problem. Yet Dilthey is one of the chief sources of historical relativism, and, in addition, he is one of the most suggestive of the philosophers who have dealt with the methodological problems of history. For these reasons we shall be concerned with him here, even though (in his case more than in any other) our necessarily brief treatment of his thought will fall far short of an adequate discussion.

It is clear that both in theory and in practice Dilthey did not consider himself as a relativist. In practice he attempted to unfold the cultural history (Geistesgeschichte) of the modern world through a series of works which, though partial and scattered, afford a glimpse into the material of this inquiry which has never been surpassed for its richness. In the field of theory Dilthey constantly reiterated his belief in historical objectivity. He held that historical relativism could be overcome by concentration on the larger, spiritual forms (geistige Gebilde) present in history; [50] precisely those forms with which he, as historian, had concerned himself. He says explicitly that universally valid synthetic judgments are pos-

---

[50] *Gesammelte Schriften* (to be referred to as *GS*) v. VII, p. 260.

sible in history,[51] and yet we find in him a deep feeling that all historical phenomena (including all philosophical systems and all historical works) are relative. He says in one place: "Everything is relative, the only thing which is absolute is the nature of spirit itself which manifests itself in all of these things. And for a knowledge of the nature of spirit there is no terminus, no final apprehension, each is relative, each has been sufficient if it has sufficed for its time." [52] Above all Dilthey holds that philosophy is relative and time-bound. The only knowledge which can save man from the flux of history is historical knowledge and a historical view of the world. But where, Dilthey inquires, are to be found the instruments which can overcome the flux of historical opinion itself? It is for the sake of a solution to this problem, he tells us, that his whole life was spent.[53] He himself believed that he had seen a way which could lead historical understanding out of anarchical relativism without relinquishing a truly historical view of the world. It is this way that we must now examine, approaching it through as brief a survey of his general philosophical position as will suffice.

Dilthey tells us that the fundamental motive of his whole philosophy was the attempt to understand life (das Leben) in terms of itself.[54] Life was for him the fundamental reality: "Life is the fundamental fact

[51] *GS* VII, 278.
[52] *GS* IV, 250.
[53] *GS* V, 9.
[54] *GS* V, 4.

which must serve as the starting point of philosophy. It is that which is known from within, it is that behind which one cannot go. Life can not be brought before the judgment seat of reason." [55] This vital reality lies at the basis of all knowledge; out of it knowledge springs. It is irrational and cannot be rationalized, it cannot be expressed. But this fundamental reality is immediately experienced (erlebt) by us.[56] Immediate experience (Erlebnis) is one with that fundamental reality which is Life; it is Life experienced within us, and experienced so immediately as to give rise to no subject-object differentiation. [57] This immediate experience furnishes us with the only direct contact which we have with reality; in it there is given the qualitative manifold of this reality. But reality is also characterized by temporality; what is the relation of immediate experience to this? For Dilthey, immediate experience is characterized by a dynamic unity, so that (although the present is always an extensionless "now," a cut through temporality) the past reaches through the present into the future.[58] It is the structure (Strukturzusammenhang) of the qualitative differences which makes this dynamic unity of an experience possible.[59] In short, immediate experience, in which we are in direct contact with life, contains a qualitative manifold grasped through

[55] GS VII, 261.
[56] GS V, 11; VII, 218; VI, 314.
[57] GS VI, 313 f.
[58] GS VII, 72.
[59] GS VI, 314 ff.

its structure as a single unified whole.[60] Behind this experience we cannot go.

But if we ask what gives this manifold the structure by means of which it is grasped as a unity, the only answer which Dilthey gives us lies in his introduction of the category of meaningfulness (Bedeutung, or Bedeutsamkeit).[61] No portion of immediate experience can be grasped or reproduced in isolation; memory selects according to meaningfulness; through this meaningfulness portions of immediate experience can be grasped as a whole. But what then is the condition of the meaningfulness of portions of experience? Dilthey answers that this meaningfulness is given by the relation (Lebensbezug) of those portions with my own condition (Zustand), this condition being interpreted in terms of my desires, goal or will.[62] But this means, according to Dilthey's theory of value, that meaningfulness is relative to individually experienced value.[63] Thus our primary knowledge of reality (Erlebnis) is dominated by value, and value is subjectively conceived. At the root then of all knowledge, even of knowledge of our own past, there is to be found that which we have characterized as a value-charged judgment. Can Dilthey escape the historical relativism which would seem to follow inevitably from such a view?

Before turning to his attempted answer we must,

[60] Cf., GS VII, 19 ff.
[61] GS VII, 73 f.
[62] GS VIII, 131.
[63] GS VI, 317; VII, 118 f., 241 f.

in fairness to Dilthey, examine his view of the second method (Verfahrungsweise) within the field of knowledge. This method is that of understanding.[64]

With understanding (Verstehen) the real problem of historical knowledge is, according to Dilthey, first begun. For immediate experience (Erlebnis) can at best give us only autobiography, and historical knowledge demands that we should have knowledge of life as experienced by others. What is this understanding and how does it proceed?

In three places, in almost identical terms, Dilthey has defined the understanding: "We call that activity 'understanding' in which we grasp an inner event (ein Inneres) through signs which come through the senses from outside." [65] In this, the understanding is a psychical act, depending on a sensuous symbol, and directed toward a knowledge of a psychical reality. This seems either a too narrow or a paradoxical use of the term understanding until we recall that the fundamental reality, life, is truly inward and psychical. With this in mind, it is clear how the goal of the understanding is knowledge of an inward sort.

But this knowledge is not to be directly attained; we grasp life best in grasping the forms in which spirit manifests its activity in the external world. This is Dilthey's doctrine of the objectification of life: [66] that in spiritual activity something of the nature of life is carried over into (hineinverlegt) its external

64 GS VII, 138.
65 GS V, 318; Cf., 332, and VII, 309.
66 GS VII, 146 ff., 319 ff.

manifestations. Thus in the comprehension of life, immediate experience (Erleben) is supplemented by this indirect knowledge called understanding (Verstehen) which grasps the nature of life through the manifestations of its activity. These manifestations possess historicity, and are in fact the historical materials. Now this indirect grasp of life, the understanding, according to Dilthey's definition of its nature, proceeds by symbols toward its goal. For that reason the problem of symbolic meaning was forced upon Dilthey, and with this problem he wrestled unsuccessfully over a period of years.

For him the symbolic expression and the thing symbolized were not two, in nature, but one.[67] But the problem of how this one could be grasped by an individual other than by him who gave expression to the symbol, never ceased to occupy Dilthey. And we can readily see how, on Dilthey's grounds, this difficult problem became inordinately complex. For the grasp of the symbolic meaning would demand the possibility of living into the experience of the individual who created the symbolic expression, since they are the same. But further this experience would have to be the immediate experience (Erlebnis) of that individual, since the symbolic expression was itself a creation of that experience. This difficulty Dilthey acknowledges, holding that understanding demands a re-experiencing (Nacherleben).[68] And this re-

[67] *GS* VII, 208.
[68] *GS* VII, 213 ff.

63

experiencing means, of course, experiencing a meaningful unity. But if meaningfulness is relative to the
valuations of the individual, and these valuations are
subjective (as we have seen), how is re-experiencing
possible? Here Dilthey brings forward the doctrine
of analogy: that we re-experience the experience of
another person because we perceive the similarity
of the external expressions of that experience to the
external expressions of certain of our own experiences.[69] But this is obviously circular, since re-experiencing has been brought in to explain communication of symbolic meaning, and a grasp of symbolic
meaning has been used to explain the possibility of
re-experiencing. The escape from this circle is furnished, however, in Dilthey's introduction of the
concept of objective spirit. For it is out of the realm
of objective spirit that we draw our own experience;
we and our language have been determined by it
from the outset.[70] Objective spirit is here a common
well from which we can only draw common symbols.
Thus the symbolic creations of the experience of one
individual can be grasped by another, and through
analogy the experience itself may be grasped. Thus
Dilthey seeks to explain the procedure of understanding. We must now see why this explanation, on
his own grounds, must break down.

In the first place, objective spirit is used by Dilthey
only in the sense of those multiform expressions of

[69] *GS* V, 276 f.
[70] *GS* VII, 208 f.

life which arise out of the common traits of individuals. But immediate experience, as we have seen, depends on subjective value factors; these factors may give rise to objective spirit whenever individuals stand over against each other as part of the external milieu. And, in fact, it is in this manner that Dilthey explains the psychological fact of communication.[71] But this, at best, means that only some experiences of other individuals can be understood: namely those experiences that we already understand because they are "just like" ours. Thus the doctrine of objective spirit (in Dilthey's works) is of no great help in making historical knowledge possible.

A second, and even more telling criticism, can be leveled against the idea that the objective spirit makes historical knowledge possible, in pointing out that since life, for Dilthey, is a constant flux, its manifestations, including those of the objective spirit, must also be constantly changing. And as a matter of fact we find (as did Hegel) that the forms of objective spirit (e.g., language) are constantly changing. This Dilthey himself recognizes, but the contradiction between the belief that individuals understand historical events through a common objective spirit, and the belief that the objective spirit, although continuous, is not the same in any two ages, was never solved by Dilthey. At best, the doctrine of objective spirit, viewed from this angle, can only give a knowledge of what our contemporaries (who share the same lan-

[71] GS VII, 207 f.

guage, and other objective forms with us) have experienced.

Thus the doctrine of objective spirit does not afford us a secure foundation for the explanation of how understanding is possible. Dilthey himself recognizes this fact, explicitly saying that there must always remain in the process of understanding an irrational, unclarified element, that, in the end, there is a final subjective feeling of certainty which cannot be transcended or rendered intelligible by logical means.[72]

We see, then, that Dilthey fails in his attempt to explain *how* historical understanding is possible, but this fact must not conceal from us the indisputable contribution which Dilthey made to the discussion of what the object of this historical understanding *is*. Herein, rather than in his theoretic contributions to a methodology of historical science, lies his historical importance and the fundamental greatness of his thought. But this greatness, in its turn, must not blind us to the insufficiencies which we have traced in his theory. To the end Dilthey was unwilling to give up the ideal of historical objectivity, yet he was forced to hold that the Geisteswissenschaften sought not to give a reproduction (Abschrift) of actuality, but rather to relate the historical materials to a value and meaning-charged whole. He sought for his desired objectivity through an emphasis on this act of relating, but his subjective theory of value made

[72] *GS* VII, 218.

any such objectivity impossible. The whole of our knowledge of the past, on Dilthey's theory, depends therefore upon present values; in this Dilthey is finally and inescapably a relativist.

MANNHEIM (1893-   )

Among the most influential of the recent upholders of historical relativism is Karl Mannheim. Although his work has probably not achieved its final form we are led to choose him for special consideration because few if any contemporary thinkers have brought to this problem the same vigor of thought, range of knowledge, and determination to follow where the argument leads.

Mannheim comes to the problem of historical knowledge through a healthy concern with its underlying issue: whether the sphere of the theoretic is or is not autonomous. Influenced by more or less activistic theories of knowledge and by the view (originally Marxian) that thought is determined by class interests, Mannheim takes up the problem of how, under these conditions, historical knowledge is possible. He attempts to hold throughout that it is possible, and he would not, as we shall see, be willing to call himself a relativist. For an understanding of his "solution" of the problem, and for a clear view of its essential untenability, we must examine the interrelated but incompatible concepts of "an ideology"

67

and "a sociology of knowledge" which Mannheim uses.

The term ideology has passed rapidly into currency, and it is one of the services of Mannheim's *Ideologie und Utopie* to have given a precise meaning to the term. According to Mannheim, when one characterizes a statement as ideological one implies that it is to be understood only by means of a reference to the conditions under which it was formulated and expressed. Thus we may view the same concrete mental content either as "idea" or as "ideology:" when we view it as an idea we are viewing it in itself, taking it at its face value; when we view it as an ideological statement we take into account the conditions under which it originated, understanding the statement in terms of these conditions. The term "ideology" taken in this sense may have either a specific or a general application. Specifically, an ideological statement contains a more or less conscious concealment of fact, due to the recognition on the part of the person making the statement that a true knowledge of the situation would run counter to his interests. A lie or a rationalization would be ideological in this specific sense. In the general sense an ideological judgment would be one the true grounds of which are not to be found in the judgment itself, but in certain unconscious presuppositions which are products of the conditions under which the person making the judgment stood. An example of this would be a historical work written under the influence of a reviving spirit of nationalism. The specific ideological judgment is thus a single statement (or limited set of statements) which conceals the truth, and such a concealing judgment can be exposed by pointing to the particular psychological conditions which led to it. A general ideology, on the contrary, is a complex of many specific judgments, the whole of which depends upon the noetic conditions (Bewusstseinsstruktur) under which it was formed. Different as are these two uses of the term "ideological" they have in common the fact that a knowledge of the conditions under which the expressed judgments were formed is a necessary step toward the "understanding" of their true significance.

The history of the concept of "ideology" throws some light on its significance.[78] Briefly, we may say that the term "ideological" was used to characterize judgments as false when their falsity was due to the interests of the person making the judgment. Thus the "understanding" of the true significance of the ideological judgment was an understanding both of its falsity and of the reasons why the false judgment was expressed. But the consideration of these reasons led to a wider consideration of the general conditions under which "concealing" judgments are formed. In this one is led from the concept of a specific to the concept of a general ideology. The difference may be found in contrasting the Machiavellian phrase that one thinks differently in the *palazzo* and the *piazza*

[78] Cf., *Ideologie and Utopie*, pp. 11 ff.

with the far-reaching Marxian analysis of all thought in terms of class interest. Yet even at the Marxian stage of analysis the falsity of the ideological judgment was emphasized. It was not until the concept of ideological judgments was also turned against the Marxists that the term ideology lost the connotation of falsity. For when all opponents can characterize each other as ideologists the question of "falsity" drops into the background, and "understanding" becomes merely the understanding of the relation between specific judgments and the points of view out of which they arise. It is at this stage of the development of the ideological concept that we find Mannheim. He is interested in "understanding" judgments (in particular, historical and political judgments) by grasping the relation of these judgments to a specific point of view.

That every judgment is related to a specific point of view in such a manner as to be unintelligible without an understanding of that point of view Mannheim holds to be a fact. This fact he calls the existential conditioning of thought (die Seinsverbundenheit des Denkens), and he makes clear its meaning in saying: "The existential conditioning of thought will pass as an established fact in those spheres of thinking in which it can be shown *a*) that the process of knowing does not develop historically according to 'immanent laws of development,' that it does not come into being led by 'the nature of the object itself' nor by 'pure logical possibilities,' nor that it is driven by an inner 'spiritual dialectic,' but that at very decisive points non-theoretical factors of various sorts (which one can call existential factors) determine the origin and form of that thought; b) that these determining existential factors are not merely of peripheral importance (are not 'merely genetically revelant') to the origin of the concrete content of that knowledge, but that they enter into its substance and form, its content and formulation, and determine the capacity and the intensity of apperception of the context of experience and observation which, in a word, we call the stylistic structure (Aspektstruktur) of knowledge." [74] It is because of this that an "understanding" of a general ideological judgment demands an understanding of the point of view which gave rise to it. Further, Mannheim places all historical works within the class of general ideological statements: "From the content of a mathematical proposition it cannot be immediately discovered when and where it was thought. As opposed to this, however, every person with a knowledge of historical writing can always, by an examination of any historical description which is presented to him, establish in what epoch, from what standpoint, out of what concrete cultural strivings the given, purely objective description was written. And this not merely in the trivial sense of the position which it assumes (Stellungnahme) but in the sense that the constitutive categories of its grasp of the

[74] *Wissenssoziologie,* pp. 660 b-661 a.

object are apparent." [75] It therefore follows that any understanding of the judgments contained in a historical work depends upon a relating of those judgments to the point of view of him who expressed them, and this point of view embraces the whole sum of the categories and the forms of his thought which were determined by existential factors. Thus, for example, to "understand" what Burckhardt has to say concerning the Renaissance we must relate his statements to the conditions of his own time. But to understand these we must go to another historian; yet the statements of this historian must then be related to the conditions of *his* time. In the end, it appears, no "understanding" of a historical statement will be possible, for the last series of statements must always be related to their times, and it is in the nature of contemporary categories to remain concealed. This essentially relativistic conclusion is a direct consequence of Mannheim's application of the concept of ideological judgments to all historical works.

Mannheim, however, attempts to escape this predicament into which his characterization of history has betrayed him by his theory of a sociology of knowledge (Wissenssoziologie). Before following him in this attempt we must inquire a little more closely into what he means by "the existential conditioning of thought."

Implicit in all of Mannheim's thought is the metaphysical hypothesis that man's nature, including his

[75] *Der Historismus, (Archiv für Sozw. und Sozp.,* v. 52, p. 22.)

rationality, emerges out of an interaction between himself as an organism and the external world. On the social level, where man is social and historical as well as biological, Mannheim recognizes that the external world is also social and historical; out of the interaction on this level arise the categories through which man grasps himself as a social and historical being. These categories of social and historical knowledge are to be understood only by relating them to the fundamental existential reality which determined their emergence; they are to be understood as an expression (Ausdruck) of the interrelation of thought and the external, non-rational, existential factors which determined it. For Mannheim, this interrelation is to be conceived in terms of valuations and will. These valuations and volitional elements have, naturally, no transcendent (non-existential) referents. Thus the categories of social and historical understanding which emerge in the historico-social process have their whole basis in the fact that an active, valuing subject (of somewhat indeterminate metaphysical nature) "lives into" an external world. In this, thought and action are not wholly disparate; thought and the modes of thinking, are brought within a larger, activistic framework. There are, therefore, three elements present in all ideological judgments: the social situation, the volitions, and the resultant thought. The social situation, the first of these elements, is not to be considered as a single entity but as the integration of many diverse factors;

Mannheim views it as the analogy of the term "constellation" as used in astrology, meaning thereby the copresence of many diverse elements all of which have bearing on the life of the individual involved. Further, the social situation so conceived is ever-changing. The volitions are individual and undergo changes and modifications according to the situation in which they are expressed; they are concrete and specific responses to situations, not to be understood in relation to any supposedly transcendent values. But it is with the third element of the ideological judgment that Mannheim chiefly concerns himself. This element, the thought which springs out of the relation of a valuing subject to an existential situation, Mannheim treats on the analogy of stylistic forms in art. This he sometimes calls "Denkstil," sometimes "Aspektstruktur." He identifies it as follows: "The stylistic structure of knowledge (Aspektstruktur) means in this sense the way in which a person sees an object, what he grasps in it and how a set of circumstances is construed by his thought. Style (in this sense) is therefore more than a merely formal determinant of thought; it is concerned with qualitative ingredients which must be neglected by a merely formal logic." [76] In short, the stylistic structure of thought is the system of categories with which a person or an age, pushed on by its purposes and limited by its social-historical situation, seeks to grasp the nature of the world.

The fact that the social situation is constantly

[76] *Wissenssoziologie,* p. 662 b.

changing leads inevitably to a plurality of ideologies, since these are but the resultants of the situation and the volitions which are aroused by it. Mannheim recognizes this: "The directly given is for us the dynamic change of the standpoints."[77] This plurality of ideologies cannot, however, be organized into a dialectical system of the synthesis of opposites; its dynamism is not of the rational type. For Mannheim the dynamic interplay of varying ideologies is to be understood only in his own sociological terms. It is his problem to show how these ideologies may be understood as the resultants of the social situation and the individual or collective will; this his sociology of knowledge attempts to do.

"The sociology of knowledge is a newly established discipline which as a theory attempts to establish and develop the teaching of the existential conditioning of knowledge, and as historical-sociological investigation attempts to expose this existential conditioning in the content of past and present knowledge."[78] Such is Mannheim's definition of a sociology of knowledge. As a method he considers it able to yield an "understanding" of any general ideology (e.g., any historical work). Such understanding, he claims, is impossible if we take the ideas expressed at their face value, for we may find other contradictory ideas equally widely held by other people. Thus the plurality of ideologies demands an indirect approach, an abandonment of

[77] *Das Problem einer Soziologie des Wissen (Archiv für Sozw. und Sozp.*, v. 53, p. 634).
[78] *Wissenssoziologie*, p. 659 a.

the method of treating ideas as if their significance transcended the situations out of which they arose. This indirection characterizes the method of a sociology of knowledge. This form of sociology proceeds by "relationism," by relating the ideas expressed to the concrete situation which led to their expression: "Relationism means . . . that it belongs to the nature of certain statements not to be formulable absolutely but only in relation to the stylistic structure determined by the situation." [79]

This method obviously opens the way for the criticism of Mannheim on the grounds of the "genetic fallacy," a criticism which Mannheim faces and attempts to overcome. His argument may merely be summarized here.[80] He holds, firstly, that the existential conditioning of certain judgments is a fact, and that it is also a fact that this conditioning is relevant to the meaning of those judgments. Secondly, he holds that the formulation of the "genetic fallacy," and its application to all judgments, was itself determined by existential elements, and must be so explained. Thirdly, he holds that the genetic fallacy is applicable only to certain types of attempts to understand judgments through existential conditioning. His philosophical justification for the second and third points in his position consists in a critical and in a constructive part. Critically he attempts to show that although the theory of knowledge is logically

[79] *Ibid.*, p. 666 b.
[80] *Cf.*, *Wissenssoziologie*, pp. 666-b-671 b; 673 b.

prior to any specific discipline, it is *merely* logically prior; that since these disciplines arise spontaneously out of a historical and social situation, without awaiting a demonstration of their possibility, they are genetically prior to a theory of knowledge. Further, he attempts to show that the theory of knowledge is always dependent for its formulation, and even for its conception of truth, on the stage of advancement of these genetically prior disciplines. With this critical "demonstration" he believes himself to have clinched his second point, and passes from the critical to the constructive portion of his justification. In this he attempts to show that the "genetic fallacy" (which was in fact brought to the forefront through Husserl's attack on psychologism) is applicable to psychologism, but not to the sociology of knowledge. Mannheim's argument here turns on his view that psychologism attempts to "explain" or "understand" the meaning of a judgment by reference to meaningless phenomena such as association. A sociology of knowledge, on the contrary, attempts to understand the meaning of a judgment by reference to a social phenomena and volitions which are meaning-charged. Thus the genetic fallacy may be applicable to psychologism, but not to Mannheim's theory.

We cannot concern ourselves with a critical discussion of this somewhat doubtful philosophical justification of the sociology of knowledge. We must, however, point out why it appears to be extremely doubtful. In the first place it is at best inconclusive,

77

for the critical portion consists merely in denying its opponent's position: if that position is correct Mannheim's argument is worthless; if incorrect, its incorrectness has not been shown. For a decision as between Mannheim and the upholders of the "genetic fallacy" one must examine both positions on a more ultimate metaphysical ground: this we cannot, of course, here attempt. But Mannheim's argument demands further criticism, since he has not attempted to show why associationism is meaningless (sinnfremd) while the social situation which molds our will and our thought is not. While the metaphysical differences between, let us say, the path of a nerve-current and the real wages of a group of laborers at a certain place and time may be very profound, we cannot assume lightly that the one has no relevance to the meaning of a judgment while the other has. This Mannheim apparently does.

On the assumption that Mannheim might have clearly established the philosophical validity of a sociology of knowledge (which he did not) we may turn to our most important problem: does the establishment of such a sociology make it possible to find "truth" in any historical work?

Mannheim insists that his position, while it is a relationism, permits of valid historical knowledge. It is not, he claims, a disguised form of relativism. He accepts a realistic position in regard to historical phenomena: the phenomena are what they are, regardless of the assertions made concerning them; it is not our assertions that determine them, but it is their actuality (Ansichsein) that determines our assertions. However, no assertion can grasp the actuality of the historical object itself, for every assertion is ideological, i.e., is determined by the social situation and the volitions of the historian. Mannheim tries to overcome the predicament which arises out of this situation by the introduction of his doctrine of perspectives. He holds that there are many perspectives on the same object, and that the historian is led, by the nature of the social situation in which he finds himself, to reveal the object through one of these perspectives rather than another. The conflict which then arises between the views of the object is not to be overcome by an appeal to a non-perspective theory, according to Mannheim, but in the attempt to show what conditioned the perspective, and therefore the view, in each case. As between these perspectives the choice will then lie with that perspective which gives the widest and most "fruitful" comprehension of the object.

To this solution of the problem of the objectivity of perspective knowledge we must take objection. It depends upon the ability not only to understand what gave rise to the perspective of your opponent, but to use his perspective, and to compare what it reveals with your own. If you are truly bound by your perspective it seems difficult to believe that this procedure is possible. Further, it holds up as a criterion a "fruitfulness" which can only be judged in terms of your own volitions, the very thing that led each of the opponents to a divergent view.

But Mannheim himself does not accept this method of gaining objectivity in historical judgments. He sees another means as possible and, although he does not seek to establish it as preferable to the first, he accepts it for himself.[81] This second way consists in establishing the relations of the judgments to their social-volitional bases, allowing each to show the merely perspective character of the other, thereby "neutralizing" them, and thus creating a wider and more general perspective that will include both.

This synthetic view, however, is also open to difficulties, for it gives us no guarantee of objectivity; the last view will always be the best. Mannheim's criticism of Troeltsch on this score [82] is equally applicable to him: he has not shown us a progress in historical knowledge. Nor is it possible, on his view, to show any such progress, for before we can predicate progress of a series we must know its goal, and this goal, the true account, is necessarily concealed from us by the perspectival character of our own knowledge. Further, it is doubtful whether the perspectives of another age can enter into our own perspective, on Mannheim's view of the matter. Even if we consider the conflicting historical accounts of other ages as part of our own situation (Seinslage) it can only be these accounts perspectively seen by us (not their own

[81] *Wissenssoziologie*, p. 676 a; *Ideologie und Utopie*, p. 164.
[82] *Der Historismus* (*Archiv für Sozw. u. Sozp.*, v. 52, p. 26 f.)

perspective) which enters into our judgments. This difficulty could only be avoided by holding either: *a*) that our situation was coextensive with these historical accounts, and therefore that they alone determined our perspective; or, *b*) that we can have objective knowledge of the perspectives of other ages. Mannheim, rightfully enough, would reject the first, but would accept the second. This raises the one fundamental difficulty in the whole of his attempt to escape the relativism implicit in his view of history as ideological in character.

It is Mannheim's underlying belief that the stylistic structure (Denkstil, or Aspektstruktur) of any general ideology may be objectively known. But, as we have seen, Mannheim means by this stylistic structure the resultant of the situation (Seinslage) and the volitions of the individual knower. Thus in order to understand this structure we would have to view it as a product of the situations and volitions. But to do this we would have to possess prior knowledge which can only come to us through the mediation of the stylistic structure itself. How then is a sociology of knowledge possible? Apparently it would be possible if we had an immediate insight into the nature of stylistic structures of thought, but in so far as we ourselves are perspectively limited in our acts of knowing even an immediate insight rather than a genetic "understanding" would not yield the stylistic structure itself. With this problem it may truthfully be said that Mannheim never wrestles: he assumes the objectivity of our knowledge of the stylistic structure of thought. But this also implies an objective knowledge of the conditions which produced it if it is to be considered as a resultant of historico-social processes. Thus in so far as the stylistic structure of thought is not a mere essence, but an actual historical product, a knowledge of it presupposes the possibility of attaining objective historical truth.

Put in another way we may say that our earlier criticism of the regress in Mannheim's theory is only escaped by a belief in the possibility of an objective knowledge of the stylistic structure inherent in the thought of an age. But this possibility involves us in holding that we ourselves are not limited by the stylistic structure of our own thought. Further, if we are to understand the stylistic structure of any thought in genetic terms we must first possess objective historical knowledge. Here we can see the ultimate incompatibility of the ideological doctrine with a belief in the sociology of knowledge. Mannheim's ideological doctrine is wholly relativistic; his attempt to substitute relationism for relativism by means of a sociology of knowledge leads him to assume what he had previously denied: the possibility of objective historical knowledge. Along with Croce and Dilthey, Mannheim thus demonstrates the ultimate futility of any attempt to escape the consequences of historical relativism once the philosophic basis of that relativism is accepted.

CHAPTER III

The Presuppositions Of Historical Relativism

In the preceding chapter we have discussed three representative expositions of the relativistic position, and it is now in place to interpret these expositions to the reader, seeking to find that which is held in common by them. In this way we shall be able to make clear the basic philosophic presuppositions on which any relativistic theory of history rests.

As a guiding thread for our discussion we may revert to our previous generalized statement of historical relativism. It will be remembered that we indicated three points at which relativistic criticism of historical knowledge might set in. Let us now examine the thought of Croce, Dilthey, and Mannheim with respect to each of these points.

It is significant that not one of the three men with whom we have dealt makes use of the first of the relativistic arguments in any of its variant forms. This is not surprising for the argument itself is based upon a fundamental and obvious fallacy. It seeks to show that a historical work cannot be held to be objectively true because it is always poorer in content than is the portion of the actual historical process with which it purports to deal. The fallacy in this consists in the attempt to identify the knowledge which we may be said to have concerning some object with all of the characteristics of that object. Such an identification is fundamentally out of keeping with the nature of knowledge in any and every field of human experience. When a person claims to have knowledge of an object he does not necessarily believe that he apprehends the nature of every one of that object's characteristics. In the knowing relationship we are always aware that the object-to-be-known transcends that which we know concerning it; we seek to grasp the nature of an object by successively apprehending various of its characteristics. We are always aware that these characteristics do not exhaust all that might possibly be said concerning it, yet with each successive step in our apprehension we feel that we have actually gained knowledge. The fact that there may be many characteristics of an object which we do not know, and which we never shall know, does not alter our conviction that we may have gained real insight into the nature of that object through the steps which we have already taken. Thus, when I say that I know something about John Jones, I mean that I know *something* about him, and I feel that what I know may be true regardless of how much there may be concerning him that I do not know. I may, for example, know that John Jones is a certified public accountant, and yet not know that he has recently undergone an appendectomy; I may know that he has a daughter Emma, but I may not know who his parents were. The fact that I do not know that he has undergone an appendectomy does not make any the less true my statement that he is a certified public accountant, and my knowledge that he has a daughter Emma is not in the least affected by my ignorance of the names of his parents, their ages, nor the number of other children that they may have had. And the same situation applies to the historian's enterprise. The historian may know that Columbus landed at "San Salvador" without knowing everything that pertained to that landing, such as the exact time at which the landing was effected. And we may gather knowledge concerning that landing from the historian's work even if his work does not state everything which he himself actually knows, for example, the approximate time at which the landing was made. And, finally, we may know that Columbus landed at "San Salvador" even if we do not experience any emotional impact from the fact as recorded by the historian, or even if we receive an emotional impact different from that which Columbus experienced, or in fact different from that experienced by any other person who has ever known the point in the western hemisphere at which Columbus did land. And, further, we can say that the historian's statement that Columbus landed at "San Salvador" remains true even if the historian ascribes to Columbus no particular emotions, or emotions which Columbus did not feel on that occasion.

The foregoing statements demand only two qualifications concerning the relation of one bit of knowledge to another. First, that although an error on the historian's part may have no bearing on the truth or falsity of another statement made by the same historian it may reveal inadequacies in his methods of investigation, and thus give rise to a presumptive doubt on our part concerning certain other of his statements. Second, there are cases in which the falsity of one statement *is* relevant to the truth or falsity of another statement. In such a case it is impossible to know that we have made a true statement concerning one aspect of an empirical reality without also knowing that we have made a true statement concerning the other. With these two qualifications made we can revert to our original contention: that the historical relativist who rests his argument on the relative paucity of content in every historical description is guilty of a false identification of the knowledge which we have of an object with the object known.

As we have pointed out, neither Croce, Dilthey, nor Mannheim is guilty of this false identification. We may say therefore that it is not one of the basic philosophic presuppositions of historical relativism, even though it has often been used to support the relativistic position. This being the case, our refutation of this particular argument affords no escape from historical relativism, and we may well turn to a consideration of other forms of argument which have been brought forward.

The second argument which we discussed in our generalized statement of the relativistic position contended that all historical accounts were falsifications of the historical process since the continuity and structure which they depicted were not characteristic of that process. This argument, it will be remembered, assumed two divergent forms. In the one it was claimed on supposedly empirical grounds that the historical process itself contained no structure whatsoever, that the structure found in historical works was infused by the historian himself. In the other it was claimed that the process itself was structured, but not in the manner which historical works revealed.

It is not surprising that none of the three men here to be considered accepts the first form of this relativistic argument, for the argument rests upon an obvious misstatement of fact. If one tries on empirical grounds to uphold the contention that the historical process is in itself structureless one is immediately faced with the problem of explaining away our apparently naïve and spontaneous discriminations. That one event is seen as having a bearing upon another is simply and directly a fact of experience. That the hammer in hitting the nail drives the nail into the board, or that recent German and Italian policy were responsible for the increased armament program of Britain—these are events whose structured and continuous aspects are given us in our immediate experience of them. Only a metaphysics (such as Rickert's) could hold that the historical material is in itself formless. So far as direct experience is concerned, that which we know as the historical process is characterized, to a degree at least, by structure and continuity. No appeal to "experience" can therefore establish historical relativism in this fashion. Since this is the case, and since it is clear that none of the three men with whom we are here dealing would accept this method of argumentation, we may dismiss this appeal to experience as providing no adequate ground for relativism.

It is now in place to examine the second form of this relativistic argument. We have seen that it has sometimes been contended on metaphysical grounds that every historical account in some sense falsifies the true structure and continuity of the historical process. We shall here attempt to show that this view, which was shared by Bradley, Beard, Bergson, and Stern, must rest upon one specific philosophic doctrine. We shall show that this doctrine is also characteristic of Croce, Dilthey, and Mannheim, and consequently may be claimed to be a basic presupposition of historical relativism. The doctrine to which we refer, and which we shall now try to isolate, holds that historical knowledge is to be understood and estimated with reference to its setting in the historical process.

This doctrine can best be understood as being one particular manifestation of that which has been called historicism (Historismus). Historicism consists in the attempt to take seriously (in a philosophic sense) the fact of change. It sees behind every particular fact the one ultimate fact of change: every particular is treated with relation to the process of change out of which it arises, and this process is seen as immanent in it. This view of the world may express itself in many variant forms. Perhaps the most common is that which holds every set of cultural values to be relative to the age in which it is dominant. This form of historicism, which we may best speak of as the historicity of values, is often identified with historicism as such.[1] However, there is also a prevalent form of historicism which we may call that of knowledge, and it is with this form that we are here dealing. With respect to knowledge, historicism claims that no statement can be considered true or false without reference to the time at which it was formulated; for it, like every other entity, must be understood in the light of the ever-changing process of history. Although this view has long been given up with reference to such statements as the natural scientist makes, it is still held to apply to historical accounts. Our task in this connection lies in the attempt to show that it is this form of historicism which is basic to the argument that the structure and continuity of the historian's work do not reflect the structure and continuity of the historical process itself.

It is obvious that the element of relativity which

---

[1] *Cf.*, Troeltsch: *Der Historismus und seine Probleme*, p. 68 f.; also, Rickert: *Probleme der Geschichtsphilosophie*, pp. 129 ff.

is introduced into Stern's and Bergson's views by the "plastic" nature of the past bears out our contention. For in so far as the past is plastic, being formed by the future, the historian's view of the past will be relative to the position at which he stands in the historical process: he will only be able to see the past as he and his predecessors have shaped it. Precisely the same relativistic doctrine is implicit in Bradley's contention that every historical object endures as far as it extends its influence. For, if a historical object endures as long as its influence endures, the historian's vision of that object is relative to his position in history; he can know its complete nature only as it is manifested up to that point in time at which he stands. It is this insistence upon viewing knowledge with respect to its temporal origin that is basic in the relativist's contention that no historical account can be adequate to the actual structure and continuity of historical events.

Such an argument might be validated on metaphysical grounds similar to those advanced by Stern, Bergson, or Bradley. The argument cannot, however, be substantiated through any appeal to empirical facts of history. Yet Beard's monistic view seems to be based upon empirical grounds. He contends that in selecting merely one segment of the historical process for consideration the historian is guilty of "cutting off connections with the universal." [2] The

---

[2] *Written History as an Act of Faith* (*American Historical Review*, v. 39, p. 228; cited above, p. 28).

implication is that *as a matter of empirical fact* the historical process is a continuous and completely interrelated "One." But such a view can not be derived from a study of history and at the same time be used to deny the possibility of historical knowledge; the relativist must establish it upon metaphysical grounds.

But here it must be pointed out that even if a general metaphysical monism is established, such a monism does not entail historical relativism. The empirical historian is not concerned with the ultimate nature of the universe, but with the concrete manifestations of history. There may be an ultimate underlying unity in the historical process, but the historian will never be able to discover it, for he is concerned merely with the actual temporal processes discernible. On empirical grounds he could at best show that these processes manifest a marked unity. Thus even the introduction of an ultimate, or metaphysical, monism could not establish historical relativism as Beard sought to establish it. Relativism follows not from monism as such, but from those more specific metaphysical doctrines which demand that every work should be estimated with respect to its position in the historical process. This conclusion can be substantiated through an examination of the thought of Dilthey.

Dilthey held that the historical process, metaphysically considered, is an ultimate ever-changing One, immanent in all of its "objectifications" (that is,

91

concrete manifestations). This ultimate and temporal One he called Life itself. To understand reality would be to understand this One, and no understanding which falls short of this goal is ultimate. However, the historian is not concerned with Life as such, but with its concrete manifestations. These are not illusory for Dilthey, and a knowledge of them is therefore truly knowledge even though it is not a direct apprehension of metaphysical truth. Thus by means of this distinction (which must be drawn if one is a metaphysical monist) Dilthey sought to escape historical relativism without abandoning his view that reality was ultimately one and continuous.

However, as we have seen, Dilthey's attempt to overcome relativism terminated in failure, and it will be of interest to note the fundamental cause of this failure. It suffices to point out that the breakdown of historical objectivity enters his thinking because he attempted to interpret the understanding (das Verstehen) as itself an objectification of this essentially irrational and unknowable Life. Having sought to save historical objectivity by a distinction between the ultimate historical process and the objectifications of that process, he reverted to a point of view which demanded that he treat "the understanding" in relation to the ultimate experience, the Life, out of which it arose. Thus in the end Dilthey fails in his attempt to save historical objectivity, for he refuses to consider the fact of understanding as it is in itself; he seeks to interpret it as a manifestation of Life.

What we have seen with respect to Dilthey can further be substantiated through a consideration of Croce. It is not metaphysical monism as such which establishes relativism in Croce's view of historical knowledge; in fact, he attempts to escape a complete relativism by an appeal to the Absolute. Relativism enters his system because the particular form of idealistic monism to which he holds demands that he should consider all knowledge as a spiritual act. He therefore insists that knowledge can only be understood in relation to its source, the absolute, immanent, historical One. This One, or Spirit, makes its object by its own activity, and the object itself, once posited, is still unreal except in so far as it is remade —posited again—by Spirit. This of course makes it impossible to separate out the objects of knowledge from the ultimate process of reality; all knowledge must be understood with reference to its origin. Since Croce conceives of the ultimate Spirit as ever-changing, every attempt to gain knowledge must be understood with reference to its own place in the historical process. It is thus that Croce establishes his relativism. Once again we see that it is not metaphysical monism as such, but a particular view as to the nature of all estimates of knowledge that gives rise to historical relativism.

This can also be seen with reference to the theory of Mannheim. Mannheim nowhere acknowledges that he is a metaphysical monist, and it seems unlikely to one familiar with his works that he would accept any such metaphysical view. Yet Mannheim's theory becomes relativistic at precisely the same point as do those of Dilthey and Croce: he seeks to understand the validity of knowledge in terms of the relation between the knower and the historical process of which he is a part. Knowledge for him is to be understood as a "living into" a particular historical situation, and it is out of this that his theory of "standpoints" or "perspectives" grows. On this view we cease to inquire whether a historical work is true or false in itself; we attempt to "understand" it with reference to the historical conditions under which it was formed. As we have seen, such an interpretation of historical works is essentially and inescapably relativistic.

It should be clear that we have now isolated a basic philosophic presupposition of historical relativism. This presupposition consists in the view that knowledge can only be understood and estimated with reference to its place in the historical process. Such a view was seen to be fundamental not only in the thought of Croce, Dilthey, and Mannheim, but to underlie the frequently expressed view that every historical account falsifies the continuity of the historical process. For we have pointed out that the latter view cannot be established on empirical grounds, nor can it be said to follow directly from metaphysical monism. It must follow from the attempt to estimate a historical work in terms of its place in the historical process. As a consequence of the pervasiveness of this attempt, and because of the inevitability with which relativism follows from it, we are justified in terming it a basic presupposition of the relativistic doctrine.

We shall not here attempt to attack the validity of this first presupposition of historical relativism. Unlike the earlier arguments with which we have dealt, this position represents a thoroughly serious attempt to deal with the problem of historical knowledge; it cannot therefore be lightly dismissed. Further, it has so much in common with the third general form which relativism takes that it will be better to defer critical comment until we are in a position to deal with both at the same time.[3]

It will be remembered that the third form of the argument in support of historical relativism is to be found in the contention that all historical judgments are value-charged and cannot therefore be objectively valid. Like the preceding point of view, this contention is central in the theories of the three men with whom we are here primarily concerned; it too may be said to constitute a basic presupposition of historical relativism.

The argument that historical judgments are not objective because they are value-charged may assume many forms. For example, it may consist in an empirical pointing-out of distortions of fact and of in-

[3] *Cf.*, Chapter VII.

terpretation due to the personal or cultural biases of particular historians. Yet such an empirical argument is not in itself sufficient to establish the position of historical relativism. To be an acceptable position relativism must rest on some general principle which shows that all historical accounts are necessarily distorted by valuational factors within them. It is now our task to inquire into the basic philosophic presuppositions of such a principle.

If we compare the thought of Croce, Dilthey and Mannheim in regard to the valuational factors in historical knowledge we find that each holds that the act by means of which the historian grasps the past is an interpretative act. By an interpretative act is here meant a unification of specific "facts" into a meaningful whole. This we can see in Croce's insistence on the distinction between history and chronicle, in Dilthey's use of the category of meaningfulness, and in Mannheim's concern with the "stylistic structure" (Denkstil or Aspektstruktur) of the thought which arises from any general ideology. In their divergent theories this interpretative aspect of the act of historical knowing plays an identical rôle. In each case we find the claim put forward that every historical account carries the impress of a unifying interpretative principle which is the product of the historian's activity. In Croce history, as distinct from chronicle, is a spiritual act springing directly from the interests of the present; in Dilthey the meaningfulness which determines the unitary

96

structure of an object of historical knowledge is given by the relation between the portions of that object and the historian's own desires, goal, or will; Mannheim interprets the stylistic structure of thought in terms of an active valuing subject "living into" an external world. Thus all three agree in this: that every historical account is the result of an interpretative act, and that the interpretative principle to be found in that act is a product of the historian's own interests.

If we examine this common element in the thought of the three relativists with whom we have been dealing, we find that it implicitly contains two basic elements. The first of these takes the form of an insistence that the "interpretation" of facts is to be understood as proceeding from the side of the subject, rather than being forced upon the subject by the nature of the material with which he is dealing. And it is only natural that if interpretation is imposed on the material by the subject that this interpretation will be a reflection of the subject's own interests.

The second of the elements implicit in this view is the interpretation of these valuational factors (the subject's own interests) in terms of a naturalistic theory of value. By that is meant the interpretation of every valuation in terms of the individual's interest in an object, and in no other terms. Such a theory is opposed to every attempt to hold that values in some sense exist independently of specific valuational judgments. We have seen that for Dilthey and for Mannheim valuation is to be understood simply as the expression of a subject's interest in an object, that there is no objective value which the subject "comprehends." Thus for them value is constituted by the fact that a subject desires an object; this is sufficient to characterize that object as a value (or, of value). The same holds true of Croce's theory of value,[4] although, for the sake of brevity, we did not in our previous treatment of Croce deal with it.

This second element, taken in connection with the first, is extremely important for the argument that valuational factors distort every historical account. For if it could be shown that the interests of the subject which guide his historical interpretations are universal and necessarily valid recognitions of some transcendent cultural values, then the historical account itself would not be distorted by the valuational factors involved. In that case every historical account, while dictated by values, would be "objective" in the sense that it would be recognized as "true" by all other historians. And this, in fact, is the chief line of argument which has been taken by the opponents of historical relativism. However, the historical relativist would with great vehemence seek to deny that any values are objectively valid for all.

To summarize our argument in the present chapter we may say that in comparing our generalized

---

[4] For the best statement of Croce's theory of value see his *"Ueber die sogenannten Werturteile"* (Logos, v. I, pp. 71 ff.).

statement of the position of historical relativism with the concrete teachings of Croce, Dilthey, and Mannheim we have found that these writers have embraced two of the traditional forms of the relativistic argument. Not one of the three has put forward his relativism on the grounds which some relativists have tended to emphasize: the "incompleteness" of the material contained in a historical account. In this respect Croce, Dilthey, and Mannheim have done well. The argument based upon "incompleteness" contains a basic philosophic fallacy and is easily overcome by pointing out that knowledge may be considered as valid even though it does not mirror the complete nature of the reality with which it deals.[5] At the same time the other two positions which are characteristic of relativism have been based upon philosophic assumptions which merit more detailed consideration. We may here restate what we take the nature of these assumptions to be.

We have examined the view which holds that the actual structure and continuity of the historical process is falsely represented in every historical work; we have found that this view can only be defended on the assumption that every attempt to gain knowledge is relative to its place in the historical process. This assumption of historicism with respect to knowledge we have called the first basic presupposition of

[5] We have therefore dismissed it as an argument for relativism. It is none the less incumbent upon us to reveal the true nature of the historian's "selective" procedure, showing on what factors this supposed "incompleteness" actually rests. This analysis is to be found primarily in Chapter VIII.

historical relativism. The second basic presupposition of relativism we have found to reside in the view that every historical account is dependent upon historically conditioned valuational factors. This presupposition is supplementary to the first; it seeks to point out the precise nature of the factors in the historical flux which most largely determine the relativity of every historical account. By virtue of the fact that this second presupposition permits the relativist to appeal directly to the historian's procedure, rather than demanding a purely metaphysical exposition, it has always been the most popular, most characteristic, and strongest argument for historical relativism.

CHAPTER IV

Four Counter-Relativists

FOLLOWING the procedure previously adopted we shall now present separately several attempts to overcome the doctrine of historical relativism. These attempts, like the relativistic doctrines which they seek to combat, have a common root; when examined together they also possess an inward dialectic. But the present chapter will merely present these views in their most logical order, leaving it to Chapter V to draw together the strands of our discussion and formulate the outcome of the present argument.

SIMMEL (1858-1915)

The work of Georg Simmel provides a fruitful starting point for our examination of some of the more important attempts which have been made to escape historical relativism. Chronologically the first edition of *Die Probleme der Geschichtsphilosophie* (1892) stands almost at the beginning of the debate, although it is not until the third edition (1907) that Simmel's essential position emerges. By virtue of the characteristic intensity with which the problem of relativism is faced this work is still one of the most readable and psychologically compelling books in the literature of our problem. Yet even its last revised editions show that Simmel's position remained unclarified, in that the examples, analogies, and aphorisms with which they abound conceal unsolved problems on every hand.

The starting point of Simmel lies in his acceptance of a Kantian theory of knowledge. Like Kant, Simmel holds that if we ask ourselves how knowledge is possible within a given field of experience we find that the mind creates that knowledge through its own activity, forming by means of its own categories the material which is presented to it. It is Simmel's view that if the categories of historical understanding were laid bare it would be seen that history as we know it is a product of our mind's activity, and that, having recognized this fact, we could the more readily give up that search for objectivity which leads inevitably to historical scepticism. Simmel, like Kant, attempts to hold that the only real objectivity to be attained in knowledge lies in the internal necessity of thought. He does not, however, hold that the Kantian table of categories is adequate to account for historical knowledge. With some justice he argues that Kant's table of categories provides only for natural-scientific knowledge, and offers no clues as to how historical description and explanation necessarily proceed. By uncovering the specific categories of historical understanding Simmel hopes to show that although historical knowledge is not a mirror-image of history it is not relative to the standpoint of the age in which it is written; on his view it is only relative to the universal and necessary categories out of which all written history springs. Thus Simmel at one and the same time seeks to undermine both the Rankian ideal of historical objectivity and the relativistic assertion that each age must create past history anew. In order to come to an estimate of Simmel's success in this undertaking we must first examine what he takes to be the material of historical knowledge and then turn to an examination of the categories on the basis of which this material is formed.

For Simmel the material which enters into historical knowledge is comprised wholly of human experience; unless an occurrence is human that occurrence is not material which can be formed into a history. On this point he goes far beyond the statements usually made concerning the material of historical knowledge. Whereas many persons delimit history (as a separate discipline) with reference to occurrences which are human in *either* character or influence, Simmel holds that the material of history is wholly human (psychological) in character; that all historical accounts are concrete descriptions and explanations of nothing but human feelings, thoughts, and acts of will; that the only external events which appear in the field of history appear as they are reflected in the inner experience of the individuals or groups who participate in them. He says, "All outer occurrences, political and social, economic and religious, legal and technical, would be neither interesting nor intelligible to us if they did not result from or give rise to psychical reactions (Seelenbewegungen)." [1] Thus all of the external events of man's life, including the forms of his social organization, enter into a historical account merely as bridges between the impulses and feeling of different individuals. This radical delimitation of the field of history transforms what is usually thought of as historical inquiry into an attempt to grasp and interpret the realm of psychological fact. But, if this be the case, what distinguishes history from the field of psychology?

Simmel is able to distinguish between the disciplines of history and psychology by means of his insistence on the individual, concrete nature of historical understanding as against the generalizing procedure of the natural sciences, among which psychology is to be numbered. To this first and major difference in the formulation of historical and psychological knowledge other differences may be added. The psychologist, for example, is not so much interested in the content of psychical experiences as he is in the process by means of which that content is experienced, whereas the historian is not interested in how it happens that a given content of consciousness was experienced but rather in *what* that content was. Simmel expresses this difference when he says, "For history it is not so much a question of the *development* of psychical content, as of the psychical

<hr/>

[1] *Die Probleme der Geschichtsphilosophie,* p. 1.

development of content." [2] However unclear this may be, he adds to it a third difference between history and psychology. He holds that psychology is interested in the genetic explanation of *all* psychical content, whereas history is interested in a description of only such content as falls under the concept of political activity, diplomacy, or the like. By this means he is finally able to separate psychology and history, even though holding that the material of historical inquiry is wholly to be found within the realm of psychical (psychological) experience.

We have now before us the nature of the historical material as Simmel conceives it, but we have not seen how this material arises into the consciousness of the historian. It is clear that a historian's material is not confined to his personal experiences. It follows therefore that he must gain that material which his mind is to form into a historical narrative by virtue of an awareness of the psychical data of others (a transsubjective awareness). Simmel explains this awareness by postulating a combination of sympathetic understanding (mitfühlen) and a direct feeling of transsubjectivity (Gefühl des Uebersubjektiven). In dealing with the first aspect of this process of awareness, he comes perilously close to the traditional view of an analogical judgment as the basis for our understanding of others: "He who has never loved will never understand the lover, a choleric temperament will never understand a phlegmatic one ... and,

2 *Die Probleme der Geschichtsphilosophie*, p. 39.

conversely, we will more readily understand the
movements, expressions and actions of others the
more often we ourselves have experienced those affections for which these are the symbols." [3] Thus, on
the basis of our own experience we apprehend the
elements of the psychical life of others, according to
Simmel. But he holds that this apprehension must be
supplemented by a further element if we are really
to understand the personality of others. It is not
enough for the historian to grasp elements of consciousness, he must also see how these elements are
fitted together into that whole which is the true personality of the subject. As the necessary supplement
to merely sympathetic apprehension (mitfühlen) Simmel brings forward the category of a direct feeling
of transsubjectivity. He means by this the apprehension of the given psychical manifold as part of
the experience of another. In order that this feeling
should be present we must be able to consider that
experience as "typical." For Simmel contends that
the only way in which we can know that a contemplated psychical manifold is not merely a part of our
own experience, but also belongs to another, is to
see that the elements comprising it fit together in a
fashion which is not explicable on the basis of the
partiality and accidental conditions of our own subjective psychical life. To make this clear he uses the
analogy of a poem: the only way in which we know
the "rightness" of a poem (the validity of its internal

[3] *Die Probleme der Geschichtsphilosophie,* p. 39.

structure) is through its "universality," that is through its "consistently imaginable character." [4] So too in the apprehension of the psychical life of another person: we are convinced of the validity of our apprehension only because we have the feeling that here is a set of psychical elements which fit together in a thoroughly intelligible fashion, that is, in a fashion which we think to be typical of the way in which the psychical life of an individual unfolds.

On this theory of the manner in which we apprehend the experience of others rests the whole of Simmel's attempt to deal with the methodology of history. Simmel holds that since the material of history is nothing but the apprehension of psychical experience in its concreteness and individuality, whatever shows us the nature of such experience gives us history. The fundamental categories of historical understanding are therefore those forms of cognition in which the unity of the concrete individuality in question is apprehended. Simmel does not, however, give us much detailed analysis of the precise nature of these categories. We may best take the classification of them given by Troeltsch,[5] according to which there are four: selection (Auslese), individuality (Individualität), totality (Totalität), and meaningfulness (Sinndeutung or Sinnbeziehung). These are the categories which form the material given in psychical experience. This psychical experience may be either

[4] For this definition of aesthetic universality, *Cf*. E. F. Carritt: *Theory of Beauty*, p. 83.
[5] Troeltsch: *Der Historismus und seine Probleme*, p. 578.

one's own experience or that of another; in either case as *mere* experience it is essentially formless, as *known* experience these categories are implicit in it. Let us take as an example the rôle which selection plays in giving form to a concrete bit of historical writing. A historian dealing with the life of a diplomat is interested in tracing the development of those psychical experiences which relate to the diplomatic activity of his subject. But to follow out such a development the historian must select from the total experience of his subject only those elements which have bearing on the particular content in question, that is, only those feelings and volitions which can be subsumed under the concept of diplomacy. In actuality these psychical experiences were crossed and recrossed by many other experiences; in a historical work they stand out as an isolated continuity. Every historical work shows just such a continuity, and thus selection may be said to be a necessary category of historical knowledge.

The second category of historical knowledge, that of individuality, can be seen to be necessary by the fact that every historical account has two characteristics: first, it springs from a theoretic interest in certain of the revealed contents of a historian's experience (e.g., Ranke's awareness of the German Reformation) and second, it must possess unity. The historian is only able to give unity to the material of which he is aware by means of linking it to the psychical experience of one individual, or by postulating a group-soul. In either case he is forming the material of which he is aware around the central core of a single individuality, and individuality becomes a category for the forming of experience into a historical account.

Closely allied with the category of individuality we find the category of totality. As we have just seen, Simmel holds that the historian must in every case gather together the psychical experience of which he is aware around the core of an individual or of a group-soul. In so doing he seeks to portray the essential character of an individual or group-individual. This attempt to understand the individual demands a synthesis of experienced elements into a totality, and this is the third category of historical knowledge. This category of totality is nothing but an expression of the historian's interest in giving a complete picture of the individual being around whom he has centered the psychical data of which he has become aware; it is nothing, that is, but the expression of a necessary attempt on the part of the mind to fill out with real flesh and blood the individual skeleton which stands at the core of a historical narrative.

The fourth category, meaningfulness, is in turn involved in the others already mentioned, since the attempt to contemplate as a single living whole an individual whose experiences are successive in time demands that we see one portion of this experience as relevant to another. It is this which Simmel apparently intends by the term meaningfulness.

Let us now see where these distinct but interlocking categories are to be found in historical writing. Let us take as an example the history of European painting. If the historian is to produce a history in Simmel's sense he cannot, it is clear, be content with giving an account of works of art merely as created objects; he must rather deal with those works in relation to the *consciousness* (Zeitgeist) of the times in which they were created. And here he must utilize selection, for it is evident that not all of the works of the times, nor all of the psychical effects of any particular work are to be considered in his history. The precise nature of the selection which the historian makes from among all the material at his disposal depends upon the three other categories with which it is connected. For the selection is made with reference to the individuality which the historian seeks to describe. In this case—the history of European painting—it is clear that the individuality in question is not that of a single person, but is a collective individuality (the European psyche) or else a succession of such collective individualities (the Mediaeval, Renaissance, etc.) Thus where the historian does not find an individual at the core of history he postulates the existence of one. But this individuality leads beyond itself into the category of totality. Once seen as the core of history the individual must be portrayed as a single whole which includes all of the elements which the historian is forced to consider. The European or the Renaissance spirit becomes more than a skeleton around which history is built, for the history becomes a history of that spirit, and all elements must be fitted together as aspects of its total development. Simmel himself recognizes that this on occasion demands a certain forcing of the material, and he is willing to admit the appeal to an unconscious will residing in the group where no other hypothesis can bring the material together into a totality.[6] This procedure, which seems to run counter to the whole notion of historical accuracy, would be defended by Simmel on the ground that only by means of some postulate could these diverse elements be rendered intelligible, and therefore that an apparent forcing is in such cases demanded by the category of meaningfulness. This last is, it appears, the ultimate category of the historical understanding, giving order to the other categories which we have been discussing. For it is evident that on Simmel's Kantian grounds the whole nature of the knowing activity is to bring intelligibility into the formless and hence unintelligible realm of mere experience. And historical understanding, which is by nature the apprehension of the development of psychical content, must proceed by selecting its material on the basis of the meaningfulness of that development as a whole. A history such as the history of European painting would therefore be so constructed as to show the significance of each aspect of the European spirit for the development of that spirit itself.

[6] *Die Probleme der Geschichtsphilosophie,* p. 20 f.

If we ask what objectivity Simmel ascribes to history as thus written we find that his answer is thoroughly Kantian. History as known is the result of spiritual activity; it is no copy of mere experience. The categories which are presupposed by historical writing are sufficient guarantees of universality for they are nothing but the manifestations of those "inner energies" which form sensuous material into knowledge.[7] Thus historical knowledge, like all other knowledge, is epistemologically objective even though it is metaphysically subjective. When Simmel comes to the explanation of this epistemological objectivity he appeals, as we have noted, to the direct feeling of transsubjectivity. In order to show how the categories which we have just been discussing provide a guarantee for objectivity we must see the relation in which they stand to the feeling of transsubjectivity.

It will be recalled that in dealing with the historian's awareness of the psychical content of another person's experience Simmel depended upon a postulated sympathetic understanding and a direct feeling of transsubjectivity. The latter, he held, is a result of our awareness that this set of psychical data belong together independently of our apprehending them together: that, as in the case of a poem, the internal consistency of the given elements provides a guarantee that the object whose elements they are considered to be is not a product of our own individual

[7] *Die Probleme der Geschichtsphilosophie,* p. 10 f.

modes of experiencing. This being the case, it can be seen that the feeling of transsubjectivity rests upon the categories with which we have been dealing, since it is they which give to our experiencing its unity and meaningfulness, that is, its internal consistency. It is in this sense that Simmel claims that the categories of historical understanding guarantee historical objectivity.

In brief Simmel's argument has been that no historical work is able to reproduce actual experience without radically transforming it. He holds, however, that such a transformation proceeds according to apriori categories, and that these categories provide a guarantee that the knowledge which results from their employment is not limited by the personality and period of the historian. This guarantee is expressed in the form of a direct feeling of transsubjectivity. This feeling is a product of the categories and is, at the same time, the test by means of which the historian measures his objectivity.

Let us now see to what extent Simmel has overcome historical relativism and presented an adequate alternative to it. Our estimate of Simmel's work on this score will necessarily depend upon a threefold appraisal: first, whether Simmel's account of the manner in which we gain access to the material of history is safe against the onslaught of relativism; second, whether the categories by means of which Simmel hopes to guarantee objectivity do in fact serve as a sufficient guarantee; and, third, whether

Simmel's account of the nature of historical knowledge is in itself, apart from all questions of relativism, an adequate account.

It is in the first place clear that Simmel's account of how we gain a knowledge of other selves, that is, how we attain to an awareness of the material of historical knowledge, is not psychologically plausible. The circularity of an appeal to an analogical judgment on which our awareness of other selves is supposedly based has often been pointed out. But Simmel, it will be recalled, held that the material for history was not derived simply from such analogical judgments. Although those judgments are the sole means by which the historian becomes aware of the content of historical events, his recognition of the historical (non-subjective) nature of that content depends upon the feeling of transsubjectivity, that is, upon the perception that the psychical states constituted a unified whole whose internal structure was manifestly different from the structure of our own self as experienced by us.

Now the relativist could argue that historical relativism is inescapable so long as the historian depends (as Simmel admits) upon analogical judgments for his awareness of the content of historical events. For any analogical judgment necessarily distorts the material which it supposedly grasps: the historian's experience, on the basis of which the judgment proceeds, cannot be identical with the experience of the historical personages who are to be understood. To this Simmel would agree, merely substituting for the term "distorts" the Kantian notion that the subject "forms" that material. But the relativist would argue further that the analogical judgments of two historians would differ as much from each other as each judgment would differ from the material which it purported to grasp. Again, perhaps more reluctantly, Simmel would be forced to agree: for if it is clear that one's own character and experiences serve as limits to one's apprehension of the psychical content of another's experience there is no guarantee that *any* two historians will have access to the same historical materials even if they have at their disposal identical records and sources. But the relativist could push this admission yet farther by pointing out that even if two individuals living within the same country and period could be said (by an act of faith) to have the same material before them, it is assuredly true (on empirical grounds) that the experience of individuals in different periods of the world's history are in some respects radically dissimilar; with respect to those experiences the identical past object would furnish self-contradictory material to different historians. This I take to be a point at which Simmel's view of historical knowledge fails to provide an answer to historical relativism.

It might with some force be objected, however, that Simmel is not interested in guaranteeing universality to any particular interpretation of historical sources; that he is, on the contrary, only interested in establishing the fact that such interpretations can ultimately be fitted together into a final and objective historical interpretation, in which each variant interpretation would play whatever part it could. It is for this purpose that Simmel introduces the apriori categories which we, following Troeltsch, have classified as the categories of selection, individuality, totality, and meaningfulness. If we examine what objectivity these categories afford we will, however, come to a disappointing conclusion.

Simmel holds that the feeling of transsubjectivity provides us with whatever clues we can be said to possess concerning the objectivity of judgments. This feeling depends upon those categories which form the material presented by analogical judgments into single individual or social wholes. We test the elements which are said to make up that whole against our notion of what its nature must be, and we find its nature through an examination of its elements. Simmel recognizes the apparent circularity of this method of attaining knowledge of historical objects, but he holds it to be the only method by means of which the historian can proceed.[8] And this in fact constitutes a valuable recognition of the inseparability of analysis and synthesis in the historian's task. But it is perfectly clear from Simmel's discussion of this problem that the whole emphasis of his thought was placed on the side of what he would term "synthesis," that is, on the construction of a whole out of

[8] *Die Probleme der Geschichtsphilosophie,* p. 28.

discrete elements. The analogies which Simmel draws between artistic construction (or appreciation) and historical understanding are so frequent as to leave no doubt as to this. It becomes important therefore to inquire how one can distinguish history from art.

The sole relevant difference between them, in the light of Simmel's discussion, seems to be that in historical knowledge we have the material given us through analogical judgments and not from the realm of our own psychical experience. But if, as we have seen, the universality of our analogical judgments is open to doubt then historical understanding seems to merge with art, for the categories cannot in themselves guarantee the uniform nature of the material elements upon which they are used. Instead of providing a basis for objectivity, therefore, the categories at best provide an explanation of how the historian's mind works in producing a history out of materials given to him by analogical judgments. But if these materials vary from historian to historian the fact that the same forms of procedure are gone through by each historian in no way guarantees the compatibility of their variant views. Between a guarantee of objectivity and the attribution of identical mental processes to all historians there is an absolute cleft so long as it is not demonstrated that the material on which these processes are employed is also an identical material. It is precisely the latter point which, as we have shown, Simmel leaves in doubt.

We have seen then that Simmel furnishes us with no guarantees of universal acknowledgement in regard to the material of historical accounts, and that as a consequence the synthesis of understanding which arises from this material according to apriori categories cannot be guaranteed but only explained. Thus it may be said that his view of historical knowledge does not escape relativism. We must now ask whether it is in itself an adequate account.

The vigor of Simmel's thought on the problem of historical understanding cannot be denied, and the concreteness with which he carries on his discussion reflects a deep personal concern with problems of cultural history. However, when one examines his illustrations one sees that it is with the problems of cultural history (as usually understood) that he is primarily concerned. The whole emphasis on the material of history as the development of psychical content, the interest in the unconscious group-will, in the periodization of history, and the continued emphasis on historical understanding as a construction of a "stylized image" (stilisierte Gebilde) [9] shows that Simmel was building his theory of history on the basis of an analysis of the problems of cultural history, and not on the basis of works narrower in scope and less philosophic in import. If, as may be the case, one should find that there is a real difference between cultural history as Simmel understands it, and historical works which deal with other historical mate-

[9] *Die Probleme der Geschichtsphilosophie*, p. 217.

118

rials, then Simmel's account is likely to be inadequate as a treatment of historical knowledge as such.

In turning now to an examination of Rickert we come to a theory of history which possesses a far broader base and is argued with greater dialectical skill. But we shall find that Rickert continues Simmel's Kantian approach, and we shall find that here too Kantianism breaks down against the stubbornness of an unexplained (and, for the Kantian, unintelligible) mass of material.

RICKERT (1863-1936)

Rickert, more than any other thinker, stands at the center of all philosophic discussion concerning the problem of historical knowledge. *Die Grenzen der naturwissenschaftlichen Begriffsbildung* which he first published in 1902, and which has undergone alteration through five editions, is beyond dispute the classic work in the field. Together with Rickert's other discussions of the historical problem, it provides a theory which in scope, consistency, and logical subtlety far surpasses all other works with which we shall be dealing. For that reason it is in a sense unfair to Rickert to treat of him at this point. Yet if we are to understand the significance of Scheler and Troeltsch it can only be through a contrast and comparison with Rickert, whose work, in its earliest form, provided the background for theirs. But we must be careful in considering Rickert here, not to discuss him merely as Scheler and Troeltsch first saw him, for each of the five editions of *Die Grenzen* has carried him beyond the position which they—not without reason—ascribed to him. And yet Rickert's position, as he himself would insist, has not changed. If we draw the full logical consequences of his thought we shall see that in spite of his many polemical assertions and denials even his later statements are defenseless against most of the attacks which they launched against him.

Rickert, like Simmel, starts from a thoroughgoing Kantian position, but unlike Simmel he attempts to show that the complete nature of a historical account is determined by values. In this we can see that he represents a step beyond Simmel, but a step taken in the same direction: for him not merely the form but the material of historical accounts depends upon non-existential factors. We must now consider closely, and in considerable detail, just how Rickert attempts to establish his view that values determine the complete nature of every historical account.

Rickert's earliest concern with the problem of historical knowledge arose out of his attempt to undermine the then prevailing view that knowledge and "the scientific method" were identical. Following in the footsteps of Windelband's famous rectoral address,[10] Rickert drew a distinction between natural-scientific knowledge and historical knowledge.

[10] *Geschichte und Naturwissenschaft* (1894).

This distinction, which is drawn in the first sections of *Die Grenzen der naturwissenschaftlichen Begriffsbildung* may here be briefly discussed.

Rickert seeks to delimit the field of the natural-sciences not through an analysis of their subject matter but through a consideration of the formal elements involved in them. This procedure is paralleled in his treatment of historical knowledge, where he first inquires into the historian's purpose on the assumption that this purpose determines the form of historical accounts. This method of proceeding has its basis in Rickert's Kantian view that knowledge can never grasp actuality without transforming it, and that such a transformation is always determined by the theoretical purpose (Erkenntniszweck) which lies behind the attempt to gain knowledge.

According to Rickert the characteristic form of natural-scientific knowledge lies in the use made of general concepts, or laws. The purpose of these concepts is to overcome the extensive and intensive multiplicity of things; to bring together and to simplify the infinite manifold of the external world. This the general concept does by virtue of its generality. It looks away from the individuality, the concreteness and the uniqueness of the manifold under consideration, concentrating on the recurring, or general, aspects of actuality.

Historical knowledge, on the other hand, is characterized by an interest in the particular. It grasps both concreteness and individuality; its purpose is to discover not the general but the individual concepts of things. The specific function of history is to call attention to the uniqueness of certain objects. This difference between historical and natural-scientific knowledge is summarized by Rickert when he says: "Empirical reality becomes nature when we regard it with reference to the general (das Allgemeine), it becomes history when we regard it with reference to the particular and individual (das Besondere und Individuelle)." [11]

This distinction between the two forms of knowledge is basic to all of Rickert's discussion of history, and for that reason he builds his argument slowly. Yet the point is clear enough, and well grounded: science is interested in the general, it strives for generalized systematic knowledge, and for it an individual thing is but the representative of a principle, an example that is used to establish a law; but history is interested in the particular, in what actually did occur, in the presentation of this or that unique happening. Rickert acknowledges that this formal distinction between the two types of knowledge is not absolute in the sense that all natural science is to be thought of as entirely devoid of historically represented things. His distinction is a logical one, and has formal validity only: there will be some crossing-over between the divisions, every object may be considered from either standpoint, and within each province there will be all degrees of generality and indi-

[11] *Die Grenzen*, p. 227.

viduality. But as a formal distinction it is not open to attack.

Our problem, however, is not concerned with a further inquiry into the validity or the usefulness of such a distinction, but rather in tracing out the consequences of this distinction for Rickert's view of history. Starting from his contrast between the generality of scientific concepts and the individuality which characterizes history, Rickert seeks to determine what makes us contemplate an object as individual.[12] At once the criterion of indivisibility springs to mind. This criterion cannot, however, show us the meaning of historical individuality so long as it is interpreted as meaning physical divisibility. If we look, however, at the difference between the Kohinoor diamond and a lump of coal, we find the concept of indivisibility taking on new significance. Both the diamond and the coal are physically divisible, but they differ in their "historical" individuality. The diamond cannot be divided without losing some of its value and for the reason we look upon it as an individual: it is considered as an individual because we believe that it should not be divided. Obviously the reason why it should not be divided is the fact that it is a unique bearer of certain values, and therein lies its true individuality. Now this Rickert carries over into the realm of history proper, a historical individual being for him the unique bearer of cer-

---

[12] Concerning what follows, *Cf., Die Grenzen*, Ch. IV, Sect. 2 (Das historische Individuum).

tain values. Goethe or Napoleon is thus a historical personage in a sense in which the average man is not, and Goethe and Napoleon enter into historical works because it is seen that in them, uniquely, were realized certain values. In this way, starting from a contrast between the generality of the natural sciences and the particularity of history, Rickert finds that historical knowledge is based from the very foundations up on the acknowledgement of values.

Now Rickert is at this point careful to draw a distinction between the act of valuing (Wertung) and the act of relating an object to values (Wertbeziehung). That which makes an object a historical individual is not, according to Rickert, the fact that the historian personally values it, but rather that he sees its value-relevance, its relation to values. A person or a social movement only becomes a historical "individual" when we see that through him or it certain transcendent values enter into the realm of the actual. While the historian may personally value some friend, that friend only becomes an object for historical contemplation if he is so related to the universal cultural values of mankind as to be irreplaceable. For the historian the average men is to Goethe as a lump of coal is to the Kohinoor diamond.

This introduction of values into the historian's enterprise enables Rickert to offer a delimitation of history according to its subject matter. For if history is constrained by its theoretical purpose to deal with value-relevant objects, the field of historical inquiry can be readily defined. The only place at which values enter into actuality is through the valuations of human beings. Thus history must be essentially human in its scope. But if history is to be knowledge it must rise above the merely subjective, and relate the objects of its contemplation to generally acknowledged values. These generally acknowledged individual values are identified by Rickert with "cultural" values (Kulturwerte), and history becomes, as a consequence, cultural knowledge (Kulturwissenschaft). The long and tortuous argument which led Rickert to this position cannot here be followed in detail. It may merely be noted that much of this argument was directed against a material delimitation of history which rested on the contrast between nature (Natur) and spirit (Geist). It is to the credit of Rickert that rather than fall in with the prevalent but vague notion of the "Geisteswissenschaften," he forged an alternative concept which, without sacrificing the value of that designation, stressed the important fact that history necessarily deals with socially significant events (Kultur).

But Rickert recognizes that this linkage of value and history does not carry him far enough, for he has up to this point merely demonstrated the relation of values to the historian's selection of his subject matter. He wishes also to prove that the form of the historical account, the method in which the historian treats his subject matter, is determined by values.

We must follow this argument in somewhat greater detail.

Rickert points out that in every historical account there is an element of selection, and it is his purpose to prove that what determines this selective process is the historian's orientation toward values. Now he takes it as an established fact that the historian selects the object of his account with reference to values. The portrayal of this object must also proceed with reference to these same values if the original choice is to have any meaning: it is inconceivable that a historian should determine what is "historical" through a consideration of values, and then proceed to leave these values totally out of account. In other words, if its relation to values makes an object "historical," the "historical" account of that object cannot fail to stress the object's relation to those same values. But Rickert does not wish to hold that the historian actually and directly relates the object of his attention to values, for this would run counter to all that we know of historical works. Furthermore, since the cultural values in question are, according to Rickert, purely formal in character (the state, art, law, morality, religion, and the like), every historical work would necessarily be empty and formal. To avoid this reduction of history to the purely formal, and at the same time to hold that values determine the inner nature of a historical account presents Rickert with some difficulties. These he avoids by the introduction of the concept of concrete "value-

structures" (Sinngebilde).[18] These value-structures are
the manifestations of the formal values in particular
situations; their nature is determined by the values,
but in contradistinction to the latter they are individual and not general. It is with these concrete value-
structures ("this particular state," instead of the
value: "statehood") that the historian is concerned;
his account is therefore neither empty nor formal.
On the other hand, these value-structures can only be
understood with reference to general values, for the
particular state would not have its being were it not
for the acknowledgement of the value of statehood.
Thus Rickert is able to save his insistence on the
relation of a historical account to universal values,
and yet not give up the concreteness of history.

This introduction of the concept of concrete value-
structures demands, however, that every historical
account have as its central core human valuations as
they appear in concrete cultural form (Sinngebilde).
But here again actual historical accounts seem to deny
Rickert's contention, and again he must seek a reconciliation of his theory and those works. For while
it is certain that valuations form part of the material with which the historian deals, it is equally certain that non-valuational, in fact non-human,
elements, such as the contour of a battlefield, also
have their place in a historical work. This fact Rickert
seeks to explain by his distinction between the pri-

---

[18] Concerning what follows, Cf., *Die Probleme der Geschichtsphilosophie*, Ch. I, Sect. 6, and *Die Grenzen*, Ch. IV, Sect. 9.

mary and the secondary historical objects. A primary historical object is one selected for consideration by the historian because of its relation to universal values; a secondary historical object, however, is not a unique bearer of universal values, but it enters into a historical account only because the historian must take cognizance of it in order to understand some primary object. Thus Goethe would be a primary historical object, while Goethe's father would be a historical object of the secondary type. Or, to take another example, the battle of Thermopylae would be a primary historical object, while the contour of that battlefield would be a secondary historical object. From these examples it can be seen that the relation holding between a secondary and a primary historical object is a causal relation. This Rickert recognizes. But we may well ask how, on Rickert's view, causal explanation can be related to value explanation. This question leads us into the very heart of his theory of a historical account.

Rickert recognizes that every historical event is temporal, that no non-enduring "event" is the subject of a historical account. Further, he admits that every historical object, like every other phase of actuality, is heterogeneous rather than simple. Therefore, if value-relevance is to be the determining factor in the nature of a historical account, it must show itself through the whole of the historical individual, that is, through all its changing aspects. This can only be the case when each of the aspects of a historical object contributes to its value. And Rickert in fact insists that it is this which determines the selection of the elements which make up a historical object: the historian, relating the whole individual to a value, selects as aspects or elements of that individual those factors which determine its unique value. In this, as Rickert admits, every historical object when viewed as a series of events has the characteristic stamp of "teleology" on it. This teleological conception in which each part seems to lead purposefully into the next is nothing but the "developmental" view of a historical object. This Rickert recognizes, and he claims that every historical narrative is the account of a development. But our question remains to be answered: how is it that Rickert can hold to some measure of causal explanation and yet embrace the view that the elements of a historical object are those of its aspects which are relevant to the values embodied in the object as a whole?

To this question Rickert gives no clear answer. He holds that history must show not merely *what* was, but also why it was, that is, what caused it.[14] The historian, according to Rickert, must place the object of his contemplation in its proper context. and since every object, no matter what its nature, is at once an effect and a cause, the causal analysis of historical objects seems to be demanded. But what, in fact, is Rickert's view? After quoting with approval

[14] *Cf., Die Grenzen*, p. 373. Concerning what follows. *Cf., Die Grenzen*, pp. 393 ff., and *Die Probleme der Geschichtsphilosophie*, p. 81.

Schopenhauer's dictum that causality is no hack that
one can stop when one will, Rickert holds that causal
explanation forms part of a historical account in
either of two ways. Firstly, one can trace the causes
of a primary historical object back to secondary historical objects. Secondly, one can trace the causal relations existing between secondary historical objects
just as far as one chooses, the limits being set either
by caprice or by the amount of material demanded to
cement together the elements of the historical account so that it can be re-experienced (nacherlebt) by
the reader. As Rickert himself admits, this answer in
its second aspect is of no theoretical significance. Yet
it serves to illustrate the inner weakness of Rickert's
entire theory.

It is certain that the historian must do more than
trace a teleological manifestation of cultural values.
But when he does more he is involved in causal explanation. Now Rickert is on safe ground when he
admits that this causal explanation demands the introduction of secondary historical objects; for so long
as the primary historical objects are selected for consideration on the basis of their value-relevance and
the secondary historical objects are selected solely on
the basis of their existential-relevance to these primary
objects, the value-oriented nature of historical accounts remains unbroken. But Rickert apparently
recognizes that no history is written in this manner,
for if it were there would be no semblance of continuity in it. A historical account of, let us say, "the

Industrial Revolution" would, according to this view, have as its elements a series of descriptions of the inventions and techniques which were relevant to that concrete value-structure (Sinngebild) known as the Industrial Revolution. The causes of each of these elements would then be traced back into the realm of secondary historical objects (the circumstances of this or that man's life, the labor market in this or that town, etc.) until the historical work would become a combination of an ideal, value-oriented, teleological development on the one hand, and a collection of rather curious, isolated causal information on the other. Thus Rickert goes on to say that the historian must trace the causal connections between these secondary historical objects, since this alone would make of the work a truly historical account. But he holds that this tracing of causal connections (far from being an irresistible vehicle) halts wherever we choose to have it halt.

Let us now summarize what we have found concerning Rickert's view of a historical account. Rickert holds that the theoretical purpose which determines the form of historical knowledge is an interest in the particular individual. The selection of which individuals are to be treated by the historian is determined by the recognition that in certain individuals general cultural values are uniquely embodied. These individuals are the primary historical objects. The historian builds his account of them with reference to the values which they embody, portraying in his account the successive stages by which the values are realized. But Rickert recognizes that the historian goes beyond such a portrayal in almost every historical work, examining causes as well as developmental consequences, analyzing as well as synthesizing. Thus he holds that the historian also traces the primary historical objects back to their actual causes. Recognizing that this would break the continuity of a historical account, Rickert acknowledges the fact that the historian also traces causal connections between the secondary historical objects, thus linking them to each other as well as to the primary historical individuals. However, he holds that the latter type of causal portrayal does not constitute a problem for the theory of historical knowledge.

His account of historical knowledge may perhaps become somewhat clearer to the reader if, before going on to a criticism of this view, we here list the general philosophic presuppositions which lie behind it. The first of these is that the facts of the past may be objectively known, whether those facts be valuations or non-valuational events. The second presupposition is that the knowledge of these facts does not in itself constitute "historical" knowledge; in order to have historical knowledge we must give these facts a particular form, dictated by our theoretical purpose. Third, that historical knowledge is similar in this respect to all knowledge whatsoever, since the true object of knowledge is never actual at all, but is always a transcendent value. Fourth, that the transcendent values are universal, demanding acknowledgment by all, everywhere. Fifth, that the only "objectivity" to be found in knowledge is the Kantian objectivity of universality and necessity: no knowledge ever reproduces actuality. Sixth, that causal explanation leads to an infinite regress, and if history is to be valid knowledge, its objectivity (necessity) must therefore depend upon some principle other than causal explanation.

Bearing these general presuppositions in mind, and remembering what has been said concerning the account of historical knowledge which Rickert gives, it will be well to conclude with a rather extensive criticism of Rickert's theory. Our criticism will fall under two headings: first, that Rickert has not actually provided an escape from historical relativism; second, that in spite of its scope and subtlety Rickert's account of historical knowledge is in itself untenable.

Rickert's answer to relativism rests on two points in his theory: first, on the distinction between an act of valuing (Wertung) and the relating of an object to values (Wertbeziehung); second, on the claim that the values which determine the nature of historical accounts are of universal validity. Now the distinction between an act of valuing and the relating of an object to values is a valid distinction. Furthermore it enables Rickert to stress a fact which relativists sometimes seem to overlook, that the historian does not always choose his subject because he likes or dislikes it. It is true that it often appears as if, from the very outset, the historian values his material in terms of his own interests. But it is also true that every historian avows a theoretic interest in his material; the presence of this theoretic interest obliges his personal attitudes to give way before the demands of the material itself (Wertbeziehung). Only after he has portrayed the nature of the historical events with which he deals is the historian in a position to pass moral judgment upon past actions. But this he does as an ethical personality, and not as a historian.

This distinction drawn between valuation and value-relevance does not carry Rickert far enough. For at best it shows that the historian seeks to be objective; it certainly does not establish the objectivity of his judgments. Rickert's claim that the values involved are universally valid seeks to advance the argument for objectivity. It will be seen that if every historical judgment is constituted by the acknowledgment of a value which is valid for all people at all times, the relativist will not be able to hold his ground. To be sure, the relativist would claim that there are no such universal values; but Rickert has attempted to establish their reality by a long and careful argument. Therefore in considering Rickert's answer to relativism, it is necessary to grant him his contention that all values are universally valid, and to see whether, even on this assumption, he has provided for objectivity.

Now by the objectivity of a judgment Rickert does

not mean that the judgment mirrors that aspect of actuality with which it deals, for, according to his view, all knowledge is transformation of actuality through concepts. What objectivity means in his system is the universal necessity of a judgment; that all persons in all times, when confronted by a given aspect of actuality will be forced (through the acknowledgment of transcendent values) to judge thus and not otherwise. If a historical judgment is objective in this sense, Rickert will have answered the relativist. Let us see how the matter stands.

Rickert has admitted that the historian does not deal directly with the transcendent values, but with the value-structures (Sinngebilde) through which these values are evidenced in actuality. The objectivity of a historical judgment becomes therefore a question as to whether the presence of universal values in a particular value-structure can force all beholders to judge identically of that value-structure (i.e., of that particular state, or of that particular religion). Now the particular value-structure must be more than a concretion of the universal formal values, for in so far as the historian deals with it, it belongs at least partially to the sphere of actuality.[15] Rickert holds that the elements in it which were actual (both what happened and what was actually valued by the person or persons in question) can be objectively known as facts. Because this factual information and the universal values are both objectively given to the historian, it seems as if the value-structures would also of necessity be objectively given. But this the relativist can and would deny.

The relativist would hold that a particular value-structure (this state, this literary ideal, and the like) is to be known neither through a set of facts which went to form part of its being, nor through the "universal" formal values which might be found represented in it, nor yet through both of these together. And his argument here would be plain. The historical object, being a particular value-structure, belongs to a realm which is an in-between realm; it is neither a mere actuality nor a pure value, but a resultant of both. To "understand" it the historian must be in a position to experience the intimate connection of these two diverse elements which went to form it. But the infinite and heterogeneous character of actuality makes such a re-experiencing of the past impossible. Therefore the historian must substitute for past actuality the contents of his own given present. This necessarily means that the value-structure which he experiences is not identical with the value-structure which he seeks to describe; it is, rather, a product of the "universal" values and his own given present. This is the ultimate basis of Troeltsch's insistence on an intuitive re-experiencing, an insistence which Rickert has failed to understand.[16]

But Rickert might answer such a relativistic con-

---

[16] *Cf., Die Grenzen,* p. xxix; p. 435, n. 1. Also, Kaufmann: *Geschichtsphilosophie der Gegenwart,* p. 26 f.

tention by saying that the historian does not seek to re-experience the past or reproduce it in any sense. He might hold that the historian's judgments are no less universally necessary because they contain an admixture of his own present actuality. But this answer would overlook Rickert's own acceptance of the fact that actuality is a sphere of heterogeneity, a fact which makes it theoretically possible, if not logically imperative, to hold that the actuality presented to different historians is different in kind. This being the case, the value-structures which are the resultants of actuality and the universal values will change from historian to historian. And we see, in fact, that Rickert's whole case for objectivity rests on his appeal to the universal values, even though the historian is concerned with value-structures which are not produced out of these values alone. The only real escape from relativism which Rickert could give would be an insistence on the ability of the historian to know all the facts which, in conjunction with the universal values, gave rise to particular value-structures. But his view that actuality presents an infinite manifold excludes any such solution: the facts of the past are themselves "selected." In this the last avenue for escaping relativism has been closed.[17] We may now

[17] It is significant to compare earlier and later editions of *Die Grenzen*. In the earlier editions relativism was in fact avoided by the appeal to the universal values. But this led to the frequent, and not unjustified, criticism that Rickert's view of history was formal and empty. To meet this criticism emphasis was placed on the concrete value-structures. But this threw Rickert back towards that relativism which we have described.

turn to our second set of criticisms of Rickert: that, in itself, his theory provides a false account of the nature of historical knowledge.

The inadequacy of Rickert's theory as a whole is to be found in the dualisms which beset it. The chief of these dualisms, and the one which we shall consider first, is the distinction which Rickert draws between factual knowledge of the past and true historical knowledge. His whole view of history rests on the assumption that objective factual judgments are possible, and that a historical account builds on these even though it then goes beyond them. However, Rickert's epistemology is of a sort that makes objective factual judgments concerning the past impossible. To this we must now turn.[18]

In regard to the validity of factual judgments concerning the occurrences of the past, he sees no special problem. He holds that factual judgments present no greater difficulties to historical writing than they do to the natural sciences. This is certainly theoretically true, but we must ascertain whether Rickert's view can account for the validity of any factual judgments whatsoever. His theory of the knowledge relationship maintains a dualism between what is known and the material of knowledge. This dualism is similar to the Kantian dualism of the given and the known, but is not identical with it, since givenness (Tatsächlichkeit) is itself a category according to Rickert. What

[18] The following epistemological considerations are based chiefly on *Der Gegenstand der Erkenntnis*.

138

we have is a dualism between the unformed and directly experienced (erlebt) sphere of actuality, and the sphere of the known, which is actuality brought under concepts. Now the act of knowing, or bringing actuality under concepts, is held to take place through a judgment, and a judgment is an affirmation or denial which is to be understood as the acknowledgment of a value or the denial of a disvalue. Bringing actuality under concepts, therefore, is an act which is value-oriented. The form of knowledge is determined by values, and the known itself is therefore to be understood only through its value determination. This is tantamount to saying, as Rickert himself would be the first to admit, that the relationships expressed in a true judgment are not derived from the material of knowledge (actuality) but from the form in which the subject is forced to express them. We could ask why, if this is the case, the concepts of science serve the practical purpose of aiding adjustment (as Rickert admits); for if the relationships expressed by those concepts were not paralleled by relationships in the sphere of actuality, it would be hard to see how adjustment could be aided by employing them. This problem, however, is left totally out of account by Rickert, due to his insistence on dealing with the form and not with the content of knowledge. For him, as he says, actuality contains no problems worthy of philosophic discussion; the subject-matter of critical philosophy is the realm of the known. But such a treatment of knowledge leaves out of account the possibility that actuality may itself contain formal relationships which the factual judgment expresses. The reason for the neglect of this possibility is to be found in the dialectical structure of *Der Gegenstand der Erkenntnis*. There he accepts the immanental copy-theory (that ideas are copies of impressions) in its destructive aspect, treating its rejection of all forms of realism as beyond question; but the crumbling of this copy-theory in his own hands was not followed by a reexamination of the possibility of realism, but by a theory of his own. However, unless the destructive side of the immanental copy-theory (its denial of realism) is free from all definitions and postulates which characterize its positive side, this procedure of Rickert's is tantamount to lifting one's immaterial soul by one's bootstraps.

The whole emphasis on form in Rickert's analysis tends to eclipse an equally important subject for reflection: the source of the concrete content of our judgments. In holding that this source can never be known in itself (since all knowledge consists in a transformation), Rickert may have thought to escape the problem. But if he is incapable of dealing with actuality in itself, it is still possible to direct attention to those aspects of a factual judgment which are not derived from the formal values. We may therefore say that Rickert's account of the factual judgment is in no wise complete, since it fails to deal with that which is of utmost importance for any account of history, namely, the relation of the content of a judgment to its referent, a portion of the flow of actuality.

But here we can go even further, and show that Rickert's account of the factual judgment is inadequate not only on the side of *what* the judgment expresses but also on the side of *why* the judgment expresses it. Rickert holds that we are to seek the *why* of a judgment in value-acknowledgments, and not in the presented material. But if this were the case, it would be hard to explain why we might not judge "this rose is red" without having a rose before us. To introduce the concept of logical validity affords no escape from the problem, because the criterion of logical validity concerns only the form and not the content of the judgment. On Rickert's view there would be no possibility of distinguishing between a true and a false judgment; every judgment in so far as it is formally valid and is made "with good will," would be the product of a value acknowledgment, that is, it would be made under a transcendent and universal obligation. But then false judgments would cease to exist. It is here in particular that the formalism of Rickert's epistemology appears to be so vacuous.

This difficulty which inheres in Rickert's account of all factual judgments manifests itself even more clearly with respect to the historian's judgment of past facts. For it is evident that no pure value-acknowledgment can furnish the criterion for the truth or falsity of a judgment unless some portion of the realm of actuality is also presented. But the historian who deals with the past does not have the possibility of getting into contact with the actuality which is relevant to a specific factual judgment concerning the past. He must therefore accept the accounts of past facts which have been handed down to him. Yet it is true that the historian also criticizes the accounts which are offered concerning past facts; through the "criticism of sources" he is often able to show that a supposed fact is untrue. Such criticism must remain forever unexplained by Rickert's theory of factual judgments.

Thus Rickert's theory of factual judgments is to be condemned from two points of view. On the one hand it fails to consider the possibility that a factual judgment may be expressive of actual relations which are independent of the act of knowing; on the other hand it fails to show how false judgments of fact are possible, and how such false judgments once made can actually be criticized. This being the case we may say that Rickert's theory of historical knowledge, assuming as it does the possibility of valid factual judgments, rests upon an insecure basis.

To this first criticism of Rickert's view of historical knowledge we may now add a second. We have already alluded to the fact that he attempts to combine causal explanation and value-relevance. These two aspects which he finds in all historical accounts are not, however, in every case compatible. For it will be remembered that he uses causal explanation not only to explain the relation of primary historical objects to secondary ones, but also to link the secondary historical objects to each other. Value-relevance, on the other hand, was used merely to link primary historical objects together. The incompatibility of these two methods of historical "understanding" lies in the fact that there is no reason to assume that the causal linkage of secondary historical objects will parallel the teleological linkage of the primary ones.[19] For example, the historian dealing with the judicial interpretations of the Constitution will be forced to take into account certain economic factors which were causally related to the cases coming before the courts. But there is no guarantee that the chain of economic events necessary to explain these cases will parallel the chain of judicial interpretations; the two sets of factors may diverge. Thus if the historian is really attempting to include the causal chain of secondary factors in his account, he stands in danger of having his material draw him off in two opposite directions. Only the assumption that all causation is somehow "valuetropic" would enable the historian to follow both the causal and the teleological lines of

[19] No incompatibility exists between value-relevance and a causal explanation of primary historical objects by secondary ones. It is only the causal sequence of secondary historical objects which may run contrary to teleological views of the historical process. Frischeisen-Köhler tends to overlook this fact when he criticizes Rickert from substantially the same point of view as is here taken. (Cf., *Wirklichkeit und Wissenschaft*, p. 166 f.)

understanding.[20] But, as Rickert would admit, such a metaphysical assumption lies beyond the province of the historian. It is apparently due to this discrepancy that he holds that the causal explanation of secondary historical objects proceeds merely as far as the historian chooses to have it proceed. As we have seen, this is to allow a theory of historical knowledge to break down at one of its most crucial points.

Our third, and final, criticism of Rickert's view consists in showing that the relating of past facts to values presupposes a full grasp of the historical material, and not merely a knowledge of isolated events, as Rickert would have us believe. Consider Rickert's view of the historian's activity: according to it, he selects the primary historical object which he is to describe because of its relevance to certain universal cultural values; he then selects as elements in his account those aspects of his object which are relevant to its manifestation of this value. Now if all historians were content to choose as the objects of their consideration such events as are unambiguously associated with certain cultural values, Rickert's view could adequately account for their historical works. A historian might, for example, say, "I shall deal only with objects in which the value of statehood resides," and then trace out the particular and concrete manifestations of statehood at various times. But let us suppose that our historian chooses to write

[20] In an interesting attempt to defend and elaborate Rickert's position in regard to historical causation Sergius Hessen admits this fact. (*Cf., Individuelle Kausalität,* p. 52.)

a history of trade-unionism. With respect to what values, political or economic, should his account be built? The relevance of a phenomenon such as the rise of trade-unionism for either political or economic values can only be known after we already know the history of that movement. Or, let us take another example. If a man sets out to write a history of the American frontier, with reference to what values should he select the elements of his account? If the work is really to be a history of the frontier (and not a study of its influence on American government, American religion, or the like) he must describe the successive migrations into new territory, the modes of life that developed in each locality, and the like. Only after he has done all this will he be able to see whether or not the elements in his account are relevant to political, moral, religious, legal, or artistic values; whether, in short, they are relevant to one or to all of the universal cultural values.

By these examples we have sought to show that the relating of a fact to values presupposes a comparatively full knowledge of the fact in its actual historical context. It has been our purpose to do this, for if this is true then Rickert is mistaken in holding that it is the *value-relevance* of facts that explains their presence in a historical account. He assumes throughout (it is implicit in the very notion of a teleological development of value) that there is one particular form of value-relevance which runs through a whole historical account and determines

its form. But a history of trade-unionism or a history
of the American frontier could not originally be
written on any such principles. In order that it might
be so written at all we should already have had to
possess a more complete history of the object in
question.

It need hardly be said that to have treated of
Rickert's work as a whole in these few pages is to
have done it an injustice. Yet the criticisms which
we have levelled against his view of historical knowledge can stand on their own strength, To summarize
them, we may say that he has provided neither a
philosophically sound answer to relativism, nor has
he advanced an independent theory which is free of
defects. The major defects which we have found in
his system are three: first, his inability to render an
adequate account of judgments of historical fact;
second, the incompatibility of causal explanation
with value-relevance; and, third, the dependence of
all value-relevant judgments on prior historical
knowledge. Yet in spite of these faults Rickert's
theory will long remain classic, for no other thinker
has envisioned the problems with the same painstaking concern, nor has any other brought to these
methodological inquiries an equal subtlety and dialectical skill. It should therefore be a disappointment
to the reader, and not merely a relief, that we now
leave the rarefied theoretical air of Rickert's speculation and return to the less rigorous atmosphere

which we shall find pervading the theories of Scheler and Troeltsch.

SCHELER (1874-1928)

In contrast to the formalism of Rickert, Scheler's approach to the problems of historical knowledge is concrete and vivid, arising as it does from a lifelong concern with the data of the historical process. Yet like Rickert, Scheler finds the key to historical knowledge in values that transcend the flux of reality. The difference between Scheler and Rickert on the score of historical knowledge lies chiefly in the difference between their views as to the nature of the transcendent values: for Rickert these are formal, and their relation to us is directive, we construct our world according to the obligation that they impose; for Scheler these values are material, and their relation to us is simply that we know them with an immediate and convincing emotional insight. The emphasis which Scheler places on the data of the historical process is a direct product of his belief in the concrete material character of these values. Unlike Rickert, Scheler does not hold that the problem of objectivity is to be solved by an appeal to a set of formal values which direct thought; for him a clear understanding of the timeless validity of material values is in itself enough to guarantee historical objectivity. In this, as we shall see, Scheler's argument lacks the subtlety and dialectical skill which one has the right to expect of so genial a philosopher.

Scheler's direct concern with historical knowledge arises from his attempt to lay a systematic basis for sociology. Influenced by the far-flung "Historismus" of his time, and yet a phenomenologist; holding to a theory of eternal values, and yet seeking to do justice to the flux of the empirical world: Scheler makes a boldly synthetic attempt. He holds that all knowledge is determined by the social conditions out of which it arises ("Alles Wissen ist ... durch die Gesellschaft und ihre Struktur bestimmt"),[21] and yet he seeks to show that it is not for that reason any the less valid. The manner in which he builds up this point of view is what here concerns us. For if it be shown that the relativist is right in holding that historical knowledge is conditioned by non-theoretical factors, and yet is wrong in holding that this robs it of ideal objectivity, the sting of relativism will have been extracted: it will have lost its epistemological significance.

The manner in which Scheler develops his point of view in regard to historical knowledge is dependent upon his metaphysics. This metaphysics is fundamentally dualistic in that it holds to the reality of two separate realms of being, a realm of ideal value-essences and a realm of existential fact. These realms parallel each other but cannot at any point be identified with one another.[22] The distinction be-

[21] *Die Probleme,* p. 48.
[22] *Erkenntnis und Arbeit* (in *Die Wissensformen und die Gesellschaft,* p. 347 f.).

tween the two realms of being is not, however, a reintroduction of the same dualism which is to be found in Rickert's metaphysics, for the realm of existence is neither unknowable nor is it a product of the mind's activity. The realm of existence is a sphere of ever-changing factual relationships; the realm of values is a sphere of timeless and valid meanings emotionally intuited. Now Scheler holds that both of these realms are presupposed in historical knowledge. He takes it to be a fact that historical writing must in a sense be explained in terms of determining social factors; and yet he holds that it cannot wholly be so explained, because it also involves an intuition of ideal values. The particular blending of these two realms which Scheler attempts in his theory of historical knowledge is peculiar to him alone, although in principle it is a perfectly natural solution.

He insists that to explain the social factors which conditioned the historian's belief is not to determine the validity of that belief. In contradistinction to Mannheim he would hold that any such attempt to estimate validity in terms of a genetic account of the origin of a judgment is the crassest sort of philosophic error. In this he extends Husserl's attack on "psychologism" to an attack on "sociologism." [23] But Scheler is unwilling to hold that the genesis of a belief is of no importance whatsoever, and, like Mannheim, he even goes so far as to wish to establish a sociology

[23] *Die Probleme*, p. 55, n. 1; p. 127.

of knowledge (Wissenssoziologie) which would examine the social conditions under which certain beliefs were held. These two apparently antagonistic
views—that the genesis of beliefs does not affect their
validity and yet that it is important to trace the
genesis of beliefs—are reconciled by means of Scheler's
dualistic metaphysics. For it is Scheler's contention
that the realm of timeless essences enters into the
content of judgments, but that th*e acts* of judging
belong to the realm of existence and are thus socially
conditioned. This being the case, social factors determine the direction of a person's thought, but the
objects of that thought are "there" independently of
any acts of judging. Scheler says: "While neither the
content of knowledge nor still less its validity is sociologically determined, the selection of the objects
to be known is determined by social perspectives of
interests, and the forms of the spiritual acts through
which that knowledge is won is always and necessarily
sociological." [24] The realm of essences is to him a realm
of possibilities out of which we, bound to time and
our interests, first select one set and then another for
consideration. Where we as historians turn the spot-
light of our attention depends upon our own sociologically conditioned valuations; what we see there is
determined by the set of absolute and timeless values
which are implicit in the past with which we are
dealing. For Scheler, both in his theory and in his
own practice, historical understanding consists in

[24] *Die Probleme,* p. 55.

tracing the configuration of the norms, purposes, and value-charged goods of a culture, and in relating this configuration to the sociological conditions which determined its appearance. The objectivity of this historical understanding he feels to be guaranteed by the distinction which he has drawn between essences and existences.

Against Scheler's view several criticisms may be levelled. It will in the first place be seen that such a view does not even raise the problem as to how the historian is in a position to discover and estimate the nature and potency of those various sociological factors in terms of which he is to explain the appearance of a cultural configuration. In this Scheler has assumed, but not explained, the primary question at issue: the nature and validity of historical understanding on its most fundamental level.

It might, however, be objected that this is not the problem with which Scheler is concerned. It might with good grounds be contended that Scheler's purpose was not to justify historical understanding of this level, but to explain and validate historical "interpretation," the value-charged estimate of an age in terms of its cultural significance. Our question then becomes one as to whether, granting Scheler the sort of primary historical knowledge which he assumes, he is able to hold that historical interpretation is objective.

In this connection it must first be noted that, as Scheler himself insists, a historical work has as its material the realm of historical fact, a temporal realm. If it is dependent for its judgments on the realm of essence, an eternal realm above all temporal facts, it can never really grasp the temporal. As Scheler says in speaking of the knowledge of essences: "It is knowledge of the determining constants (Sosein-konstanten) of all objects that we call knowledge of essences or Ideas—i.e., it is knowledge of mere structures (Zusammenhänge) of essences or Ideas. Therefore nothing specific and differentiated about the chance actuality of the world follows from this knowledge, since it is valid and applicable apriori to all possible chance actuality (zufällige Weltwirklichkeit)." [25] Thus, by definition, Scheler's attempt at a resolution of the problem which faces him seems hopeless; for that which should guarantee the objectivity of historical knowledge through its timelessness is valid for any possible historical judgment. It cannot therefore provide any guarantee whatsoever.

This first purely dialectical objection—which might after all be interpreted as a verbal quibble—can be supplemented by a more pointed attack. The first concrete argument which can be brought against his view is at once obvious and decisive. Scheler held that the historian's range of values was determined by his sociologically conditioned interests, but that his judgments concerning those values as embodied in specific past valuations, norms, and purposes were none the less valid. However, as we have pointed out

[25] *Erkenntnis und Arbeit*, p. 285.

in a previous chapter, the historian must rely largely upon the testimony of others for his material. The nature of this testimony, according to Scheler's view will always be limited in scope by the interests of him who recorded it. But later-day historians will discover in the original source only what their own sociologically conditioned interests permit them to discover. Since they themselves have no direct access to the past, their interpretations will only yield a series of perspectives upon one perspectival portrayal of what has happened. Although every historical account is in truth limited by the sources available to it, Scheler's view calls for a constant revision of our estimate of a source with reference to those of its aspects to which our own present interests are relevant. But this dissolves the value of a source, for its significance can not then be estimated with reference to what it says but only in terms of what it means to each successive historical generation. Thus Scheler's theory fails to account for the true usefulness of historical sources, turning them from instruments of knowledge into objects to be known.

What happens to the sources in Scheler's view of historical knowledge is symptomatic of what happens to the past as a whole: it is dissolved into a series of perspectives, and then into a series of perspectives of perspectives, *ad infinitum*. Like Mannheim, Scheler accepts the doctrine of perspectives; [26] like Mannheim also he seeks to overcome the dissolution of the his-

26 *Die Probleme,* p. 181.

torical object which this entails by surreptitiously introducing a non-relativistic standpoint for the historian. In Mannheim this non-relativistic element, it will be remembered, was a direct semi-artistic stylistic intuition. In Scheler it is the fact that the historian (unique among men!) can apparently intuit not only the whole range of eternal values but also the whole range of value-charged norms, purposes and goods; he can understand each age in terms of its own interests. But this is to halt relativism just when it becomes of philosophic importance, when the judger admits (as does Beard) the relativism of his own judgments. In this respect Scheler's theory lacks that consistency of thought which we have a right to demand.

A second concrete criticism may be levelled against the theory which Scheler brings forward: Scheler assumes that all judgments which interpret an age in terms of a set of eternal value-essences are valid judgments. This is to assume that because all values are (by definition) concordant, all such judgments regarding an age must be concordant. Scheler never attempts to prove this assumption, and its truth is far from self-evident. For it will be seen that although there is no conflict within the realm of essence between personal religious morality and economic value, yet the interpretation of the fall of Rome as given by Augustine and the interpretation given by a Marxian would be in conflict. Now Scheler would have to hold that both were right, although both were partial, due to the sociologically determined interests out of which they sprang. This, however, leads to the not wholly desirable conclusion that all historical interpretations are true, although all are also false in the sense that they are partial. Thus Scheler comes to a Crocean solution in which all historical manifestations (including not only the "truths" of historical knowledge, but also those of religion, ethics, and art) are partial and relative, and only the one "eternal, objective Logos" embraces ultimate truth.[27] To this view we may say that if it is sound metaphysics it none the less fails to provide any possibility of telling how true any particular "truth" really is. In this "escape" from relativism, as in so many others, the ultimate conclusion that we are forced to reach is that relativism is a fact stronger than much metaphysical theory: in the end it will break its way through any tissue of speculation which once affords it tenancy.

TROELTSCH (1865-1923)

Chronologically, Troeltsch's attempted answer to historical relativism precedes that of Scheler, but succeeds that of the other philosophers considered in this chapter.[28] Yet Scheler's attempt to transcend relativism is cut from the same cloth as that of Rickert, and Troeltsch's dissatisfaction with his pred-

[27] *Die Probleme*, p. 14.
[28] Troeltsch does in fact discuss Scheler (*Der Historismus und seine Probleme*, pp. 603 ff.) but he had not, of course, access to the works with which we have primarily been concerned.

ecessors applies no less to Scheler than to them. In criticism of all previous attempts to link the historical material to transcendent values Troeltsch says: "If one starts out from Ideas and standards one falls into an unhistorical rationalism and loses contact with empirical history and its practice. If one starts out from the historical-individual and thereby remains in harmony with research, a limitless relativism and scepticism threaten one. If one attempts to come close to both through ingenious concepts of development the two aspects always break asunder." [29] Troeltsch's own approach to the problem of relativism, a problem which he saw with exceeding clearness and tried to meet without equivocation, springs from this realization of the failure of his predecessors; he says: "The concrete situation demands concrete standards." [30]

Troeltsch, like the other philosophers of history who have been considered in this chapter, emphatically rejected all attempts to deny valid historical knowledge. As a historian of religion, the problem of how such knowledge is possible was forced upon him. He saw it in the light of the still broader question as to how *any* historical (and therefore changing) phenomenon can lay claim to universal validity. It is this broad problem of the relation of change to validity which underlies all of Troeltsch's thinking on the subject of history. As a historian of religion

[29] *Der Historismus und seine Probleme,* p. 162.
[30] *Ibid.,* p. 193.

he saw the foundations of Christian belief threatened; as a theologian he could not but affirm the validity of Christianity. He saw that this dualism which must be faced in the case of a historical religion must also be faced with respect to other historical phenomena such as historical writings: how can such time-bound products of a given historical situation present us with valid knowledge of their material?

Troeltsch's answer to this question, in so far as historical writing is concerned, consists in holding that, in the first instance, the historical understanding of any past age depends upon viewing it in the light of its own dominant value or values. This he deems possible, and speaks of "immanent standards of measurement," [31] and of "immanent criticism" [32] which proceeds with "the greatest possible faithfulness, accuracy, objectivity and withdrawal of the self." [33] He speaks of "the sought after objectivity of measuring each structure only in terms of its own volition and content (which has also been called immanent criticism). It presupposes the most unprejudiced penetration (Einfühlung) of foreign meaning-structures (Sinntotalitäten), separating them from the personal wishes and ideals of life which the observer possesses. Although this can only be approximated, it can nevertheless achieve tremendous success and deep power, as has been demonstrated beyond con-

[31] *Ibid.*, p. 177.
[32] *Ibid.*, p. 171.
[33] *Ibid.*, p. 177.

tradiction by many of the masterpieces of historical investigation." [34]

However, Troeltsch insists that this impartial immanent criticism is rendered suspect by the fact that a non-theoretic valuational element always seems to accompany it. He is inclined to hold that immanent criticism is not the whole of historical knowledge, and that the valuational factor in historical understanding is worth extended consideration. He identifies the source of this non-theoretic element in the historian's undertaking with the demands which the future places upon him. The future enters into a historical work through the historian's interpretative activity; it enters by the fact that the standard of interpretation for the past is drawn from the present, and the present is always forward-looking. Troeltsch says: "The creation of standards in respect to historical objects arises out of the contemporary structure of life, and is at the same time its criticism and its continuation. Just as in the natural sciences all calculation of motion is dependent upon the standpoint of the observer, so too in history every standard is ineradicably determined by the standpoint out of which it springs. And it always springs out of a living connection with the formation of the future." [35]

Yet Troeltsch seeks a path out of this relativism; and like the other philosophers of history referred to, he seeks to find his way out by means of that which

[34] *Ibid.*, p. 119.
[35] *Ibid.*, p. 169.

brought him in: the valuational element in historical judgments.[36] But, unlike Rickert and Scheler, he does not seek objectivity by elevating to a transcendent level the values which, according to him, determine this judgment; it is his opinion that such a procedure creates an unbridgeable gap between actuality and value. Instead, he acknowledges the historical flux of these values, seeking objectivity not in value-transcendence but in value-immanence. His attempt must here be discussed.

He firmly holds that all individual valuations, such as those which form the standards of a historian's judgments, are partial and unstable. The source of this belief may be traced back not only to the general intellectual and cultural situation out of which Troeltsch's book arose, but also to his theology. In regard to the relation of his theological interests to the problem of the relativity of all historical values, we may quote his own words: "If one starts out from Heraclitus and from the prophetic Christian idea of the world as the creative living actuality of God's will which can never be exhausted by concepts... then all the urge to characterize any human truth or ideal construct as absolute disappears; but we retain

[36] This statement and all that ensues demands qualification if it can be shown that the position taken by Troeltsch in his article "Historiography" (Hastings: *Encyclopaedia of Religion and Ethics*) is consistent with those later discussions which are here under consideration. In itself the theory there presented is extremely sketchy and not proof against all criticism, yet due to the sharp distinction which it draws between "scientific history" and "the philosophy of history" it appears to be in many ways superior to Troeltsch's later writings.

the possibility of grasping divine existence (göttliches Leben) in the relative truth and the relative ideal." [37]

Troeltsch opposes Rickert and Scheler in contending that no cultural values transcend the flux of actuality. In so far as he holds that every culture is determined by the presence and absence of certain valuations, no culture has more than a relative significance: "Here there is nothing non-temporal or universally valid except the urge and duty to produce culture as such." [38] Behind all specific cultures lies the historical process itself. In conformity with his view that this process is the concrete actuality of the divine will, Troeltsch insists that it is to be monistically conceived. This insistence, as he recognizes, is merely a postulate. He says: "The empirical historian will find his task in the knowledge and presentation of these individual developments, and will merely describe as facts their perhaps tenuous connections and continuing threads.... But he himself will not escape putting his own present and future into these connections and recognizing behind and under them a deeper movement. This movement may perhaps be only inadequately and brokenly actualized, but the practical will can draw it out, strengthen it, bind it up anew and introduce it into the system of contemporary forces. He will work towards a universal conception of development, energetically drawing it out of the thin and fragile continuities which exist be-

[37] *Ibid.,* p. 184.
[38] *Der Historismus und seine Ueberwindung,* p. 30.

tween the empirically given spheres of development in order that he may link to it his own situation and the future.... But in the end he needs for this a metaphysical faith which will carry him high above empirical ascertainments and characteristics and let him believe in a real continuity at the basis of events." [39] And of this faith Troeltsch says: "But the unity and meaning of the whole can only be surmised and felt, it can not be theoretically expressed or theoretically constructed." [40]

The metaphysical faith which allowed Troeltsch to affirm the underlying continuity of the apparently broken and unreasonable historical flux arose out of his religious view of the world. According to it all cultural values, although they are transient, form necessary parts of the one necessary process; no historical phenomenon can outlive its own time, but each event has its place in the one abiding continuity. It is in this sense that Troeltsch seeks to escape the dualism of the theories of Rickert and Scheler: for Troeltsch the essential value of any cultural product lies wholly within that product, arising and perishing with it. However, since every part of the historical process is a necessary stage in the whole it cannot be said that any cultural phenomenon is without its value and truth. We must now ask whether this succeeds in answering the question as to how historical knowledge is possible.

[39] *Der Historismus und seine Probleme*, p. 174 f.
[40] *Ibid.*, p. 183.

It will be remembered that our first criticism of Troeltsch lay in the fact that he had failed to give an account of how objective immanent criticism is possible. Leaving this criticism aside, we must make clear why at two other points Troeltsch's theory appears to break down under scrutiny.

The first of these is to be found in the fact that Troeltsch's theory would demand that historical writing be something which it is not: a description of value-continuities. Troeltsch recognizes that the historian's procedure carries him beyond immanent criticism to the delineation of continuities. If this were not so the historian's view of the past would simply be a series of static images without relation to each other. But the nature of immanent criticism being what it is (the viewing of an age in the light of its own dominant values) the connections between the ages must be a connection of values. Otherwise events would be interpreted in terms of value elements, while the connections between these events would be external to values. If this were the case the historian would not be led on, as Troeltsch holds that he is, to search out greater and greater continuities.

It will, however, be seen that if the continuities within history are really held to be value-continuities, then Troeltsch's theory runs counter to the facts of historical writing. Even the history of philosophy could not be said to conform to the view that a history is a description of value-continuities:

162

in philosophy a large measure of continuity arises from accidents of terminology, of nationality, and of technical progress in the sciences. Historical writing, whether in the field of the history of philosophy or elsewhere, is not concerned (except incidentally) with tracing what happened to the hopes and expectations of an age; its task lies in showing how the future of an age or group grew out of the whole of its actuality.

We may then summarize this criticism of Troeltsch in saying that however one interprets his theory of immanent criticism, it demands that historical writing be something which it is not. For the theory demands either: *a*) that the historian give merely a series of static views of the past; or, *b*) that he connect these static value-oriented views by non-valuational elements, thus making every historical work a chain of two disparate kinds of links; or, *c*) that he connect these static views by means of value-continuities. Not one of these three alternatives appears to be in conformity with the facts of historical writing; of the three Troeltsch definitely rejects the first and inclines toward the third. In so far as it is inadequate to the facts, Troeltsch's theory as a whole must remain inadequate.

Our final criticism of Troeltsch's theory of historical knowledge is perhaps the most serious: if Troeltsch's view of value-immanence is correct it becomes impossible to distinguish true from false historical judgments. For Troeltsch held, it will be remembered, that no historical phenomenon is without its truth and value, since each event is but an aspect of one great continuity. But this leads us up into the arms of the Crocean Absolute, where the only truth in history is the inaccessible mystery of God's truth. In this light all attempts to understand history become in a sense "true" (or false); when this occurs it becomes impossible to find the truth in any given case. If, as Troeltsch suggests, the essential part of every historian's activity is dictated by his own situation and the demands which the future makes upon him, and if, as Troeltsch also maintains, there is no element in any such situation which is valid beyond its own historical limits, it should follow that all history must ever be written anew. But Troeltsch at the last possible moment avoids what seems to be the inevitable relativism of his position by means of an act of faith: he appeals to the "conscience" (Gewissen) of the individual historian.[41] But it is precisely the possibility of "conscientiousness" (in this sense) which has been called into question by the relativist. As Scheler says: "We shall not escape this relativism ... by doing what Troeltsch, for example, strangely enough wishes: by affirming our European position—in spite of our knowledge of its relativity—with a mere postulate, that is, with a 'sic volo, sic jubeo.' "[42]

We see therefore that his attempt to escape relativism while still holding to a valuational element in

[41] *Der Historismus und seine Ueberwindung*, p. 39 f.
[42] Scheler: *Die Probleme einer Soziologie des Wissens*, p. 13 f.; *Cf.* Mannheim: *Der Historismus*, p. 26 f.

historical judgments is no more successful than were the attempts of his predecessors. It was his contribution to the solution of the problem to have abandoned the attempt to view historical knowledge and the data of that knowledge in terms of transcendent values. Yet in the end the fundamental issues emerge from his analysis more confused than clarified. What he assumes at the outset in the way of an objective immanent criticism is the point over which the issue should be fought; what he takes as historical explanation—a tracing of value-continuities—is merely part of the material to be explained; and, finally, where we should have a criterion of truth we have an article of faith. Thus we find once more that the attempt has failed to save both an all-pervasive valuational aspect of historical judgments and the objectivity of those judgments.

CHAPTER V

SUMMARY AND INTERPRETATION

I

FEW people familiar with the literature of our subject would be inclined to contest our selection of Simmel, Rickert, Scheler, and Troeltsch for discussion, for their theories represent dominant landmarks in the path which counter-relativism has followed. In treating of their works we shall find that instead of being merely parallel developments of a single basic set of presuppositions—as was the case with Croce, Dilthey, and Mannheim—the thought of these counter-relativists is marked by an inner dialectical movement. As a consequence, our comparison of their systems will emphasize the manner in which each attempted to overcome the weaknesses of the view that preceded it. We shall find that as each theory emerges it corrects the major fault of its predecessor only to fall into new error. At the end of the movement historical relativism arises from the ashes of the traditional attempts to overcome it. It will therefore be necessary to uncover the basic failure in all four attempts, so that we can then proceed with greater assurance to justify the historical enterprise.

Simmel's work, the first edition of which dates

almost from the beginning of the struggle over historical relativism, is a characteristically early attempt to meet a new form of argument. It envisions the new argument concretely, yet fails to appreciate all of its ramifications; while it takes the argument seriously, it attempts to overcome the new position by the elaboration of an old and widely accepted doctrine. This can be seen when we recall that Simmel thought it possible to show on the basis of the Kantian doctrine of universal and necessary categories of the understanding that the interpretative aspects of historical accounts, while "subjective" (proceeding from the subject, and not from the material) were objectively valid (necessarily accepted to all). For in this attempted answer to relativism Simmel fails to see, first, that the emphasis on interpretation is but one aspect of historical relativism, and, second, he fails to see that it is of the essence of that relativism to deny the universality and necessity of any particular categories.

Nor is Simmel's theory adequate in the manner in which the basic Kantian contention which it embodies is developed. We have seen that he cannot account for the way in which the historian becomes aware of his material, and thus he cannot truly distinguish history from a work of creative art. Further, even granting the historian his experience of the historical material, Simmel's theory of the historical categories in no wise serves to guarantee objectivity to a historical account. For these categories merely name the procedures which, according to him, are basic in the historian's activity; in what fashion they shape the particular material with which the historian is dealing is left wholly indeterminate. For, as we have seen, even if we assume two historians to have the same material presented to them, we have no guarantee that they will form that material in a compatible manner even if they use the same categories. Is it not possible that one historian may interpret his material in terms of the developing self-consciousness of the national will, while another may interpret this same material as the death-struggle of an economic class? How then is any objectivity to be guaranteed merely by the fact that formal categories such as selection, individuality, totality, and meaningfulness are employed? [1]

It was with this question that Rickert took up the problem. Starting from Kantian assumptions, Rickert did not go back to the problem of how the historian becomes aware of his material; merely to ask such a question is, in the Kantian theory of knowledge, to demand an answer to mere words. "Whence comes the material of knowledge?" is an illusory problem (Scheinproblem) for the true Kantian, since it is a problem which in its very statement defies any intelligible answer. But the other problem which Simmel left, the problem of how the categories of historical knowledge can guarantee objectivity, was taken up by Rickert with vigor and dialectical skill.

[1] *Cf.*, Rickert's criticism of Simmel's too-psychological approach, *Die Grenzen*, p. 272 f.

We have seen in our discussion of Rickert that the basis of his position is to be found in his interpretation of the formal elements in knowledge as a species of value-acknowledgement. Because of this Rickert is able to make the categories of historical understanding more concrete than were those categories which Simmel found in historical works. In addition, he was able to account for the subject-matter of historical works by an appeal to the same values which determine historical categories, rather than delimit the field of history in Simmel's "psychological" fashion. As a consequence of this delimitation of the historical field through cultural values, Rickert avoided Simmel's constant appeal to unconscious will, group-personality, and the like. All these facts, following from Rickert's value-oriented view, mark a decided improvement over the thought of Simmel. Further, so far as the history of our problems is concerned we find in Rickert the clear recognition that a treatment of historical relativism demands a consideration of the value-consciousness of the historian. This is again an advance over Simmel's formulation of the problem. But in spite of these many advances Rickert's attempt to answer the historical relativist lacks the necessary concreteness of approach: as in the case of Simmel, too much is here taken for granted.

Simmel failed to explain how the material of historical accounts can be objectively apprehended by the historian. Rickert assumes that "the facts" which he believes are the material of the historian can be objectively known. None the less, as we saw in the preceding chapter, Rickert's epistemology does not really afford him the right to this belief. Yet even if we grant him the historian's right to these facts, the theory of historical knowledge which follows is still woefully inadequate to account for the claimed objectivity of historical judgments. For he fails to show that an understanding of the concrete value-structures (Sinngebilde), which he holds to be the goal of the historian's enterprise, is made possible by the acknowledgment of the universally valid formal values. This situation is strictly analogous to Simmel's failure to guarantee objectivity by the introduction of his historical categories: both theories break down because they attempt to separate form and content in historical works, an attempt which is prohibited by the concrete method of the historian. If we turn now to the theory of Scheler we find that his goal is essentially defined by the striving to keep form and content together, and yet to save historical objectivity by an appeal to transcendent values.

The manner in which Scheler attempts this is by means of his phenomenological theory of value, which holds that values are ideal essences, and yet are not formal, that they are, on the contrary, emotionally intuited material essences which are valid for all. This being the case, Scheler can claim that when the relativist argues that all historical interpretations are value-charged he is in no wise indicting their validity, since these values are valid for all.

Likewise, when the relativist claims that historical knowledge is relative because it springs forth at a given moment in the eternally flowing historical process, Scheler can claim that it is not therefore relative, for what it grasps is outside of the historical process altogether, being a concrete essence and not an existent at all.

This argument of Scheler's would provide an escape from relativism if he were able to show that it is really with the ideal essence that the historian deals. On the contrary he can be forced to admit that these timeless essences are to be found embodied over and over again in the historical process. Thus they are not the real material of a historian's work. In this he has fallen into the same predicament as did Rickert: he attempts to guarantee the objectivity of the historian's account by an appeal to something other than that with which the account is concerned. Although Scheler turns Rickert's formal values into concrete essences they are still remote from the historian's material. It is in this that Troeltsch's criticism of Rickert also applies to the theory of Scheler.

Troeltsch's own theory of historical knowledge marks the last point, the complete breakdown, in the development of traditional answers to the historical relativist. Accepting the theory that all historical knowledge is value-charged, and holding that the values which permeate it are not eternally valid, Troeltsch seeks an escape from historical relativism by assuming that a certain sort of objective historical knowledge (which he calls immanent criticism) is possible; he then argues that all values, even if not eternally valid, are part of an absolute immanent Unity, and are therefore in some sense "true." Such an escape is impossible. The point at issue is whether objective historical knowledge (immanent criticism) is possible. It does no good here to appeal to the "conscientiousness" of the historian. And to say that because all historical judgments are based on immanent values they therefore represent "partial truths" is merely to substitute for concrete historical relativism the relativism of metaphysics, wherein we say (to comfort ourselves) not that all beliefs are false, but that all beliefs are partially true. With this we are once again back in the absolute relativism of a thinker such as Croce.

II

Having now traced the inner dialectic of counter-relativism we are in a position to compare this movement with that which it was designed to combat. One historical consideration forces itself upon us in any such comparison, and that relates to the chronological sequence of relativists and counter-relativists. From the chronological point of view, the relativists do not antedate the counter-relativists. Simmel, for example, struggled to overcome historical relativism almost as soon as it appeared, yet Rickert was still fighting the same battle within the last years. Of those philosophers whose work has here been treated only two,

Croce and Mannheim, are living, and they belong, as we have seen, within the relativistic group. If the reader is willing to grant us our choice in the philosophers who have here been discussed, the only conclusion which can be drawn from these chronological considerations is that counter-relativism has not established its case. This fact becomes even more apparent when we recall that such well known American historians as Beard and Becker have recently espoused the relativist's cause. This, then, is a historical consideration which throws light on the struggle: the chronological order of important relativists and counter-relativists shows that the struggle has not been won unless the victory can be said to fall on the side of the relativist. Nor is this situation surprising, for counter-relativism has failed not merely in certain formal ways, but has failed in essence. It has not come forward with any arguments radical enough to undermine the relativistic position.

Simmel and Rickert, starting from a Kantian position, gave up the ideal of objective knowledge in its usual sense. For them our knowledge need not—and could not—be a copy of reality; they felt it sufficient to show that somewhere in knowledge there was an apriori valid element. Unfortunately they could not demonstrate that this element was contained in the historian's account of the material itself. Scheler tried to find the apriori within that material, but his dualism between the realm of essence, to which the apriori belonged, and the realm of existence, which

173

is the true historical realm, caused a complete theoretical breakdown in his view of historical knowledge. Troeltsch, having learned that if historical knowledge is to be termed objective it must contain its valid elements within itself (and not in some other realm), attempted by simple faith to affirm all values which are found within the historical process, and thus to justify every historical work. In this set of failures one lesson should be clear: that unless we go back to the usual view of objectivity and say that historical objectivity resides in the historian's ability to portray the real character and relations of historical events, we shall find no escape from relativism.

Such a return to an apparently discarded notion of objectivity is the major lesson which should be learned from a survey of counter-relativism. But before this can be accomplished it must be shown *a*) that the validity of knowledge is not to be understood or estimated by an appeal to the historical conditions under which it was formed, and *b*) that valuational judgments do not of themselves determine the content of historical accounts. If these two demonstrations are successful, the position of historical relativism will have been undermined, for it was on these presuppositions that its doctrine was expounded. Undercutting relativism in this fashion, and returning to the discarded ideal of objectivity, we shall be in a position to show how historical knowledge in an objective sense is possible. With this the sequel will be concerned.

PART II

HISTORICAL KNOWLEDGE

"Truth follows reality and leaves it undisturbed in taking possession of it. Hence there can be science of everything in so far as things are revealed or adumbrated for us."

S. ALEXANDER.

CHAPTER VI

JUDGMENTS OF FACT AND JUDGMENTS OF VALUE

THE task of overcoming historical relativism is now before us, since the doctrines of the counter-relativists have been shown to be inadequate. This task can only be completed by pointing out the fallacies in the basic philosophic presuppositions of the relativists, and then by proceeding to show how the ideal of objective historical knowledge is in fact possible of at least partial attainment. The present chapter will be devoted to a consideration of the two philosophic presuppositions which we have found to be basic in the arguments of the historical relativists.

Let us first turn to the relativistic assumption that the validity of knowledge is to be understood and estimated with reference to the conditions under which it was formed. Such an assumption, as we have previously pointed out, involves an infinite regress which makes knowledge impossible. For it will be seen that if I estimate a statement of fact with reference to the conditions under which it was formed, then my own statement must itself be estimated with reference to its own conditioning factors, and this entails a further statement which must also be thus estimated, and so on indefinitely. No escape from absolute scepticism is justifiable on any such theory; any belief in knowledge on the part of its upholder is simply an admission of fatigue or a surrender of the position adopted.

However, in a recent article Beard and Vagts have raised objection to such an interpretation of the relativist's position.[1] They insist that they espouse "a limited relativity, not a chaos" with regard to historical interpretations.[2] They base this view upon the theory that there is not an indefinitely large number of points of view with respect to which each statement must be estimated; each statement, they hold, is relative not to the individual who gives rise to it, but to the type of social order in which that individual has his existence. They insist that "the number of social orders is limited," [3] citing as examples of social orders such politico-economic forms as fascism, communism, and democracy.

Against this view we may urge that it has in no wise saved Beard's doctrine from the absolute scepticism which is implicit in his original attempt to estimate the validity of knowledge with reference to the conditions under which it is formed. For it should be clear that the conditioning factors of a historical judgment are not confined to specific underlying politico-economic structures; the historian is not simply a representative of these typical structures,

---

[1] Beard and Vagts: *Currents in Historiography (American Historical Review,* Vol. 42, pp. 460 ff.).
[2] *loc. cit.* p. 481.
[3] *loc. cit.* p. 481.

nor need we assume that he remains uninfluenced by the alternative structures of which he is aware. Further, Beard and Vagts are not sufficiently explicit as to what they take these politico-economic structures to be. It would appear that they construe them as abstract "ideal structures," for otherwise the number of alternative structures would not be a strictly limited one. Yet the authors say: "Neither the content nor the purpose, nor the implementation of American historiography can be the same as that of historism in Germany or its counterpart in other countries of Continental Europe, unless we are to believe that an encompassing social environment makes no impress on written history."[4] This statement would suggest that the underlying types of social order are not abstract, that there are an indefinite number of differing social environments on the continent of Europe; yet why, then, should England be omitted from the list? The dilemma which faces the authors in interpreting what they may mean by an underlying social order, or by the social environment, may be put concretely as follows: if the types of social order (social environment) are strictly limited then they must be abstract and "typical" politico-economic forms; if they are not abstract and "typical," but concrete, then there would seem to be an indefinitely large number of them. In the first case it would seem necessary to say that American historiography should share its characteristics with,

[4] *loc. cit.* p. 477.

let us say, English, French, and Czechoslovakian historiography; in the second case an unlimited relativism would seem to be demanded. Finally, we may say in opposition to Beard and Vagts that they assume that they themselves, or other historians of historiography, possess objective knowledge of the underlying politico-economic forms. If they are really caught in their social environment is their classification not a relative one? In that case it would be essential to acknowledge that the specific "limited relativity" to which they attach themselves is simply an expression of one point of view. In this we would again be caught by that which they would term "the chaos" of unlimited relativism.

Thus we may reiterate that once it is held that the validity of knowledge must be understood and estimated with reference to the conditions under which it was formed, complete relativism is unavoidable. It is therefore necessary to characterize this belief as a basic presupposition of relativism.

Now the fallacy in this view is one which is not hard to discover, and it has often been pointed out in the philosophic literature of our times.[5] It consists in confusing the content of knowledge with the act which formulates and expresses that knowledge. In our own terminology—which we shall here use—we must say that it confuses "a statement" with "a judgment." This terminology may be unique but it is not arbitrary, for it attempts to start out from the con-

---

[5] Cf., Husserl: Logische Untersuchungen, Erster Theil, # 46-48.

crete meanings which these words possess in ordinary
reflective usage. That it is not entirely consistent
with general philosophic usage is readily granted, for
philosophic terminology has often the undesirable
characteristic of overlooking some of the aspects
which concrete meanings possess. Let us now try to
show the fallacy which resides in the confusion of
statements with judgments.

When we pick up Pareto and commence to read
we find: "Human society is the subject of many researches." This is a statement. It is something said.
It is a concrete, explicit, directly given, meaningful
unit which indicates something, tells us something,
and purports to be true. Now from this statement we
can abstract out that which we call the "proposition." [6]
The proposition is the same set of meaningful words,
but when considered as a proposition it is treated
merely as a logical entity which may or may not be
true, but which is not asserted to be true. The *proposition* "Human society is the subject of many researches" is in this sense merely a logical essence; it

[6] Our use of the term "proposition" differs from the usual philosophic usage in holding that propositions are not in themselves
true or false. The reason for our divergent use of the term resides
in the fact that in so far as propositions are distinguished from
"sentences" they are abstractions from statements, the latter being
concretely expressed propositions which purport to be true. If, as
Broad holds in opposition to McTaggart, beliefs cannot be said to
profess to be true (or, as we should say: statements cannot purport
to be true), then our distinction between statements and propositions cannot be maintained. (*Cf.*, Broad: *Examination of McTaggart's Philosophy*, v. I, p. 70. For the usual view of propositions
Cf., Broad *op. cit.* v. I, pp. 58-64; Cohen and Nagel: *Introduction
to Logic and Scientific Method*, pp. 27-30; Eaton: *General Logic*,
pp. 12-24. The view of W. E. Johnson—*Logic*, v. I, pp. 1-4—is somewhat nearer our own usage).

is in itself nothing more. A proposition is thus *what* a statement says considered in abstraction from the fact that the statement has said it. A proposition is therefore that aspect of a statement with which we can deal according to principles of logic without raising the question of whether the statement itself is true. Thus, illustrations in textbooks of grammar and logic are to be understood as propositions and not as statements. A statement is intended to say something, to indicate something, to be true.

We must now distinguish a judgment from a statement. A judgment is usually defined as the affirmation or denial of a proposition. This definition is in conformity with general reflective usage so long as we underscore the terms "affirmation or denial": a judgment is an affirmation or denial. To revert to the statement which we have already chosen as an illustration, we may say that when we consider this as an affirmation or denial we are considering it as a judgment. Thus the *judgment* is: "Pareto holds that human society is the subject of many researches." In itself "Human Society is the subject of many researches" is not a judgment in our sense of the term, for it is not *explicitly* an affirmation or denial. It says something which purports to be true—*it* says something. In order to be aware that *Pareto* affirms this, we must go behind the statement itself to questions of its origin: we must consider it as the affirmation of a particular person. But when we consider it in this light, that is, as a judgment, as an affirmation on the part of particular person, we are immediately led to consider when that person made this judgment and on what grounds it was actually made. The understanding of a judgment in other words involves a genetic consideration of the statement in which it terminates. The understanding of a statement, on the other hand, is merely—on this theory as well as in common usage—the understanding of what is said, what is meant, along with the awareness that what is meant purports to be true.

Now it should be clear from this distinction between statements and judgments that the understanding of a historical work consists in an understanding of the statements which it makes, and does not primarily involve an understanding of the author's judgments. And the truth of a historical work consists in the truth of its statements, not in the fact that the author judged as he did on such-and-such grounds. To consider historical truth, therefore, as a function of the conditions on which the historian judged the statements which he made to be true, is a totally irrelevant procedure. It arises out of a confusion of statements with judgments, which is one of the basic errors committed by the historical relativists.

It might, however, be objected to what has just been said that it is sometimes important to check the judgmental processes of a historian in order to see whether or not his statements are sound. How else, it might be asked, are we to know that the historian has not been indulging some imaginative streak at our expense? This objection is of course justifiable, although it does not touch the distinction which we have drawn between statements and judgments, nor does it invalidate the contention that he who wishes to estimate the truth of a historical account must estimate it by the statements which constitute it. Let us make this clear.

If we find that a particular statement made by a historian does not concord with the facts which we believe to characterize the event with which he is dealing, we cannot merely disregard that statement. In such a case we attempt to find the grounds for his judgment, that is, we attempt to determine what conditions of his thought led him into error at this point. But we can only do this by an acceptance of some other statements as they stand: we are not led back through an infinite regress of judgments. Furthermore, we do not say that the statement is false because it was based upon these grounds. Rather, the statement is false because it does not concord with the facts. The reason that it does not concord with the facts is then found to lie in the grounds of the judgment which gave rise to it. Thus the truth or falsity of a statement depends, as we pointed out above, on whether or not what it says holds of the facts with which it purports to deal. No sociological understanding of the conditions under which the statement was made bears the slightest resemblance to an estimate of the truth or falsity of the statement itself.

This view of historical knowledge leads us to assume the philosophic correspondence theory of truth. This assumption must now be justified.

It seems clear when we examine actual historical works that they all presuppose a correspondence theory of truth, no matter how relativistic the theories of the historians themselves may be. It is strange to witness workers in a field denying in theory everything which they assume in practice. Such a dichotomy between theory and practice should trouble a philosopher even more than it should puzzle the historian himself. This situation, which is also current in fields of knowledge other than history, must spring from desperation itself. In history this desperation seems to arise from the fact that historians fail to see how they can make any correspondence theory of truth work.

Choose at will any historical statement and ask how it can be said to correspond to the facts which it purports to grasp. It is at once clear that it is not a "copy" of those facts: the statements "Caesar crossed the Rubicon," or the statement "Goethe failed to appreciate the temple at Paestum," are not "like" the facts with which they deal. And if we say that these statements "correspond" to the facts in each case we do not mean that they themselves resemble the facts. In this, the correspondence theory of truth is not a resemblance or copy theory of truth.[7]

What we do mean when we say that a statement is

[7] Cf., McTaggart: *Nature of Existence*, v. 1, p. 11 f.

true because it corresponds with the facts is that the statement expresses a relation between its terms which holds between the real objects symbolized by those terms. The word "Caesar" symbolizes the real Caesar, the word "Rubicon" symbolizes (in this context) a real river, the word "crossed" symbolizes a certain real type of action done: the whole statement "Caesar crossed the Rubicon" is true if the relation which it expresses did in fact hold of the objects with which it is concerned, if the action which it states was done was actually done. The correspondence theory of truth means this and nothing more: that a statement made "concords" with the fact with which it purports to deal.[8] There is no mystery here, so long as we remember that statements are couched in language and that it is the property of language to refer to non-linguistic entities. And we find that actual historical works all assume this theory of truth: that statements are true when they do refer to real facts, to actual relationships, and that they are false in so far as they fail to do so. We must only remember that not all historical facts are "facts" in the narrowest accepted sense of the term (spatio-temporal facts) in order to be fully aware of the truth of this statement.

The historian who is sceptical of his own work may still ask, however, to what purpose he assumes a correspondence theory of truth when the facts which

[8] *Cf.*, Broad: *Examination of McTaggart's Philosophy*, v. I, p. 77f.

his statements assert are all past, and his statements are therefore unverifiable.

It is true that the pastness of most historical facts places serious limitations upon the historian, for it forces him to accept the recorded statements of other men without direct verification. But these limitations have often been overemphasized. The methods which historians have found to corroborate these statements by independent testimony and by indirect evidence have greatly increased the certainty which the statements possess. However, in regard to the unverifiability of historical statements something further needs to be said.

In the first place, verifiability is not the essential factor in the discovery of the truth. For the act of verification itself must always depend upon hypotheses drawn from past facts, and these facts are no longer verifiable, even though, in many cases, "essentially similar facts" may be adduced to bear out the hypothesis. Further, the act of verification is but one step in the validation of knowledge, and it has no meaning unless an accurate observant insight has already given it clues on which to work. The "repeatable" character of many scientific events and the process of verification itself do provide checks on the accuracy of insight, but they are not substitutes for this insight. The mere repetition of events is not itself responsible for scientific discovery: if we could not find a real relation between events in some one instance, no number of repetitions would show us any such relation. In all of this we can see that verifiability is not the essential factor in the discovery of truth.

In the second place, however, if we examine the material of a historical account we can find certain reasons why the historian does not stand in need of repeated verifications of his statements to the same extent as does the natural scientist. For the historian deals with events which are the common property of many men, while the natural scientist deals with events which usually are observable only under the conditions which characterize the methods of his laboratory. Historical events are therefore observed, and not only are they observed they are in many instances also recorded, by many men in many countries, and this is analogous to the repetition to which the events in the natural sciences are subjected. Thus, from the fact that historical events are everywhere to be found, and from the fact that they are of direct and compelling significance, there arises in historical knowledge a type of "contemporary verification" which is analogous to the "verification by repetition" which is to be found in the natural sciences. The so-called historical "methods" outlined in the textbooks such as those of Bernheim, Langlois and Seignobos, and Bauer, make the most of this type of possible verification.

From these considerations it should be clear that the pastness of historical events, and their unrepeatable nature, does not make historical knowledge impossible, but merely places upon the historian limitations which serve to determine his procedure. In so far as this is the case, the pastness of historical events does not entail a surrender of the correspondence theory of truth which we, along with the practicing historian, have found it necessary to adopt.

The sceptical historian may, however, still challenge the correspondence theory of truth on another ground. For he may inquire how it is possible that his knowledge can correspond to historical events when his access to those events is severely limited by the materials at his disposal. In answer to this question we need merely recall what has previously been pointed out in our discussion: that the correspondence theory of truth only implies that a statement is true when it expresses a relation between its terms which did in fact hold between those terms in actuality. Thus a statement is none the less true because it deals merely with one aspect of an event, so long as it states something of this aspect only.[9] The only consequence of this limitation of source materials is, therefore, one which all historians recognize: that where materials are lacking statements should not be made, or if statements are made the grounds of judgment should be given.

[9] A "historian" of the Spenglerian type might insist that this contention is false because all events in a given culture interpenetrate. But it seems evident that no practicing historian (in contradistinction to a philosopher of history) works on this monistic assumption. It must, however, be acknowledged that in some cases aspects of a historical event so interpenetrate that a statement made concerning one aspect is false because another aspect is not known at the time.

With these considerations we may now close our treatment of the correspondence theory of truth in its relation to statements of historical fact. We have seen that it is essential to draw a distinction between statements and judgments, and that the problem of valid knowledge is a problem of the truth of the statements given, and is not concerned with the judgments out of which those statements originated. The defense of this position forced us to go to some length in a discussion of the correspondence theory of truth in relation to statements of historical fact. If this defense and the distinction which called it forth are acceptable we have overcome the first of the relativist's basic assumptions in regard to historical knowledge.

It will be remembered that the second philosophical assumption of the historical relativist consisted in the view that valuational factors entered into and determined the content of historical knowledge. This assumption, it will also be remembered, was shared by Rickert, Scheler, and Troeltsch, although each of these attempted to escape relativism by affirming a theory of values different from the naturalistic theories of the relativists. It will be our aim in the present discussion to show that regardless of the theory of value which one accepts [10] it is fallacious to hold that valuational judgments determine the content of historical knowledge. Preparatory to

[10] The chief recognized types of value-theory which we shall have in mind in the succeeding discussion are those which hold: 1) that values are concrete ideal essences (the *materielle Wertethik*

this, however, it will be well to single out those aspects of the historian's enterprise which are in fact value-determined.[11]

If one inquires what leads the historian to write a historical account certain determining valuational factors spring immediately to view. For almost any historian would answer, when asked why he undertook to write this or that history, that it appeared to him to be a desirable thing to do. Now the term "desirable" always signifies that a thing so designated is of value, no matter what type of value-theory one holds. Thus we can say that the historian acknowledges (in most cases) that the prime reason for his undertaking is a valuational one.

This general valuational reason for the historian's undertaking may assume an indefinite number of forms. It may, for example, be desirable for the historian to undertake his investigation in order to further his professional ambitions. On the other hand, it may seem desirable to him to satisfy his curiosity concerning these specific events, and once having achieved some measure of satisfaction he may find it desirable to impart to others the understanding

of Scheler and Nicolai Hartmann); or, 2) that value is a quality or non-natural property of objects (the realistic theory of J. Laird and of G. E. Moore); or, 3) that values are "objectives," formal entities which are merely valid, entities which we acknowledge ought-to-be (the Neo-Kantian theories of Rickert and W. M. Urban); or, 4) that value is constituted by a natural relation between a self and its objects, or between two objects neither of which need be a self (the naturalistic theories of R. B. Perry, D. W. Prall, and S. Alexander).

[11] A point of view essentially similar to that here adopted is to be found in B. Schmeidler's treatment of the rôle of values in historical accounts (*Cf., Annalen der Naturphilosophie*, v. III, p. 54).

which he has gained. Or it may appear desirable (as it did to Polybius) to render an account of certain events so that future generations may profit by knowing of them. Or it may be that the historian finds it desirable to preserve for posterity the account of noble deeds, as was the case with Thucydides. The historian may even attempt to render his enterprise intelligible to us by appealing to the ultimate value of truth. These and many other reasons might be given by historians if we questioned them regarding their purposes in producing historical accounts. All these reasons, it will readily be seen, are of a valuational nature, which is merely to say that the historian embarks upon his work because he deems it of value to do so.

This situation is of course not surprising, for it is the common characteristic of men to act in this way. If we ask either the natural scientist or the man-in-the-street the reason for his activities we find that he answers in an analogous fashion. Sometimes the appeal to valuational elements lies deeper, sometimes it is near the surface and readily appears, but wherever men seek to give a justification of their activities it is done by an appeal to those values which that activity fulfills or toward the fulfillment of which it serves. Thus we must acknowledge that the historian is a historian because of the values which to him appear implicit or explicit in his activity.

When we push our inquiry further and ask not merely why a given man is a historian, but also how it is that he wrote of certain events rather than of others, that he dealt with the history of Rome, let us say, rather than with the Industrial Revolution, we find other valuational factors at work. To one historian it may appear preferable to deal with Roman history, because he finds it of greater significance or because his background and talents promise him greater success along that line; [12] to another just the reverse may be the case. But whether these reasons or others are ascribed, we always find that in the choice of the events with which he deals the historian is motivated by valuational factors. We must therefore admit that in this sense also historical works are conditioned by what appears as valuable to the historian himself.

Now the investigation of these determining valuational factors provides an interesting field for that which Mannheim and Scheler have called the sociology of knowledge, for it is certain that judgments concerning the desirability of particular forms of historical inquiry, and even judgments concerning the desirability of historical inquiry as such, are in part determined by the sociological conditions under which the individual lives. Yet this fact in no wise justifies the historical relativist in his claims. For it is one thing to say that a particular historical work would never have been written except for certain valuations, and it is quite another to contend that

[12] Gibbon's choice of the decline and fall of Rome for his subject matter is interesting in this respect, coming as it did after his prior unfulfilled plans.

these valuational factors determine the content of the historical work itself. Thus we are not involved in a relativistic position by our acknowledgment that every historical work contains implicit within its very existence the fact that the historian deemed it desirable to produce such a work.

One further fact must also be pointed out in order to avoid misunderstanding. It is undeniably true that not only the existence but the content of some so-called "historical acounts" is determined by valuational factors. These historical accounts are what is known as propagandistic history. In propaganda, as we know, the purpose which determines that the work be undertaken also determines what that work will contain. Thus, a man may, for some ulterior motive, pretend to describe social events and yet falsify and distort them in order to serve his own political purposes. One thinks immediately of accounts such as Mussolini's autobiography, or history as it is written and rewritten under the guidance of a Ministry of Propaganda and Enlightenment. Such propagandistic history is, of course, not merely a contemporary phenomenon, but has often passed as history in the past. But this type of "historical" writing in so far as it is a deliberate fraud has no right to be called history at all. Even though readers have sometimes accepted such works as true we must define historical knowledge in terms which are consonant with the historian's activity; it would be as foolish to call propaganda "history" as it would be for an economist to call counterfeit coin "money" when he is interested in monetization. The fact that either propaganda or counterfeit coin can "pass" does not alter the situation, for we are asking what history is, and we are not asking what people have accepted as truth in this or that instance. "Everything is what it is, and not another thing," as Bishop Butler has it. And history is history, not propaganda.

Now the relativist would admit that the fact that there are instances of propaganda which are accepted as history does not lead to historical relativism. As Mannheim pointed out, it is only when the valuational aspect which is consciously recognized in propagandistic history can be shown to be an all-pervasive, unconscious, determining factor in every historical account, that relativism follows. And it is precisely this which relativism attempts to establish: that the only difference between propaganda and history lies in the fact that the former is a deliberate, the latter an unknowing, falsification of the nature of historical events. It is this contention that we must therefore attempt to refute.

It should be clear that no matter what theory of a value one adopts, a person cannot be said to value a particular object unless he knows something of the nature of that object, or believes that he does. An object contemplated as good must first of all be an object; it must have a certain reality or it could not be contemplated at all. Thus the relativist cannot mean that the objects which the historian contemplates are merely valuational entities; before they are evaluated they must be objects which are supposedly known.

Now the same situation holds true even where the objects to be known are intimately connected with past valuations. In fields such as the history of religion, of the arts, or of government, and wherever human motives come directly into play, events are very largely value-determined. In these fields events would not have been as they were had not men sought to bring about what to them appeared as a desirable outcome. Some persons may even hold that all historical events are alike in this, that they are at least partially determined by human volition. Our problem, however, does not consist in an attempt to find the place of valuations in history; we are concerned with the place of valuations in the statements of historians. And if we examine the situation we can see that even if historical events are dependent upon human valuations, the judgments of historians concerning those events are not determined by valuational elements. This can be seen from two considerations. In the first place, in so far as the historian attempts to describe these value-determined events he is concerned not with the valuations themselves but with their consequences. In order to discover these consequences he need have no recourse to the valuations out of which they arose: the events are embodied in the historical materials at his disposal, and, in most instances, it is with these events that the

196

historian is primarily concerned. Thus the fact that certain events were at least in part determined by the valuations of a historical personage does not change the historian's mode of procedure, for his objective is to show the nature of these events and their implications with reference to other events. In the second place, even when the historian seeks to relate an event to the valuations out of which it arose he does not appeal to his own set of values. If we attempt to determine why Luther made his break with the Papacy we do not appeal to what we would have done under the same conditions: we attempt to find out on the basis of documentary evidence why Luther (concerning whose behavior quite a bit is known) did that which he did. It is of course true that such explanations are inferences based not only upon the documentary evidence but also upon the historian's knowledge of human behavior, just as every historical statement is based not only upon the documents but upon some insight into the nature of events as they unfold in the real world. The important aspect of the situation is, however, not that valuations are known through inference, but that this inference proceeds on non-valuational grounds. For it will be seen that the historian's knowledge of human behavior lays claim to be true of all subjects, whether he views these subjects as praiseworthy or blameworthy, whether they are sympathic or antipathic to him. A principle of human behavior cannot be established on the grounds of what a given historian would find to be a desirable state of affairs. And historians in fact criticize the attribution of motives to historical personages, just as they criticize any other historical inferences, on grounds of plausibility, that is, whether or not the inference is based on documentary evidence and insight into the real constitution of things.[13] Before valuational elements can come into play something of the nature of the motives must be inferred; thus, here as before, the judgment of fact must precede the judgment of value, and if the historian is not a propagandist his statements will express his judgment of fact.

Perhaps one of the reasons why this situation has been overlooked by the relativists may be found in the tendency of historians to go beyond their statements of fact to statements of value. Thus we have historical accounts which moralize, and we have partisan history in all its varieties. But even in many of these historical works the relativist can find no support for his contention that statements of fact reflect value judgments, for in introducing valuational elements the historian usually attempts to make them so explicit that any reader can discern when the historian's statements express judgments of fact and when they express judgments of value. Few historical works are perfect in this respect, and even fewer are perfect when considered as narrations of actual facts. The relativist too readily pounces upon the presence

---

[13] *Cf.*, what Broad says concerning the "noetic framework" of a belief (*Examination of McTaggart's Philosophy*, v. I, pp. 73-76).

of these imperfections, postulating that behind every historical statement there lurks a malignant spirit of valuation. This postulated spirit cannot be exorcised by any direct evidence on our part, for in belonging to the realm of the unconscious he is too subtle to be caught. We have therefore been forced to adopt a roundabout procedure. We have attempted to show that it is theoretically impossible to hold that one can value that which one does not know. If this be accepted we can say that a judgment of fact is always prior to a judgment of value, and a statement of fact, if it be not propaganda, that is, deliberate deception, expresses a judgment of fact and therefore is not even "implicitly" valuational.

So much would probably be admitted by most historical relativists. Yet the relativist would still cling to the view that implicit in every historical account are the valuations of the historian himself. These thinkers admit that "the facts" are objectively ascertainable; it is their contention that the historical account *as a whole* is nevertheless permeated by the historian's valuations. It is here that the distinction between historical facts and historical interpretations is drawn. While admitting that the facts are accessible to the historian through his own observations and through the testimony of others, the relativist will insist that these facts can only be transformed into a historical account by the historian's own value-determined point of view. This contention, as we have seen, characterizes the thought of Rickert and

Troeltsch, as well as that of the relativists themselves.

Now any such distinction between the historian's discovery of facts and his interpretation of those facts is a wholly fallacious distinction. For the facts themselves, which on this view are objectively "given" or discovered, are not different in nature from the sum and substance of the historical account itself. Every recognized historical account is a tissue of facts, and if these facts are objectively ascertainable by research then they are not dependent upon the historian's activity. This the relativist might grant and yet hold that while the facts remain untransformed in the final work, their inter-connections come from the historian himself.

This, then, is the crux of the matter: those who maintain that valuational elements enter into the actual constitution of historical accounts believe that it is only through some unrecognized valuational judgments that the historian orders and arranges his facts. However, if we examine historical works as they stand we find that this contention is false. For every historical fact is given in some specific context in which it leads on to some other fact. If the historian tells us that "Caesar crossed the Rubicon" his statement calls forth questions concerning the consequences of that act. Now for any one familiar with the context of that event these consequences are political, and it would be meaningless for the historian to describe Caesar's itinerary on his journey to Rome. If the historian says that "Bluecher crossed the Rhine with so and so many troops," the context of that event demands that we should look to the consequences in the battle of Waterloo. Thus when a historian makes a statement of fact it is not with an isolated fact, but with a fact in a given context that he is concerned. And in that context the fact itself leads on to further facts without any intermediation or selection based upon the historian's valuational attitudes, class interests, or the like. If this were not the case, that is, if the relativist were correct in his assumption, we should have to appeal to our knowledge of the historian himself or to some general cultural value to determine how one fact is related to another in his historical account. That we do not do this, but consider the concrete facts as themselves possessing a definite meaning, significance, and order, testifies to the non-valuational character of that which binds the facts into a historical account.

The same point may be brought out through another approach. If we ask ourselves why certain historical accounts which contain no mistakes in chronology (and the like) appear to us to be inadequate we find that certain relevant facts have been omitted or that the interconnections between the facts given are forced. Now if the historical relativist were correct in assuming that it is simply the historian's own personality, or that of his age, which determines the connections between facts in a historical account it would be perfectly impossible to criticize a historical work on the grounds that something relevant had been omitted or that connections between events were not what the historian claimed them to be. Since these are the grounds of our criticism of historical works it seems clear that the theory of relativism does not conform to the data which it seeks to explain. This is the more serious since the relativist tries to explain why one historian criticizes the work of another, finding the reason in some difference in their unconsciously accepted values. But the actual grounds of historical criticism are quite different, as we have pointed out; they consist in showing that the historical material itself demands another arrangement of the facts set down.

We have seen, then, that an actual examination of historical works and of historical criticism leads us to doubt the relativistic contention that the arrangement of facts derives from the historian's valuational attitudes. The facts seem to have an arrangement and order of their own. But if valuational judgments do not enter into historian's arrangement of facts they do not enter into the content of historical knowledge at all, for we have already seen that the relativist must admit that the knowledge of the facts themselves does not depend upon such judgments.

Our argument here, however, remains still incomplete, since we have not demonstrated what is meant by the statement that concrete facts possess a definite meaning, significance, and order of their own. It is with this problem that our next two chapters will be concerned.

CHAPTER VII

Relevance and Causation in History

Since Hume and Kant it has often been assumed by philosophers that whatever traits of structure the objects of our knowledge possess must be attributed to the activity of the human mind. According to such a view the real events of the world, if we could ever perform the impossible and see them in themselves, would present us with a mere flux, devoid of all order, coherence, and meaning. The structure which we find in reality as it is known is attributed to the transformation which data undergo in being made objects of knowledge. It will readily be seen that historical relativism falls into line with this assumption in claiming that the content of every historical work, in so far as its structure is concerned, depends upon the valuational interests and attitudes of the historian.

In the present and succeeding chapters it will be our concern to offer a theory which can explain the structure of historical works without appealing to valuational interests. This theory will start out from an assumption diametrically opposed to that commonly made by philosophers. We hold that the order to be found in nature and history as they are known by us may really characterize the events of the world independently of the mind's activity.

We shall not attempt to justify this assumption, for such a justification would run far beyond the limits of the present work. We may, however, be permitted to point out two factors which would be relevant in such an attempted justification. The first of these factors is positive, and may be stated as follows. If we find the characteristic activity of the human mind to be an ordering activity, then in so far as the human mind belongs to the realm of nature we may say that there is at least one element of nature which somehow has order implicit within it; to deny that any other elements may share this characteristic would be in effect to cut the mind loose from nature. He who wishes to leave the mind outside of the realm of nature may do so, and accept the consequences which this entails for his psychology and his metaphysics (not to mention those which it would have for theology).

The second factor which seems to point toward a justification for the assumption that order is implicit in the events of nature is negative and appears to us to carry even more weight. It may be stated as follows. If we hold that the order found in objects as known is due to the mind's activity, we are faced by the problem of why it is that the mind attributes one form of order to certain of the elements in its experience and another form of order to certain other elements. On any assumption such as the Kantian this

204

problem must remain to the end of time what Windelband calls "a sacred mystery." Let him who will, accept such mysteries as the ultimate terminus of philosophic discussion. To us it seems preferable to start from mysteries and conclude with some definite knowledge, rather than to start from grounds of which we feel ourselves to be sure and proceed to a point where the very search for an answer becomes meaningless.

Such lines of approach, then, would be those adopted by us were we attempting to justify the assumption that events may possess an order, coherence, and meaning independent of the activities of the human mind. It seems more profitable, however, to proceed to an account of what we mean by this assertion rather than to engage in a polemic on so ultimate a metaphysical problem. And in truth it may be said that the most effective fashion of refuting a false metaphysical position is to be found in a clarification of that which the false and the true positions entail. For no metaphysics can be true which denies the data on which it rests, and every metaphysical judgment must rest on some data given in concrete experience. Now we have already attempted to show that historical relativism is incompatible with the set of data which it attempts to explain, and that such alternatives to relativism as are presented by Rickert and others are equally unsatisfactory in so far as their conformity to historical practice is in question. It now remains, therefore, to show in what sense the presence of order, coherence, and meaning in historical events makes the historian's enterprise intelligible and historical criticism valid.

In attempting to do this we shall find it necessary to use the twin concepts of relevance and causation. Before showing their applicability to the historian's procedure it will be well to make clear what we take the meaning of these concepts to be.

In criticizing concrete works which purport to give us knowledge in some field of research we often say that a certain statement is "relevant" or "irrelevant." The same terms are also applied to the logic of arguments which arise in ordinary discourse, and, in given contexts, to propositions (i.e., to statements considered merely as logical entities). In all of these cases the concept of relevance expresses some definite relation between a statement, or a judgment, or a proposition, and the context in which it is being considered. The assumption has often been made that this relationship which we call relevance holds between statements (or judgments, or propositions) merely because the mind judges, or finds itself "forced" to judge, in a certain way. According to this assumption the relation of relevance pertains between statements, or judgments, or propositions, because of some "inner" necessity, and not because of any objective relations implicit in the material with which the statements, judgments, or propositions deal. We shall here attempt to show that relevance cannot be explained in terms of any "subjective" necessity; that, on the contrary, we can only attach meaning to the terms "relevant" and "irrelevant" if we recognize that there are relations within the material dealt with which demand one statement (judgment, or proposition) rather than another.

Since, in the interests of brevity, we cannot attempt to deal with the problem of relevance in all fields, we shall confine the discussion which follows to the question of the relevance of one statement to another. This limitation excludes from consideration the problem of the relevance of one judgment to another: for example, why it is that an argument *ad hominem* is said to be irrelevant. Furthermore, it excludes the relation of relevance which pertains between two propositions considered in a given context: for example, two mathematical propositions in the context of a given proof.[1] We assume, however, that a demonstration essentially similar to that which follows might be made to show that logical relevance in judgments, and propositional relevance in deductive proofs, likewise depend upon the nature of the material involved. The present exclusion of these problems may, however, be defended not merely on the grounds of brevity. We have already seen that historical understanding is almost wholly concerned with statements considered as statements, and it is with the problem of historical understanding that we

[1] On the view previously taken in regard to the nature of propositions, it seems impossible to hold that propositions can ever be relevant to each other outside of a given context such as that furnished by a deductive proof.

are here concerned. In those cases in which the historian must consider a statement as a judgment, the traditional logical treatment of "material inference" provides an adequate groundwork on which to proceed. It is only crucial therefore to give an account of the relevance of statements to each other.

General usage points unmistakably to the fact that when we say one statement is relevant or irrelevant to another we intend to express some relation which holds between the entities with which the statements are concerned. If we characterize a statement concerning human freedom as irrelevant to a statement concerning the behavior of electrons, or if we characterize a statement concerning Newton's first law as irrelevant to a statement concerning the course of the French Revolution, it is on the basis of the belief that these entities have nothing to do with each other. What we mean by characterizing such statements as irrelevant is that the fact which is asserted by one statement has no bearing on the facts asserted by the statements which form its immediate context. In this, relevance is a category of facts. When we say "the acceleration of gravitation depends upon mass and distance. Everything else is indifferent to it. The freezing of water depends on temperature and pressure, and nothing else is relevant," [2] it is clearly with relevance as a category of facts that we are dealing. Likewise, when it is said that "the qualities of a term

2 M. R. Cohen: *Reason and Nature*, p. 151.

are *relevant* to the relations in which it stands," [3] relevance must be taken as a category of facts, and not as a product of our apprehension and description of them.

Objection to this argument from general usage might be raised on various epistemological grounds. It might, for example, be held that relevance can be claimed to be a category of facts only because facts are "made" by the mind's activity, that, ultimately, the relevance of one statement to another is merely the way in which the mind "works." Against such an epistemological objection it is possible to raise an adequate empirical line of defense. Let us suppose that the relevance or non-relevance of statements is a function of the mind's activity; on what grounds will it then be possible to characterize any given statement as irrelevant? If an individual contends (as it has often been contended) that a statement concerning some physical law is relevant to a descriptive statement concerning the fate of a given civilization, on what grounds will we be able to show him to be mistaken? If we disregard the nature of the facts with which the statements purport to deal, and turn our attention wholly to the mind's activity, every statement included in any description would have to be acknowledged as somehow relevant for him who made the statement. Whether we did or did not understand the place of that statement in the whole descriptive account we could not call the statement irrelevant; we

[3] A. C. Ewing: *Idealism*, p. 126. (*Cf.*, p. 127, n. 1).

could only say that for us it was irrelevant. But even this assertion, that a statement is "irrelevant for us," cannot be explained except by assuming relevance to be a category of facts. For in saying this we must mean either a) that we do not see how the nature of the facts justifies it, or b) we must mean that we cannot understand it. But obviously a) gives away the whole case. And no less so does b). For in saying that we cannot understand a statement in a given context we must mean that we cannot see the connection of the fact which the statement asserts with the facts asserted by the other statements. Thus, here again, we see that relevance must be admitted to be a category of facts, and not merely a category of our "subjective" apprehension of those facts. No matter what metaphysical status we attribute to "facts," this contention still holds. We may say, then, that relevance is a relational term, which, whether it be applied to facts themselves, or to our statements concerning facts, must be assumed to be grounded not in our "understanding" merely, but in the facts themselves. It is only by virtue of the relevance of facts to each other that we can understand the relevance of statements made concerning them.

To have stated this point of view does not, of course, show us the precise nature of the relationship called "relevance." In attempting to point out the nature of this relationship we shall again confine ourselves to the problem of the relevance of one statement to another.

The relation of relevance between facts (or statements concerning facts) may, I submit, be stated as follows: One fact is relevant to another when they are so connected that the mind cannot apprehend the nature of the latter without an understanding of the former. Applied to statements concerning facts, this means that one statement is relevant to another only in those cases in which the facts dealt with are so related that the apprehension of the nature of one of them is impossible unless we take into account the fact dealt with by the other statement. Thus, we cannot understand the fact that water freezes without taking into account the facts of temperature and pressure. On the other hand, we can understand the behavior of electrons without taking into account human freedom, just as we can understand the course of the French Revolution without taking into account Newton's first law of gravitation; thus, in each case, these are irrelevant facts. In order to avoid misunderstanding, two further points in regard to this relationship must be made clear.

In the first place, we must point out that we have not attempted to "reduce" the relationship of relevance between facts. Nor have we attempted to "define" this relationship, if by "definition" is meant anything more than stating what we mean by a term. The relationship of relevance cannot be reduced, nor can it be defined in the usual sense, for it is an "ultimate" in our common apprehension of the world.[4] This can be seen from the fact that in characterizing the relation of relevance we were forced to appeal to human insight (understanding) while at the same time pointing out that relevance was not an addendum furnished to the facts by the operations of the human mind.

In the second place, it must be noted that our characterization of the meaning of the term relevance laid stress on the "nature" of a fact. We did not say that any fact was relevant to another whenever the "existence" of the latter could not be understood without reference to the former. At first glance it might seem that the two terms should, in this context, be interchangeable, but this view can be shown to be mistaken. First, however, we must attempt to clarify this terminology.

It should be noted that a fact is not the same as an event.[5] What we mean by a fact is the occurrence of a specific event at specific time and place. Thus, a flash of lightning is an event; *that* the flash of lightning occurred is a fact. Facts, therefore, do not exist; their reality depends upon the existence of events. We must therefore rephrase the problem which we have raised before we attempt to discuss it.

Our problem rephrased asks whether facts are relevant to each other whenever the events about

[4] This is merely to say that it is an ultimate characteristic of our phenomenal world, and is in that sense irreducible. Further philosophic analysis can show, as we hope to make clear, that whenever the relationship of relevance *does hold* (that is, when statements about it are veridical) we are dealing with a causal relationship.

[5] *Cf.*, Broad: *Examination of McTaggart's Philosophy*, v. I, p. 57.

which they are asserted are so related that the one could not have occurred had it not been for the *previous* [6] existence of the other. Stated concretely, we may ask: are all of the facts which are concerned with the presence of water at this place and at this time relevant to the fact that this water freezes? To this our answer must be negative. Whatever facts are necessary to the *nature* of a given fact (that the water freezes) are relevant to it. Whatever facts are necessary merely to its being a fact (to there being water here to freeze) are not relevant to it. Unless, in accordance with common usage, we confine the concept of relevance in this fashion we are bound to render it useless for historical as well as for scientific purposes. Ample justification for this view will be found in much that follows; here it is sufficient to have called to the reader's attention that one fact can only be said to be relevant to another if it is essential to an understanding of the latter's concrete nature.

Having thus attempted to point out the meaning of the concept of relevance, and having attempted to guard against serious misunderstandings of this meaning, we shall now turn to a discussion of causation. This represents no abrupt shift in our argument, for it must be acknowledged that the concepts of causation and of relevance cannot be divorced from each other. One need only recall Mill's discussion of "relevant" conditions in his treatment of the Canons

[6] The significance of this qualification will come out in our discussion of causality and the relation of "existential dependence."

of Induction to see that this is the case. As we proceed
we shall actually find that the relevance of one fact
to another depends upon a causal connection between
the events asserted by the facts. A discussion of this
point must, however, be preceded by the attempt to
render explicit what we take the causal relation to be.

Before attempting to point out the precise meaning
of the term "causal relation" as we shall use it, it will
be well to draw certain distinctions. In the first place
it should be clear that any attempt to determine the
meaning to be ascribed to the term "the causal relation" is not an attempt to determine the nature of
any particular causal relationship. When we inquire
into the meaning of a term we are not attempting to
point out the particular nature of some instance of
it. Such illustrations may be helpful, but, as every
reader of Plato should know, they do not solve the
problem. Now this warning is so obvious that it would
seem impertinent were it not for the fact that many
philosophers have committed the error in a somewhat
disguised form.[7] For they have been content to define
the causal relationship in terms which restrict its
applicability to one particular set of instances, for
example, instances of causation within the sphere of
mechanics. But the use to which the causal relationship is put in other sets of instances, for example, in
physiology, makes any such restricted statements of

[7] I regret to say that Professor Alexander's treatment of causality
seems to border on this fallacy. (*Cf., Space, Time and Deity,* v. I,
pp. 279-299). For a clear instance of the fallacy, however, one can
turn to Gustav Heim: *Ursache und Bedingung.*

the nature of causality a mere statement of a specific causal principle. In order to be sure that we are not substituting a statement concerning one particular causal principle for a statement concerning the meaning of the causal relationship itself, we must not confine our illustrative instances or the course of our argument to any one science nor to any one type of science.

It should also be clear that when we discuss the meaning of the causal relationship we are not discussing what generally goes under the name of "the law of universal causation." The law of universal causation holds that every event must have a cause. But it is obvious that before we can make any such sweeping statement we must know what we mean by the causal relation. Only then would it be fruitful to inquire into the nature of the grounds for such a judgment, or into the truth of the statement itself.

This second distinction leads us on to a third. It has sometimes been claimed that the world is constructed in such a manner that it would be possible to foretell any future state of its existence if we knew the state of its existence at some particular time and knew, also, the law (or laws) which are inherent in its structure. This view, of which the prime example is afforded by Laplace with his hypothesis of an omniscient spirit, may best be called "the deterministic view of nature." Now it should be clear that this extreme form of determinism rests on a complicated assumption whose parts are the following: a) that causal relations are real; *b*) that every event in the world is causally determined; *c*) that causal determination can always be stated in terms of one law, or in terms of several laws which bear a definite systematic relationship to each other; *d*) that this law (or these laws) holds throughout the whole universe, now and forever. If the full content of this deterministic assumption is once grasped it becomes evident that the problem of the nature of the causal relation is not identical with the problem of determinism. In fact, an analysis of the deterministic assumption makes clear that it presupposes a certain view of the causal relation, namely, that causal relations are real and are statable in terms of natural law.[8] But such a view cannot be arrived at (unless it be inherited from one's predecessors) without an examination of diverse instances which are termed instances of causal relation.

Thus we are thrown back to the concrete problem of the meaning of causation. We shall, to be sure, have to determine whether the meaning of the causal relationship necessarily involves that cause and effect be linked together by natural laws, but we shall be spared an examination of both the principle of universal causation and of the principle of determinism as a whole. With this our problem is at once clarified and simplified. To it we may now turn.

Everyone must be aware that there has been in recent years an increasing scepticism regarding the validity of causal analysis in the natural sciences. Such

---

[8] *Cf.,* Ducasse: *Causation and the Types of Necessity,* p. 21, 40 f.

scepticism must of course rest on a prior notion of what is meant by causality. It will be illuminating to examine the notion of causality held by those who reject its applicability to nature.

The scientifically oriented thinkers who reject the concept of causality have generally taken that concept to mean the production of a thing, or the production of a change in a thing or its states, by some previously existing object. That which produces the thing, or change in the thing, has been called the cause, and the new result has been called the effect. This view of causation as applied to events in nature has been open to criticism on various grounds.

It has, in the first place, been pointed out that such a view of causation is based upon a certain primitive animism. Thus, Professor Cohen says: "When we popularly speak of a thing's causing something else, we undoubtedly tend to attribute to the thing something analogous to human compulsion, something of muscular tension or the feelings of activity and passivity when we wilfully push or are pulled contrary to our will. Such animism is out of place in modern scientific physics.[9]

In the second place it has been pointed out that the notion of causality which we are discussing is never in fact used by the natural scientist. The natural scientist states the results of his investigation in non-causal terms. Again Professor Cohen points out: "Technical and mathematical language . . . is

[9] M. R. Cohen: *Reason and Nature*, p. 224.

surely, if slowly, replacing expressions of causal relations with mathematical functions or equations." [10] When a physicist speaks of heat or gravity as "causes" he is merely slipping back into an "anthropomorphic" way of speaking due to the great pressure of popular usage, or due to the need of vivid metaphorical expression.[11]

A third source of dissatisfaction with the notion of causality (as interpreted by its critics) is also evident in Professor Cohen's rejection. He says: "The whole tendency of modern experimental as well as mathematical physics is to eliminate the notion of matter as an *ultimate* substance. . . ." [12] But this means that "the power to produce" has really lost its habitat, for where can this power lie if not in a material substrate? The popular notion of causality, as it was usually interpreted, demanded that all events be regarded as derivative from ultimate substantial entities. When the ultimate substantial nature of matter began to disappear under the bombardments of physical research, the popular notion of causality was seriously undermined. For "the power to produce a thing or some change in a thing" is most easily understood as being due to some quality (visible only in its effects) which is to be found in the ultimate substantial core of a previously existing thing. In the physical science of today, in which there exist only events, or as some choose to call them, "occurrents," wherein lies the

10 *Ibid.,* p. 224.
11 *Ibid.,* p. 224.
12 *Ibid.,* p. 225.

power to produce *this,* rather than some other, effect?

Now something must be said in regard to each of the above reasons for rejecting "the popular notion of causality." It should first be noted, however, that the objections to it are well-founded in the field of current theoretical natural science, and thus are not to be lightly disregarded. For it would be meaningless to give an analysis of causation which is out of joint with precisely those instances of explanation which we are accustomed to think of as the most certainly causal in character. We must therefore conclude that the specific notion of causality which is currently attacked by the physicist does not provide a tenable definition of the causal relationship. However, it will be well to draw what we can from an analysis of each of these objections.

When the critic of that which we shall call "the popular view of causality" points out that this view is animistic (and therefore vicious in this enlightened age), he has in mind only one thing: that such a view is, as Professor Cohen has said, "out of place in modern scientific physics." He does not say that the popular view of causality has no place anywhere in the modern world. If he said this he would be guilty of gross error. There is nothing animistic in saying with McTaggart that "an east wind may be the cause of a bad temper. And the ambition of Napoleon may be the cause of bullet-holes in the walls of Hougoumont." [13] It is also perfectly possible to say that the

13 McTaggart: *Philosophical Studies,* p. 168.

motion of one billiard ball is the cause of the motion of another without being guilty of "anthropomorphism"; but in saying this we must be aware that we are not speaking "scientifically." And here is precisely the crucial point: the popular view of causality is not adequate when it is introduced into the realm of the natural sciences as they exist today. But this does not preclude the possibility that it is in some sense meaningful when employed within some other restricted field of experience. This fact should put us on our guard against taking every criticism of the notion of causality as universally applicable.

In regard to the second objection which has been made to the popular view of causality we must point out that "in studying the logic of the natural sciences, we tend to forget that they have a history." [14] While it is true that at the present level of advancement in some of the natural sciences the relationship between events is expressed in terms of mathematical functions or equations, it by no means follows from this that the notion of causality need be discarded from these sciences. Although this notion may not appear in any mathematical statements to which a science attains, it may be the case that in the earlier stages of the development of a science the notion of causality was necessary, and that this notion is still in some sense implicit within those mathematical statements. It would be folly to prejudge the issue as to whether science is merely concerned with mathematically

[14] R. M. Eaton: *General Logic,* p. 484.

formulable laws before we had attempted to substitute for the popular view of the cause-effect relationship some more adequate notion of causality. The adequacy of any such notion must be tested against the actual procedures of those natural sciences on the basis of which causality has been denied, and we must be careful not to overlook the aspects of those procedures which led to the formulation of the mathematical laws. By means of this method we shall be in a better position to judge whether or not those who reject the notion of causality on the basis of the current attainments of the natural sciences (in this case chiefly physics) are justified in doing so. Until we have attempted to put forward an adequate view of the causal relationship we must leave the question open as to whether the incompatibility between the popular view of causal explanation and the ideal of mathematically expressed physical laws makes the concept of cause meaningless.

In regard to the third objection raised by the critics against the term causality as they understand it, something more definite needs to be said. We have pointed out why the rejection of "substances" in favor of "events" makes the popular view of causality more difficult to maintain. This difficulty may not, of course, be insuperable, and since we have found other grounds for rejecting the popular view of causality, there seems to be no reason why this criticism should be stressed. However, it will be well to inquire briefly into what the scientific use of the term "events" implies for our knowledge of the nature of the world.

By "an event" the scientifically oriented philosopher generally means "anything that endures at all." [15] Now such an entity may be either qualitatively alike or qualitatively different at adjacent points in its history, but whatever its qualitative nature may be it is clear that it must be "pervaded by a certain special unity and continuity." [16] Otherwise it would not be *an* event, distinguishable from other events. But this unity which characterizes an event is not merely another name for absolute simplicity, for events generally (and perhaps always) possess a certain complexity; their unity is in some sense a unity of pattern. Thus events are usually spoken of as "strands of history," for they possess multiple factors bound together into *one* event. Now these factors, according to the scientific view, are themselves events, since they too are entities which endure. Thus events may have subevents within them, and may themselves be subevents of other events. On such a view, the world as a whole (if we may speak of it as a whole) is made up of various strands of history, which are termed events, and these strands possess definite relations to each other by virtue of the fact that the subevents included in one strand are themselves strands of history, and also form part of other, independent strands.

Such, in brief, being the view which science, for its own purposes, seems to accept in place of the tradi-

[15] C. D. Broad: *Scientific Thought*, p. 54.
[16] *Ibid.*, p. 408.

tional view of substances, their qualities, and their relations, we may now inquire as to what significance this view has for the meaning of causation.

It will readily be seen that the relation between cause and effect is a relation between events, since these are all that truly exist in the scientific world-picture with which we are dealing. Nor is it difficult to discover precisely what relation between events is to be denominated as the causal relation. For the term causation is inextricably bound up with the origin of an event or with some qualitative change within an event. This we already noted in connection with the popular view of causation. However, the popular view of causation tends to look upon these changes in terms of "productive activity," and to differentiate between that event which "produces" the change and those events which are merely accessory to the exercise of this productive capacity. The former event is then called the cause, and the latter set of events are called "conditions." But this distinction between cause and conditions breaks down as soon as we attempt to make any rigorous causal analysis. Within science the notion of cause is strictly confined to the set of events which are sufficient and necessary conditions for the existence of a new event or for the existence of a new quality within an already enduring event. These conditions may best be termed the "determining conditions" of an event; and the complete set of these conditions is spoken of as the cause of the event in question. The relation between "cause and effect" is thus a relation of *existential dependence,* the cause of the event being the complete set of those events "without which the event would not have occurred, or whose non-existence or non-occurrence would have made some difference to it." [17]

Now it may seem to the reader that we mean more by the causal relationship than is contained in this apparently empty relation of existential dependence. A single reminder should serve to allay such doubts: we are attempting to deal with the meaning of causation and not with specific causal connections. To go beyond the relation of existential dependence would be to substitute some particular causal relationship for the meaning of causation itself, and we would thus be put in a position where no general signification could be attached to the term in question.

It should already be clear that the concept of existential dependence is as applicable to cases of causation which fall within the sphere of everyday living as it is applicable to scientific instances. The succeeding chapter will undoubtedly serve to make this even more apparent. Here, however, we must note the differences rather than the similarities between the popular and the scientific uses of the cause-effect relationship. As we have already seen, one important difference lies in the fact that the scientist does not seek to reduce this existential dependence to a simple, unanalyzable transference of productive power from

<hr />

[17] Cited from Joseph: *Introduction to Logic,* p. 401. *Cf.,* L. S. Stebbing: *Modern Introduction to Logic,* p. 271.

one event to the other. Yet existential dependence maintains its meaning within scientific analysis in spite of this refusal to consider the cause as a productive agent. For the concept of an event as a strand of history fills out this apparently empty relationship with a wealth of concrete meaning. When we consider an event as an enduring entity, pervaded by a specific unity, and at the same time comprised of multiple subevents, the relation of existential dependence becomes that which binds the event to its subevents. The complete set of these subevents, without which the event itself could not exist, becomes the cause of the event in question.[18] The subevents are literally the determining conditions of there being any event at all, for where there are no fibers there can be no strand of history. And thus we see the manner in which the scientific view of events does not rob causation of its meaning, but on the contrary makes this meaning more clear than it would otherwise have been.

Yet an objection to this meaning might be raised on the ground that it overlooks the temporal character of the causal relationship. And here we find that the scientific view of causality differs from the popular view in yet another respect. In the latter that which is the cause is apparently antecedent in time to the effect, and the causal relationship is held to be the production of an effect by some power residing in a

---

[18] This analysis does not hold (and would absolutely deny) that the complete set of subevents is itself the event; thus we may speak of the set of subevents as the cause of the event.

temporally prior substance. But when, as in the scientific treatment of causality, we treat the cause of an event as the set of conditions which determine that event, we find that these conditions are contemporary with the effect. The cause of a disease, for example, is not antecedent to the course of the disease, if by antecedent we mean that it produced the disease and then ceased to determine it. The presence of certain micro-organisms which may be spoken of as a determining condition (i.e., "cause") of the disease is contemporaneous with the disease itself. This fact has been overlooked by those who hold to the popular notion of causation, and its full consequences have also been overlooked by many who attempt to hold to a scientific view of the causal relationship.[19]

If one asks the layman what caused the death of Alexander, King of Jugoslavia, he will answer promptly, surely, and correctly, that an assassin in the crowd at Marseilles shot him. Yet if one asks the same question of a physician who was in attendance, the answer, if given in a professional capacity, would be quite different. The physician would not trace the death of Alexander to the firing of a pistol shot: the determining conditions of the death would be found within the king's body. Thus the layman would apparently attribute the death to an antecedent cause,

[19] R. L. Saw in an interesting article starts out to inquire "How can two characters be necessarily related in time," and concludes that this topic should be examined with respect to the following question: "What is the relationship of a pattern of related elements to the events which may be said to sustain the pattern." (*Cf., Proc. Aristotelian Society*, v. XXXV, p. 112.)

while the scientist would find its determining conditions to be contemporaneous with what is called dying.

This apparently irreconcilable divergence in approach between the popular and scientific views of causality must, of course, be overcome if we are to be able to include instances of both views within one meaning. But it is not this with which we are at the moment concerned. What we wish to make clear is the fact that the scientific analysis of determining conditions does not make the causal relationship one of temporal sequence. To be sure, no event which postdates a given event can be called a determining condition of that event, for clearly the relation which we have called existential dependence would not hold in such a case. But there is no reason why we should not call an event a determining condition of another event even when it did not actually antedate that event. Thus, one of the determining conditions of the actual path of a given projectile may be an event which had its origin at a point in time later than that at which the projectile's trajectory had begun; to use an absurd but clear-cut illustration, the repercussion of a cannon-shot might be a determining condition of the path of an arrow, even though the arrow was shot first. It would of course be possible (and in some cases it would be desirable) to treat the path of the arrow as two events, one up to the point at which the repercussion altered its course, and one after that point. Yet if we are interested in the determining conditions of the actual path of the arrow, we cannot avoid saying that the effect of the repercussion was among them; and this holds true no matter at what moment in time the cannon was fired. Thus we can see from this illustration (and from any number of analogous ones) that we must not look upon the cause of an event as being (in its entirety) prior to the event of which it is the cause.

This, however, raises the question as to whether the cause (in its entirety) is ever prior to the effect. And here we can see, if we again adopt the criterion of existential dependence, that if it is meant by "prior" that the cause does not temporally overlap the effect, then no cause is prior to its effect. For it must be remembered that by the cause we are here referring to the set of determining conditions of an event, and if the whole of this set of events had ceased to be before the "effect" existed, then these events could not be held to be its determining conditions. Of course, the determining conditions of an event need not be coterminous in time with it, that is, they need not be of exactly the same duration as it is. In fact, if they were coterminous with it, this event would stand isolated in the whole of nature, having no connections with anything outside of itself. Our argument leads to no such absurdities, but holds that in order to be a determining condition of any other event, a given event must be at least partially contemporaneous with it, that is, their durations must overlap. To give up this view would be to return to the popular view of causation, where the cause produces the effect at a definite point in time, and we would thus fall prey to the Humian analysis which derives much of its strength from the fact that the cause had been considered as separable in time from the effect.[20]

It might, however, be objected that to make the determining conditions of an event necessarily contemporaneous with it would be to rob the causal relation of much of its significance. We could not, for example, speak of a "first cause" or "remote causes" as actual causal factors in an event unless they were considered as present determinants of that event. This must be acknowledged to be true; yet as we shall attempt to show, this does not really rob the causal relationship of any vital significance. What we say on this point will, furthermore, serve to overcome the divergence which was apparent between instances of causation as seen by the scientist and by the layman.

When the doctor speaks of the cause of the death of King Alexander, and finds the cause to be a certain definite set of events occurring within that person's body, he is not contradicting the layman who says that the cause of the death is the assassination, nor is he contradicting the historian who may say that the cause of the person's death was his tyranny (or else the machinations of a foreign power). For the events with which they are dealing are in a very real sense different events. The doctor is speaking of the event

[20] Cf., B. Russell: *On the Notion of Cause; Proc. of Aristotelian Society*, v. XIII, p. 5.

which we might call "dying"; the layman is speaking of the event which might be called "the fatal shooting of Alexander"; the historian is dealing with "the political assassination of Alexander." Now these "three" events are very different in scope; they are, so to speak, on different levels of discourse. They do, however, have a definite connection with each other, as can be seen from the fact that the third embraces the second, and the second embraces the first.

If we take other illustrations we can see in them equal differences between the events dealt with by the scientist and the directly experienced events of the layman. Take McTaggart's statement that an east wind may be the cause of a bad temper, which we have already cited as a non-scientific instance of a causal relation. I take it that McTaggart means: remove the influence of the east wind and my bad temper will disappear. In this the presence of the east wind is a determining condition of bad temper, and thus can be referred to in causal terms. Now the scientist does not (presumably) speak of the east wind as the cause of a case of bad temper, for "bad temper" to him is not the same event as is one's directly experienced bad temper. Let us call the event X the scientific equivalent of bad temper. The scientist then attempts to find the determining conditions of X. If both he and the introspecting layman are correct in their causal attribution, then the scientist will find that among the determining conditions of the event X there were events of the class Y which are the scientific equivalents of what our introspectionist would call "the east wind" (or are existentially dependent upon these scientific equivalents of "the east wind"). Here again, then, the scientist is dealing with "a different event," or, if one prefers, with the same event at a different level of discourse. Thus the scientist is not contradicting the layman, so long as it is clear that the scientific events and the events of ordinary experience bear an assignable relation to each other.[21]

With these illustrations in mind, it should be evident that we have not turned the whole realm of causal relationships over to the scientist, and thus robbed the term "cause" of its vital significance. We have, to be sure, attempted to raise a barrier to the attribution of a causal relationship between a Deistic deity and the universe, and we have attempted to rule out of meaningful investigations the search for remote causes. In respect to both of these points we can do no better than again quote McTaggart, who says "If A is the cause of B, then the existence of A determines the existence of B. And it determines it in some way which does not hold between all things in the universe, so that it is possible for A to be the cause of B, and not the cause of C." [22]

We have, then, seen that the causal relation is one

[21] This relation is again that of existential dependence. It is one of the objects of psychological investigation, and also one of the objects of a phenomenological investigation of scientific procedures, to establish this relation. (*Cf.*, our discussion of *"phenomenal"* and *"scientific"* objects, below, note 23.)

[22] McTaggart: *Philosophical Studies*, p. 156.

of existential dependence between events which are contemporaneous but which are not necessarily co-terminous in time. We have seen that this is precisely the meaning which the causal conception has when it is used by the scientist; and we have also seen that the instances of causation with which the layman is concerned are of the same type. The apparent use of the popular "anthropomorphic" conception of causality, in which a prior cause produces the effect, is easily, and without distortion, brought within the framework of the scientific use. For it will be seen that the difference between lay and scientific causal explanations is due not to incompatible *conceptions* of causality, but results from the difference between the *instances* of causation which each chooses. This difference may appear at either of two points. In the case of the death of Alexander, the layman was concerned with a longer-enduring event than was the scientist: the layman was speaking of the fatal shooting of the king, while the doctor was speaking of the death of the king, which was an event included in that fatal shooting. In our other illustration, that of the east wind causing bad temper, the events dealt with by scientist and layman were of equal duration, but they were "the same event seen from two different points of view," that is, the layman was dealing with "phenomenal objects," while the scientist was dealing with "scientific objects." [23] It is in this fashion that

[23] I use the term "phenomenal object" in this sense in which it is used by the Gestalt psychologists; in this sense a tree as a phe-

one can see that instances of causation which seem to depend upon the popular notion of causality do not run counter to the meaning of causation as it is used in science. The popular notion of causality, as we have already seen, must be discarded as giving the meaning of the causal relationship; but we can now see that it may be valid in dealing with instances of causation among phenomenal objects. Its validity within this field is only to be restricted by the proviso that when we say that one phenomenal object "produces" another, or some change in another, we must admit our ignorance as to how this "production" is possible. And, in fact, those who use the popular notion outside of science do not believe that they have explained the productive power; they either accept it as inexplicable or they are inclined to turn to the scientist for such explanations (that is, to explanations in terms of scientific and not phenomenal objects). The notion of production holds, therefore, within the realm of phenomenal objects, and is to be considered merely as a phenomenal relationship.

These considerations should suffice to show that the notion of causality need not be considered as "anthropomorphic" either within science or outside of it. Furthermore, from these considerations it can be seen that the scientific abandonment of matter as

nomenal object is the tree that I perceive. I use the term "scientific object" in preference to "physical object," in order to include not merely the tree as dealt with by the physicist, but also as dealt with by the biologist. This distinction is in line with Eddington's well-known distinction between his "two" tables. (*Nature of the Physical World,* p. ix.)

an ultimate substance, in favor of the concept of scientific events, does not in the least affect the validity of this view of the causal relationship. Thus our discussion, which has found the causal relationship to be a relationship of existential dependence, has avoided two of the three objections which have been raised by "science" to the notion of causality. We must now turn to the remaining objection which falls within this set: that science deals with mathematically formulated laws and not with causes.

We must remember that science does not find its mathematical laws already formulated and at its disposal. These laws have behind them a history of observation, and usually of the controlled type of observation which we call experiment. Laws are generalizations based upon observation of particular instances. "Everywhere the particulars of the actual world suggest generalizations; and these generalizations are subsequent to, and dependent on, the particulars. That there is a realm of particulars which confronts all its generalizations, and to which these generalizations must conform, is the condition accepted by a natural science when it takes the actual world for its subject-matter." [24] Thus scientific laws depend upon scientific observation. This observation is precisely what might be called causal,[25] for it seeks to establish the determining conditions, or some

[24] R. M. Eaton: *General Logic,* p. 483.
[25] *Cf.,* L. S. Stebbing: *Modern Introduction to Logic,* p. 260.

aspect of the complete set of determining conditions, for a given event.

It must not, however, be assumed that the scientific law tells us in regard to two events which is "the condition" and which is "the effect." On the contrary, scientific laws are reciprocal, or as is sometimes said, they represent "necessary" and not merely "sufficient" conditions of an event: in propositions which are necessary one can argue as well from effect to cause as from cause to effect. This characteristic reciprocal relation between two events which fall under a scientific law can be seen in Boyle's law: given either the pressure or the volume of a gas we can calculate the other. If this reciprocal relation did not characterize the events which we call condition and effect we could not, in fact, state their relation in terms of a mathematical formula.

Although this characteristic of reciprocity between two events which enter into a scientific law is merely one of the features which we might point out concerning such laws, it is a highly instructive characteristic. For it should be noted that one could never attain to the statement of such a law without having gone through the most careful causal consideration of the events themselves. One scarcely needs to point out that before such a reciprocal relationship can be established the scientist must determine in specific cases that one event depends for its existence upon the other. This, as we have seen, means that it is causally related to the other. But such an examination does not in itself give sufficient data for the formulation of a scientific law. Beyond the first discovery of a causal relationship the scientist must show in a variety of instances not merely that one event depends upon the other, but also that whenever the latter exists it is followed by or "necessitates" that the former should also exist. Without this further step no scientific law can be formulated.

This position bears out what we have already seen: that it is not causation as such, but the formulation of causal relationships in terms of scientific laws, that gives rise to the principle of determinism. The "overthrow" of determinism in contemporary theoretical physics does not, therefore, necessarily run counter to attempts to elucidate causal relationships. In fact it has been made clear by various investigators that the "overthrow" of determinism in contemporary physics does not even invalidate the concept of physical laws.[26] The whole weight of "indeterminism" falls not on the conception of physical laws, but on the deterministic principle that there is one physical law, or one set of physical laws which stand in such a relationship to each other that there is no element of contingency in the universe. But it is not with the principle of determinism that we are here concerned. What we wish to make clear is the fact that the formulation of scientific laws depends upon causal analysis.

This dependence of scientific laws on causal an-

[26] Cf., Philipp Frank: *Das Kausalgesetz und seine Grenzen.* Also M. R. Cohen: *Reason and Nature,* p. 151 f. on contingency.

alysis, that is, on the analysis of specific relations of existential dependence, should already be clear from the little that we have said concerning the subject. It should be no less clear that a scientific law can always be translated back into causal terms, and thus the causal relation is not merely a presupposition of its existence, but also remains implicit within it. It is this which Eaton doubtless had in mind when, in a previously quoted passage, he said of science that "there is a realm of particulars which confronts all its generalizations, and to which these generalizations must conform." [27] For the only empirical testing of a scientific law lies in retranslating it into causal terms, and seeing whether it holds of further particular instances.

The fact that causal analysis is implicit in scientific law, as well as being a presupposition of its formulation, should not conceal from us the fact that the causal explanation of a particular instance may be quite different in kind from anything into which a full-fledged scientific law gives us insight. For it lies in the nature of a scientific law to deal with only certain causal aspects of particular instances. One could not, for example, discover a full causal explanation of an object's fall from the law of gravitation. As is commonly said, "Other factors, aside from gravitation, enter into the situation." To take all of these factors into account would be to attempt to formulate a law for one instance only, which is absurd. A scien-

[27] Eaton: *General Logic,* p. 483.

tific law purports to hold of all instances of a given "type." [28] On the other hand, a full causal explanation attempts to deal with the complete nature of one instance. In much of science we find that such a full causal explanation of any event is not a major objective of investigation. The physicist, for example, deals with the particular event as "an instance," rather than as an event to be examined wholly in itself. Such examination is, as we have seen, causal in character, for those generalizations which we call scientific laws can only be formulated on the basis of causal analysis. Such scientific laws yield what might be called a skeleton of causal explanation when they are applied to particular instances, for they indicate one or more determining conditions of the event in question. But they do not indicate all of the determining conditions of an event (unless we assume the principle of universal determinism). Thus they are not substitutes for full causal explanations: their task is different in kind, and their dependence upon causal analysis must not be allowed to conceal this difference.

We can, however, see that in some cases the scientist is concerned with a comparatively full causal explanation of a particular instance. This is, for example, the case in the practice of medical diagnosis. Yet the main theoretical objective of science undoubtedly lies in the formulation of scientific laws. On the other hand, the historical enterprise, as we

---

[28] It is for this reason that "universals" are presupposed by scientific laws. *Cf.*, Eaton: *General Logic*, p. 496.

pointed out in our introductory chapter, lies not in the formulation of laws, but in concrete description. This concrete description, as we shall attempt to make clear in the succeeding chapter, is causal in character. Before proceeding, however, it will be advisable to review and integrate what has been said in the present chapter.

Rather than assume that the order and structure to be found in our knowledge is a function of the mind's activity in knowing, we have assumed that events in the real world possess a determinate structure of their own, which is apprehended, but not transformed, by the mind. We indicated at the outset of the present chapter two considerations which seemed to justify this assumption. In the course of our discussion we have found that the relevance of one statement to another can be adequately explained on this basis, whereas any "subjective" attempt to explain the meaning of relevance is bound to fail. Our discussion of causality can likewise be regarded as justifying this assumption, since the causal relationship was seen to lie in the determinate connection which exists between events. To have established this realistic assumption, or at least to have rendered it plausible, constitutes one of the chief contributions of this chapter to the general argument of which it is a part. For, as we have seen, historical relativism derives much of its vigor from an uncritical acceptance of the mind's "transforming" activities.

The second addition which the present chapter

has made to the course of our argument is to be found in its discussion of the meaning of causation, brief and scattered as that discussion was. We have seen that the causal relationship can be defended both in the realms of scientific explanation and phenomenal description. We have seen, further, that the causal relationship may be said to consist in the relationship of existential dependence between events. By means of attributing this meaning to causation, we have been able to bridge the gap between scientific and phenomenal instances of causal attribution. We have found, for example, that the discrepancies between causal explanation in science and in phenomenal description are due not to two meanings of the term causality, but to the fact that the scientist and the lay observer are occupied with different events, or with the "same" event seen from different points of view. Not only have we thus bridged the gap between scientific and phenomenal instances of causation, we have also pointed out that a thorough-going acceptance of the scientific concepts of "events" enables causal analysis in science to escape both the meaninglessness of an infinite regress and the attacks levelled against it by those who accept the notion of the temporal discreteness of cause and effect. In the following chapter we shall again take up this problem in more detail with reference to historical causation.

The third contribution of the present chapter to the whole course of our argument is, however, the most important. It lies in the fact that we have in effect brought together the concepts of causation and relevance. As we previously pointed out, the relevance of one statement to another can only be understood through acknowledging that the facts about which the statements are made are themselves relevant to each other. Thus, while we saw that the term relevance may be applied to statements as well as to facts, we found relevance to be a category of facts. The word category in this discussion was simply taken to mean a pervasive character of facts.[29] But, as we saw, facts are not events. The relation of relevance between facts must, unless based upon the functioning of the mind, be dependent upon some characteristic of the events with which the facts are concerned. Since we have already rejected the former alternative, the latter alone remains. And when we come to examine the nature of the causal relationship between two events we find that it corresponds to the relationship of relevance between the facts which are concerned. This point demands some further notice.

One fact was held to be relevant to another when an understanding of the latter demanded an understanding of the former. Thus the fact that the air is of a certain temperature is relevant to the fact that the water freezes. Now the events concerned, the temperature of the air, and the freezing of the water, can be seen to be causally connected: the latter is related to the former by the bond of existential de-

[29] *Cf.*, S. Alexander: *Space, Time, and Deity*, v. I, p. 184 f.

pendence. This dovetailing of the causal relationship between events and the relationship of relevance between facts (or between statements concerning facts) is of the utmost importance if it can be fully substantiated. In the succeeding chapter we shall attempt to substantiate it within the realm of historical knowledge. At the same time we shall uphold the contention that a causal analysis of the historical process is possible.

CHAPTER VIII

Relevance and Causation in History, (Cont.)

In order to overcome historical relativism and to substitute for it an alternative theory it was necessary to show first, that historical statements could not be understood or evaluated merely in terms of their origin, and, second, that the arrangement and order of these statements was dependent upon the historical material and not upon the historian's personal or social standpoint. The first of these tasks was completed in our sixth chapter. The second demanded that we examine the concepts of relevance and causation and determine their applicability to the material with which the historian must deal. The immediately preceding chapter, of which the present is but a continuation, sought to deal with the general meaning of the concepts of relevance and causation. In its argument it was brief, seeking to avoid many of the long controversies into which a truly adequate treatment of the concept of causation must enter. It is to be hoped that some of the deficiencies which were entailed by its brevity may be compensated for by the present chapter, in which we shall seek to make clear in detail how the twin concepts of causation and relevance are applicable to historical events.

Before attempting to justify the historical enterprise through showing the place which causal analysis occupies in it, it will be well to consider what the methodologists have said concerning the historian's procedure. We have already mentioned the fact that most of the discussions which deal with the historian's method draw a distinction between "fact-finding" and the "synthetic" aspect of historical knowledge. Within the realm of analysis (fact-finding) is usually included all that pertains to the documents with which the historian works. Within the realm of synthesis is then included the use to which the historian puts this material. But the realm of analysis is itself divided into the "external" and the "internal" criticism of documents. It will be of considerable importance for us to show that in so far as analysis is made to include internal criticism there is no distinction between it and synthesis. In order to prepare the ground for this we must first discuss the place of external criticism in the historian's procedure.

The criticism of documents which is called external criticism consists mainly in the technique of determining the place and date of origin, and the authorship of document. In addition it consists in textual criticism and in the attempt to determine whether or not different documents are independent of each other; in cases in which they are found not to be independent it seeks to establish which of them is the original source. This type of criticism may well be called analysis. Furthermore, such criticism is indispensable to the historian who seeks to deal with a period of human history in which the documents have not been preserved in a wholly satisfactory condition. It goes without saying, for example, that our knowledge of the Middle Ages would be incomparably less than it is, had it not been for the technical skill with which this type of analysis has been pursued. But the invaluable aid which has been rendered to the historical enterprise by external criticism must not blind us to the fact that such criticism is an accessory tool for the historian. Every methodologist recognizes that it is not the whole of historical knowledge, but its merely accessory character is usually not made clear.

That the external criticism is merely an accessory technique in historical understanding can be seen from two considerations. In the first place, it is evident that in dealing with many periods of human history it is almost wholly without significance. The problems of the authorship of documents, their places and dates of origin, and even their dependence upon other documents, have tended to become less and less controversial as time has gone on. Almost the last period in history in which such matters are of great importance is encountered by the historian who deals with the intellectual history of the eighteenth century. From that time to the present the conditions under which books have been published, and the fashion in which historians have learned to cite their authorities have tended to make external criticism superfluous in the majority of cases. That external criticism is still necessary for historians who deal with earlier periods of history does not in any sense nullify the inference which is to be drawn from this fact: in so far as history can be written without employing the technique of external criticism it can not be regarded as an indispensable step in the historian's procedure.

Methodologists have for the most part held that the external criticism of documents is more than an accessory technique because they have almost universally assumed that such criticism is in fact the first step of historical investigation. This, however, is not the case. Before one can determine the place or date of origin, or the authorship of a document, one must be in possession of an enormous amount of knowledge concerning the whole context in which the document belongs. One cannot start from scratch and determine whether a document pertains to one century or another or to one locality or another. Without having some genuine historical knowledge concerning the events referred to in the document, or without knowledge concerning literary and epigraphic styles, no document could even be dated. External criticism is thus a means by which the historian is able to enlarge the range of his historical understanding, bringing new materials into an already established historical context; it is not the primary source of historical knowledge. It is this which was intended when we spoke of the technique of external criticism as "an accessory tool" in the historian's enterprise.

In so far as the technique of external criticism is referred to by the methodologists under the head of analysis, one can have no quarrel with the distinction between analysis and synthesis. For we have just seen that external criticism differs from the historian's primary apprehension of historical relations, and it is the latter which usually goes under the head of synthesis. The difficulty with a distinction between historical analysis and synthesis arises only because the methodologists include under the former that which they call "internal criticism."

"Internal criticism" is a term applied to the attempt to determine the truthworthiness of a document. It usually includes such problems as the attempt to determine whether the author of a document was in a position to judge of the events with which his account was concerned, and whether there were any factors in his personal or social situation which tended to negate the value of his testimony. Taken in this sense, "internal criticism" attempts to "establish the facts" through separating reliable from unreliable sources.[1] Let us see how it hopes to proceed.

Langlois and Seignobos hold that the historian

---

[1] I exclude from "internal criticism" the interpretation of the meaning of a document. This is a problem usually termed "hermeneutic." Langlois and Seignobos classify it under internal criticism, distinguishing it from the "negative internal criticism" with which we are here concerned. Bernheim includes it not under internal criticism, but under "Auffassung" (synthesis). I should hold that the interpretation of documents (hermeneutic), like external criticism, is an accessory tool of the general historian.

must start with "methodical doubt": "All that has not been proved must be temporarily regarded as doubtful. . . . The historian ought to distrust apriori every statement of an author, for he cannot be sure that it is not mendacious or mistaken." [2] The historian, it is contended, must use this methodical doubt upon every statement in the document with which he is concerned, and seek to determine in regard to each statement both what the author believed and whether his belief was true. To guide this Herculean labor Langlois and Seignobos offer two sets of questions which the historian may use, one to test the sincerity of statements, the other to test their accuracy. An examination of these questions shows that each of them is concerned with factors which may have influenced the judgment out of which the statement arose. But one is never able to determine the truth or falsity of a statement if one first doubts it apriori and then concerns one's self wholly with factors which may have influenced the judgment. The most prejudiced or self-interested historian may give out true statements; a historian remote from the objects of his description may present us with a report which is no less reliable than that of some other historian who was an eye-witness of the events. The only way in which one can determine the probable validity of a historical statement is to examine it in the context of other historical statements, and to accept it as true

[2] Langlois and Seignobos: *Introduction to the Study of History,* p. 156 f.

248

in so far as it is not denied by these statements, nor controverted by what we accept as truth in other realms of inquiry. It is only in the cases where conflicting historical statements are offered that one need look into the probable grounds of the judgment. However, we must already be in possession of a great deal of historical knowledge in order to carry on such an investigation; in it methodical apriori doubt has no place. To doubt each statement in a historical work would make the historian's task not only practically but theoretically impossible. The reason why Langlois and Seignobos overlook this is to be found in their contention that statements may be *proved* by corroborative testimony. Yet it should be clear that if we actually doubt each statement apriori, corroboration loses all of its meaning: we should be proving one doubted statement by means of another statement which we also doubt.

The basic fallacy in this doctrine of "internal criticism" is to be found in the atomistic view of historical statements which it presupposes. To set "internal criticism" apart as a separate procedure which is concerned with establishing the reliability of a source, and thus with establishing "the facts," is to attempt to make it function in a void. Unless one can place a given source, or some statement made by a given source, in a germane context of other independent statements, one can never reach any conclusion regarding the reliability of the source or of the accuracy of its statements. An explanation of the probable

reasons for the existence of a distorted statement has
no significance until we know, or have adequate
grounds to suspect, that the statement is a distortion.
But this knowledge can only be gained through comparing it with other statements. Such a comparison
implies that the historian who makes it is already
involved in bringing his materials together into that
which the methodologists term a synthesis. Thus
internal, unlike external, criticism is not a separate
aspect of historical understanding; it is not "analytic,"
but is part and parcel of the historian's integral grasp
of historical events.

The emphasis on a separate internal criticism takes
diverse forms in the various methodologists. Langlois
and Seignobos, it must be confessed, represent what is
probably the most unsatisfactory view of the procedure. Yet in almost every methodologist there is
to be found the same tendency to atomize historical
facts through the doctrine of internal criticism.[3] It
is almost universally contended among the methodologists that by means of external and internal criticism
the historian "establishes the facts," and only then is
the vital problem of how he can "synthesize" these
facts allowed to arise. It is precisely this cleft between
establishing the facts and actual historical understanding that paves the way for historical relativism.[4]

The extreme form of the atomistic view of historical facts is again to be found in Langlois and

[3] John M. Vincent provides the only exception.
[4] F. J. Teggart affords an example of this (Cf., *Theory of History*, p. 28).

Seignobos. They hold that "historical construction has thus to be performed with an incoherent mass of minute facts, with detail-knowledge reduced as it were to a powder." [5] On any such basis historical construction would indeed be liable to the charges which relativism levels against it, for how could "an incoherent mass of minute facts" be brought together into a historical narrative except through value-charged selection? To hold to this atomistic doctrine is not to make historical writing "scientific"; on the contrary, it robs the historical materials of the order and structure which they must possess if history is to be more than a value-charged myth. But Langlois and Seignobos partially rectify the error when they characterize the "incoherent mass of minute facts" more fully. They then speak of it as "a heterogeneous medley of materials, relating to different subjects and places, differing in their degree of generality and certainty." [6] Facts thus differentiated can scarcely be called an incoherent mass; the latter shows itself to be but another (and exceedingly loose) way of referring to the heterogeneity of the facts.

In order to show that the atomistic view of historical facts is untenable, let us put ourselves in the place of a historian writing the political history of the German Republic. The materials with which such a historian must deal are chiefly to be found in newspapers, memoirs, state-documents, letters, and prior

[5] Langlois and Seignobos: *Introduction to the Study of History*, p. 214.
[6] *Ibid.*, p. 214.

251

historical studies of the same subject, or of phases of that subject. These materials do not constitute an incoherent mass; they are not a mere heap of data. In the first place, they have chronological order. In the second place, the materials fall into natural groups: some concern parliamentary elections, some concern foreign policy, some concern party-programs, some concern the machinery of the state, to mention but a few. In the third place, the chronologically ordered materials which belong to different groups dovetail at many points. Thus, party programs, parliamentary elections and foreign policy, may, at any given moment, be interrelated. This dovetailing of heterogeneous materials shows that it is impossible to think of facts as unrelated and atomic units. Likewise it should be clear that whether or not external criticism is demanded of the historian, that which is called internal criticism can not be considered as a separate methodological procedure. For internal criticism, which in this case would consist in examining the trustworthiness of memoirs, previous historical works, letters, and the like, could not proceed except on the basis of prior assumptions concerning the true nature of the events depicted. Such an estimate of trustworthiness can only take place step by step as the historian proceeds to grasp the events; it is not therefore an "analytic" procedure which seeks to lay bare single, isolated facts.

Having thus shown that external criticism is an accessory tool to historical knowledge, and that internal criticism is not a separate analytic procedure, but is part and parcel of the historian's whole grasp of his subject matter, we may now attempt to render intelligible that which is called the historian's synthesis of the facts. In pointing out that historical facts are not atomic, unconnected units, we have opened the way for that discussion. It will be necessary, however, to push this inquiry further, showing that the facts with which the historian deals are "events" in the sense which we have attributed to that term.

It will be remembered that Broad defines an event as "anything that endures at all." [7] Enduring entities, which Broad then terms "strands of history," were found to be pervaded by "a certain special unity." This unity was not found to be equivalent to absolute simplicity, but was, rather, dependent upon the pattern of those multiple factors of an event which may be termed its subevents. That which bound the subevents to the event in question was called (by us) the relation of existential dependence. It was pointed out that no event could be considered as a subevent of some other event unless this relation of existential dependence held between the latter and the former. This in turn entailed that no event could be considered as a subevent of another unless the two were contemporaneous. Contemporaneity, however, was not interpreted as meaning that the two events in question were necessarily coterminous in time.

[7] C. D. Broad: *Scientific Thought*, p. 54.

On the basis of this discussion the general characteristics may be held to be three: first, an event is an enduring entity; second, it is not simple, but contains as part of itself certain subevents to which it bears the relation of existential dependence; and, third, subevents are contemporaneous with the events which are related to them by the bond of existential dependence. Let us now attempt to show that each of these three characteristics is fulfilled by a historical "event."

When we view certain historical events, such as the Reformation, there seems to be little doubt that these are enduring entities. The precise limits of their endurance may appear to be somewhat vague, depending for exactness upon the taste of a historian. Yet that the Reformation was an entity which had a certain continuant existence is a proposition which could only be denied by a nominalism which would render all apprehension of non-physical realities impossible. For the Reformation has historical reality no less than has an event such as a parliamentary debate. The latter can not be reduced to a set of sound waves, nor to single speeches which happen to be given by several different personages. A parliamentary debate is a set of speeches which possesses a definite context supplied by the function of parliament, the governmental program, forthcoming elections, and the like. This is what a parliamentary debate means, and this meaning is directly apprehended by the historian. In the same fashion the movement which we call the Reformation possesses historical reality in its proper historical context; it cannot be resolved into events on a physical level. And it should be clear that this historical event known as the Reformation is an enduring entity even though it is not the sort of enduring entity with which the natural scientist deals.

When we turn from historical events such as the Reformation to specific political or social acts on a smaller scale, there may be some doubt as to whether or not these are to be called enduring entities (events). Can we say, for example, that the enactment of a law possesses temporal duration? That it does seems to be obvious at the very first glance. As any witness of the procedure can testify, roll-calls in a legislative assembly take time; even in the case of a dictator some (perhaps indefinitely small) time intervenes between thought and command. These examples, however, are not in themselves satisfactory answers to the question. When it is asked whether the enactment of a given law possesses temporal duration, the enactment of the law may be considered not as a specific procedural event (which certainly takes time), but as one of the significant points in a long-enduring event such as child-labor reform. From the point of view of such a context it would seem that the enactment of the law was an "instantaneous" happening. However, it is only because of the scale on which the historical process is in this case regarded that the enactment of the law is considered as instantaneous. The fact that we can consider the enactment of the law as a procedural process which possesses a definite duration, and which can be accurately localized in time within longer-enduring events, shows that it is an enduring entity which, so far as its endurance is concerned, may be spoken of as an event. Precisely the same condition holds in the spatial realm: it is futile to deny that any perceived point is non-spatial merely because its spatial components are not made clear on the scale which we have adopted, for if we change the scale (for example, through a microscopic examination) the spatial character of the point becomes immediately obvious.[8] Thus we may say that even those historical occurrences which seem not to be enduring entities but instantaneous happenings, turn out to be temporal as soon as we change the scale of our observations.

The foregoing illustration of the temporal character of all historical events leads us on to a consideration of the second characteristic which events possess: that they have component subevents within them. We have seen that from the point of view which regards child-labor reform as an event, the enactment of a specific reform bill is but one step in the process. Yet the enactment of such a bill is itself

[8] An analogous use of the concept of scale is to be found in K. Milanov: *Die Gesetzesbildung, das Verstehen und die anschauliche Abstraktion*, pp. 75 ff. This work, which is strongly oriented toward Gestalt psychology (as well as toward the philosophy of Heinrich Maier) came into my hands only after the major portion of the present book had undergone revision. I wish, however, to acknowledge at this point the value which I attach to the confirmations which I have found in Milanov's work.

an event. We may in such cases say that the particular reform bill is a subevent of the child-labor reform movement, for the relation of existential dependence here holds between the events in question.

In the same fashion as the enactment of a bill may be a subevent of a larger historical movement, so the enactment of a bill has many components within it. These components (such as the voting of each legislator) may not be of great intrinsic historic interest; on the other hand, they too may be analyzed into subevents which do appear as "important" to the historian. For example, the historian may find as a component element in many of the subevents which together form "the opposition" to the bill, that there is one common subevent which all of these share: the economic interests of some section of the nation. Such a subevent is, as everyone would grant, of major importance; it is a long-enduring subevent which is related to much besides this specific vote. However, the historian can only attain a full knowledge of it in all of its manifold relations by examining (within the political field) such "minute" subevents as an actual vote on actual measures. This should be sufficient to show that there are no short cuts to historical understanding; furthermore, it should show, that which we shall have further occasion to emphasize, that the historian does not proceed by selecting "the important facts": he painstakingly follows where his material leads.

The foregoing illustration should serve to make

clear that in historical events, as in events in the natural sciences, a subevent is not coterminous with the event which depends upon it, that, in fact, it may be of far greater duration. It is no more strained or arbitrary to call the economic condition of one section of a country a subevent in the balloting of a particular legislator than it is to call the influence of the earth's magnetic pole at a particular spot a subevent in the swing of a released compass needle.

Having thus pointed out that the material with which the historian deals conforms to our analysis of the nature of "events," we are now in a better position to deal with the problem of the historian's "synthetic" activity. The nature of this activity is clear: the historian always selects his material in such a way that his account presents a unified structure and pattern, each of the parts being seen in its relation to the whole. Historical relativism makes the most of such selective activities, arguing that the structural unity of historical accounts represents the distortion which reality undergoes in being made an object of historical knowledge. It will however be seen that if our previous discussions of relevance and causation are applicable to the historical materials, and if historical synthesis proceeds through causal analysis, the last of the arguments for relativism will have been overcome. For we have attempted to make clear that the concept of relevance has meaning only if it is held to be an objective relation between facts. The precise nature of this relation we found to be based upon the causal connection of events. Our analysis did not suggest that such a causal connection was in any sense a product of the mind's activity; on the contrary, if our analysis was correct it would be impossible to interpret causality in any subjective terms whatsoever. Therefore, if we can show that our view of relevance and causation explains the historian's synthetic activities, we will have justified our assumption that historical events in themselves possess a structure which the historian apprehends and does not invent.

We have just seen that the facts with which the historian deals are "events" in the same sense as are those which are dealt with by the natural scientist. There seems, therefore, to be no reason why historical relevance may not also be explained in terms of causal factors. In fact we find that all serious attempts to discuss the problem of the relevance and irrelevance of historical statements include a discussion of causal relations in history. Max Weber, for example, uses the terms "relevant" and "conditioned" in such a fashion that both express the causal relationship.[9] Furthermore, in spite of the influence of Rickert on his methodological inquiries, Weber finds the essential problem of historical understanding to lie in that which he calls "adequate causation."[10] And not only

[9] Cf., *Gesammelte Aufsätze zur Wissenschaftslehre*, pp. 162, 163, 165.
[10] Cf., *Gesammelte Aufsätze zur Wissenschaftslehre*, pp. 266-290. Many of the conceptions of Weber in regard to the problem of historical causation are identical with those to be developed in the present chapter. It is unfortunate for the present work that an adequate examination of Weber's views cannot be included within it. A section designed to present those views was written but was

Weber, but every methodologist or theoretician who holds to the possibility of objective historical knowledge, must, at one point or another, seek to justify the historian's selection of facts on the basis of causal relationships.

The question as to how causal analysis is possible in historical investigations is identical with the question as to how the historian can ever establish that the relation of existential dependence holds between two events. For, as we have seen, it is the essence of the causal relationship to be formulable in these terms. It should be clear that the establishment of this relationship offers no difficulties in many cases. We have already noted that many historical events may be said to "dovetail"; where this is the case the relation of existential dependence holds. Thus, the history of the League of Nations could not be written without a consideration of the Corfu incident or the Manchurian question. These events are imbedded in that history, and any concrete historical description of the League cannot overlook them.

It might be objected, however, that the course of the League's history would have been "substantially the same," even without these crises. It might be claimed that the actual international rivalry between

subsequently excluded because it failed to render a true appreciation of Weber's thought. No brief and yet fair analysis of Weber is possible, due to the diversity of his thought and the many misleading positions which he "adopts." Only a thorough-going analysis of the basic concepts which he employed (both in theory and in practice) could do justice to the man. Such an analysis would have swallowed the whole of the present work.

France and England in the post-war years would, of itself, sooner or later have led to the same end. However, this line of attack possesses a grave defect, for it overlooks the concrete nature of historical investigations. The historian is not concerned with setting up hypothetical cases and saying that the end result "would have been the same anyway." [11] Historical understanding attempts to give a descriptive analysis of that which actually occurred. The actual history of the League of Nations would not have been the same without these crises, for they form a part of that history itself. Thus, we can see that in many cases the historian need merely look at his material in order to find ties of existential dependence.

The relation between tracing the bond of existential dependence and the historian's synthesis of facts here becomes immediately apparent. Synthesis demands that the historian select his facts in such a manner as to portray both the unity and variety in a particular segment of history. When the historian chooses to deal with the history of the League the unifying strand of his account is thereby given. But since the history of the League is not an ultimately simple fact, he must view it in terms of its many contributing components. These yield the variety in his account. But he does not select these components at will; they are determined for him by the actual course of the League's history: they are to be discov-

---

[11] For another illustration of the fact that the historian is not concerned with hypothetical cases, Cf., H. Butterfield: *The Whig Interpretation of History*, p. 44.

ered in those subevents upon which the history of the League as a whole depends. These subevents, as we have pointed out, are in many cases immediately present in the historian's direct apprehension of the League, for the League is not an abstraction independent of its deliberations.

It must be admitted, however, that there are also many cases in which the bond of existential dependence between two events is not immediately clear. These cases test the historian's penetrative insight and provide a standard against which to measure his greatness. It is here that the framing of hypothetical cases serves as an indispensable tool in historical inquiry.

The historian who is dealing with so complex an event as the history of the League of Nations can not rest content in his knowledge of those events upon which that history can, by the most superficial examination, be seen to depend. To find other events which shared this characteristic becomes the goal of his investigations. It is here that the interpretation of hypothetical questions concerning "what might otherwise have happened," becomes of significance. Such questions may provide the historian with a working hypothesis concerning where to look for further connections between events. It was not this, but the attempt to substitute possibilities for actual occurrences, against which we took objection.

It should be clear, however, that in order to know how to frame working hypotheses the historian, no less than the natural scientist, must possess a sound theoretical understanding of his materials. It is only on the basis of previous investigations that one can ever satisfactorily abstract from the actual nature of events and entertain possibilities about what "might" happen. The natural scientist has the good fortune to be able in most cases to put such working hypotheses to direct experimental tests which establish the principle once and for all; the historian can only find confirmation of his hypothesis in individual instances which are often ambiguous and are rarely complete. It is for this reason that historical "principles" are so much less satisfactory than are scientific laws. But we must not be led by their comparatively unsatisfactory nature to overlook the great rôle which they play in actual historical investigations. Even when they do not attain the status of "laws," they are indispensable as working hypotheses. In so far as they are specifically "historical" principles, they can only be gained through a comparison of historical instances; [12] it is for this reason that we always insist (or should insist) that a historian have a wide acquaintance with historical events of the most diverse types. But the principles themselves need not always be "historical." It is a truism that the historian must understand "the principles of human motivation"; and in many fields of historical investigation it is no

---

[12] *Cf.*, M. Ginsberg: *Explanation in History (Aristotelian Society,* Supplementary Vol. 14, pp. 142 ff.). Such was Max Weber's method of establishing the partial dependence of capitalism on protestantism (*Cf.*, R. Aron: *La sociologie allemande,* pp. 141 ff.).

less essential that he understand the principles of economics, of politics, or of ethnology.

It should be clear from what has already been said that when the historian traces the bonds of existential dependence beyond the unmistakable instances which the materials themselves place before his eyes, he must use what Max Weber has called the category of "objective possibility." [13] For this, as we have seen, he must have a wealth of background in historical phenomena and in the phenomena of the social sciences generally, since it is only by means of such a background that he can form "principles" which serve to define the realm of objective possibility.[14] However, the formulation of such principles is not the goal toward which the historian, as historian, strives; on the contrary, these principles serve merely as working hypotheses in concrete descriptive analysis.[15] It is here that the difference between history and theoretical social science emerges.

(It has often been a subject of discussion whether sociology might not one day replace history. Such a question involves a fundamental misconception of the relation between history and the theoretical social sciences, among which sociology is to be numbered. The debate on this question would never have attained the proportions which it did had it not been for the imprecisions which at the time marked the

[13] *Gesammelte Aufsätze zur Wissenschaftslehre,* pp. 266-290.
[14] It is a similar emphasis on the need for "comparative studies" that constitutes the most important contribution of F. J. Teggart to the theory of historical knowledge.
[15] *Cf.,* Weber: *Gesammelte Aufsätze zur Wissenschaftslehre,* p. 178.

field of sociological inquiry. Today a more or less general agreement has been reached which recognizes that history and sociology are mutually dependent, and yet are separated with respect to their immediate aim. History, as we have shown, depends for the furtherance of its analysis upon principles which only sociology and the other theoretical social sciences can disclose; sociology depends upon historical investigation for the material upon which it works, examining and comparing historical instances in order to discover the laws which may be implicit within them. Such mutual dependence again demonstrates that historical analysis is causal in character, for if it were not the sociologist could never generalize from historical data, setting up laws which hold of the historical process. This fact is even clearer in those realms of theoretical social science which lie outside of sociology, for example, in the relation between causal analysis in economic history and the laws formulated by economic theory).

We have now seen that causal analysis is not an impossibility in historical investigations. The bond of existential dependence is in many cases immediately given with the materials, and in other cases can be established through working hypotheses based upon empirically derived "principles" of social science. The confirmation of such working hypotheses is not always satisfactory, and the bond of existential dependence which is said to tie two events together is in these cases no stronger than the principle itself.

Yet the working hypothesis derived from such general principles does not always lack confirmation in the historical realm. A historian may start from some general principle and then uncover a new document which will show that the relation of existential dependence did actually hold. The principles may thus, in some cases, find confirmation in particular instances, just as scientific principles are confirmed through experimentation. The rôle of the working hypothesis is in such cases identical in history and in science, for the principle upon which the working hypothesis is based points the way for the investigator's researches.

Having thus seen that in many cases a knowledge of causal relationships can be attained in historical studies, only one crucial problem remains to be discussed in the present chapter. This problem may be stated as follows: How is it possible to give an adequate causal description of any historical event when every such event is composed of an indefinitely large number of individual factors? Many thinkers, among them Max Weber,[16] see in this problem the crucial question for a theory of historical understanding. Because of the apparent insolubility of the problem on any empirical grounds they flee, as we have seen, either to historical relativism, or to an appeal to transcendent values, as did Weber himself.

As a matter of empirical fact, the historian does

---

[16] *Gesammelte Aufsätze zur Wissenschaftslehre*, p. 177. *Cf.*, Ed. Meyer: *Kleine Schriften*, v. I, p. 51; A. Grotenfelt: *Die Wertschätzung in der Geschichte*, pp. 119 ff.

not enter into a description of every detail which forms a part of his narrative; the scale on which he works dictates the detail which is introduced. The question therefore is what precisely dictates the scale which is found in a historical work. It is Milanov's signal contribution to the theory of historical understanding to have pointed out that the historical scale of a given work depends not upon valuational factors, but upon the level of abstraction implicit in the historian's choice of a subject matter. From the point of view which we have adopted in regard to the nature of events we are in a position to render this concept of levels of abstraction somewhat more clear.

We have seen that every event possesses subevents upon which it is existentially dependent, and that these subevents, in their turn, are further analyzable. With this in mind we can see why it is that the historian does not proceed indefinitely with his causal analysis.

Let us suppose again that we are writing a political history of the German Republic. In order to understand that history we must, of course, be aware of the terms of the Treaty of Versailles, for the conditions imposed upon Germany by that Treaty enter into political events of the time with unmistakable clarity: to use our former expression, they "dovetail" with such phenomena as foreign policy, party programs, and electoral campaigns. On the other hand, the historian of the German Republic is not at the same time a historian of the Peace Conference, for it suffices him to know *that* the terms were imposed; he need not inquire into *why* they were imposed. Thus, while statements concerning the conditions imposed upon Germany by the Treaty are relevant to an understanding of the Republic, statements concerning the framing of the Treaty are not thus relevant.[17] In the same way, the historian of the Peace Conference is not a biographer of each of the individual statesmen of the Conference; the historian is here only concerned with the characters of the statesmen as they influenced the negotiations, and does not attempt to show how these characters were formed.

From these illustrations we can see that the historian does not embark upon an infinite regress when he attempts a causal analysis of specific historical events. In history, as in science, adequate causal analysis possesses successive stopping-points, beyond which, in any instance, the investigator need not go. These stopping-points, to be sure, do not represent the ultimate limits of causal investigation, for (so far as we know) every subevent of a given event may itself be analyzed further. The stopping-points are not, however, arbitrary, for they represent answers to questions posed. The historian asks "what set of events constitutes the cause of this event?" and when he reaches an answer he is entitled to stop without having the charge of arbitrariness laid against him. It does not matter that each event in this set of events can itself be causally analyzed, for the historian, by

[17] *Cf.*, Quigley and Clark: *Republican Germany,* p. 55.

virtue of the problem which he has set himself, has not sought to determine the causes of each of these partial causes. Only a historian who posed for himself the insoluble problem of writing a *complete* history of the world would be betrayed into such an infinite regress.[18]

We may say, then, that the acceptance of the view that historical events possess the same general characteristics as do events in the realm of the natural sciences, provides an answer to the problem as to how it is that objective causal analysis does not fall into an infinite regress from which only a valuational standard can save the historian. With this, the last defense of historical relativism disappears.

It will be well to stop at this point and recapitulate the argument of the last three chapters in order to show precisely how it is that historical relativism as a whole may be said to have been overcome.

In our survey of historical relativism it was seen that the two basic presuppositions of the relativist consisted in the attempt to hold that the validity of knowledge must be understood and estimated through an examination of the historical conditions under which it was formed, and that valuational judgments themselves determine the content of historical works. In regard to the first of these presuppositions it was shown that historical statements must be considered as statements and not as judgments if we are to understand actual historical practice. Further, it was

[18] A complete history of the world is not of course a "universal history" ("world history") such as Ranke undertook to write.

pointed out that in treating historical statements as statements the historian assumes a correspondence theory of truth. We saw that the acceptance of such a theory of truth is thoroughly defensible, and does not entail a surrender to attacks which might be made by the historical relativist.

In regard to the second presupposition of historical relativism we found two reasons why it is impossible to claim that the content of historical works is determined by valuational factors. The first of these consisted in showing that in so far as "the facts" of history are concerned, the historian must understand something of these facts before he takes up a valuational position: one can not value (even "unconsciously") that which one does not know. The second reason consisted in our attempt to show that the concrete structure and continuity to be found in every historical work is not a product of valuational judgments, but is implicit in the facts themselves.

In order to establish this second contention we were forced to go at some length into a discussion of the problems of relevance in regard to statements and causal connections in regard to events. We have found that the relevance of one statement to another depends upon causal factors which relate the events to which the statements refer. Such causal connections, we held, are objectively ascertainable in the nature of the events themselves. Thus, we may say that the relevance of one statement to another is determined by factors inherent in the material with which the historian deals. The intelligible nature of a historical account does not rest upon valuational factors which are introduced by the historian; we understand a historical work only because the determinate connections which characterize events in the history are capable of being understood. The historian finds these connections and singles them out for others to see.

The psychological processes of historical understanding may present problems of significance to the psychologist, but, from the point of view of experience, there can be no doubt that we possess the power to apprehend the connections between historical events. This understanding is implicit not merely in academic historical works, but in many of the common experiences of everyday life. Whatever the psychological explanation of this understanding may be, it is true that events of the historical type possess determinate interconnections which are rooted in the events themselves, and are not addenda contributed by the mind. From the point of view of naïve experience every historical event possesses its appropriate context which rests on the nature of the event itself. Through the analysis which we have given of the causal relationship it should be clear that that which presents itself to naïve experience as an appropriate context is simply the place of an event in a causally related pattern. The naïve experience of historical events thus presupposes the ability to see causal dependencies. In the uncovering of such causal dependencies lies the goal of technical historical investigation. Thus, we may say that technical historical investigation is essentially similar in character to the layman's ability to see some event of his past in its appropriate context.

Once one recognizes that technical historical understanding has its roots in the common soil of everyday experience the arbitrary distinction between historical analysis and historical synthesis must disappear. This distinction, for which handbooks of historical methodology are to blame, is basic to historical relativism and to those theories which attempted to combat relativism by an appeal to transcendent values. Neither the relativist nor his traditional opponent denied that the facts of history could be determined through analysis; it was their contention that historical synthesis introduced valuational points of view. The ultimate disappearance of the distinction between establishing the facts and giving a concrete picture of the facts in their contextual relationships has left the field open for a new interpretation of historical understanding. We have attempted to give this interpretation through analyzing the concepts of relevance and causation, and showing how they apply to statements of historical fact. We must now turn our attention from this attempt to prove that objective historical knowledge is possible to a consideration of what this analysis entails for the special intellectual discipline which is called history.

CHAPTER IX

HISTORICAL PLURALISM

UP TO this point our consideration of historical knowledge has been directed toward showing that the ideal of historical objectivity is not an illusory one. We have attempted to put forward an argument which would not only justify this ideal, but would once again bring the theory of historical understanding into conformity with the practice of historians themselves. In these considerations we have focused our attention upon the problems which beset the individual historian in his attempt to gain knowledge of specific events. It is now in place to consider the significance of the views which have been developed for the field of historical inquiry taken as a whole.

It need scarcely be said that no short account can do justice to the main controversies which have emerged regarding the function of historical investigation. Almost every generation of historians has had its own set of problems, "programs" have been formulated, and polemics against the "older" tendencies have been the rule. In the present chapter we shall seek our way through the maze of these controversies by singling out for discussion only those problems which, from the point of view which we have developed, appear to be crucial. This point of view can best be called historical pluralism. We shall attempt to show that on the basis of pluralism many of the traditional controversies which have beset historians readily disappear.

Historical pluralism consists in the view that the grand sweep of events which we call the historical process is made up of an indefinitely large number of components which do not form a completely interrelated set. According to this view, whether we take the historical process as a whole or segregate out any particular portion of that process, we shall always find that in themselves all of its components are not related to each other in any save a temporal manner.

Such a view of the historical process differs from many other views, as will readily be seen. It differs from any all-inclusive theory of historical teleology, since it denies that every event is related to every other event. It differs also from all organismic theories of history, since it contends that even within a nation or civilization two contemporary events may not, in themselves, be related to each other by any bond save that of temporal connection. Our first task in the present chapter must lie in the attempt to show that historical pluralism not only follows from our investigations of the nature of historical understanding, but also that it can substantiate itself against the claims of historical monism. Only then will we be in a position to deal with some of the problems which have developed concerning the nature and scope of history.

If one recalls what has been said regarding the nature of historical understanding it will be seen that every historical attempt endeavors to trace the relation of existential dependence between two or more events. When the historian seeks to give us a descriptive analysis of a single event he seeks to establish the complete cause of that event, that is, he attempts to discover all the events upon which a given event is existentially dependent. When, on the other hand, he attempts to show the historical significance of a given event he endeavors to uncover the complete set of events which are existentially dependent upon it. Thus, whether he is concerned with descriptive analysis, or with the significance of an event, he always proceeds by means of uncovering the existential dependence which binds events together.

Our analysis of the relation of existential dependence brought to light two facts which demand that the historian conceive the historical process in a pluralistic fashion.

In the first place it was seen that the subevents upon which any given event depended were themselves to be considered as events, and as such they had an autonomy that could not be denied. We noted that their durations were contemporary with the event in question, but were often not coterminous with that event. They had, as we saw, their own component subevents as well as their own durations.

But this fact means that the subevents upon which any given event depends are not themselves related: two events may be relevant to the same event without being relevant to each other. This consideration, forced upon us by an analysis of the nature of historical understanding, leads inevitably to that which we have called historical pluralism. For it is obvious that if the events upon which a given event depends are not themselves relevant to each other, we have no grounds for establishing the monistic view of history. We have, on the contrary, every right to treat the historical process as if its elements did not form a completely interrelated set, admitting only such interpenetration of events as we in fact uncover in our concrete investigations.

The second aspect of existential dependence which forces historical pluralism upon us lies in the fact that we have found that this relation is not in every case a "necessary" one. A necessary relation entails that whenever A is necessarily connected with an event B, the occurrence of B demands that A should also be present. The relation of necessity, as we have found, is implicit in scientific laws. On the other hand, we have seen that historical descriptions do not always succeed in uncovering laws of the historical process. The historian may, for example, hold that the disaffection of a military class has in fact led to the establishment of a dictatorship in some one instance. Yet we have seen that the historian does not go beyond this statement to hold either a) that in every case the existence of a disaffected military class will (unless other factors forbid it) give rise to a dictatorship, or *b*) that the dictatorship would have followed even if there had been no disaffection in military circles. That is to say, the historian is neither interested in establishing laws of historical events from the observation of one instance, nor is it his primary task to consider hypothetical cases which permit him to establish or reject some proposed law of the historical process. This being the case, the historian can be said to be concerned with the concrete nature of actual events without seeking to establish a necessary relationship between those events. But this entails that the historian give up historical monism, for it is essential to monism to trace necessary relationships: without a necessary relationship between events one cannot hold that the events form a completely interrelated set. Thus, we see that the relation of existential dependence as it is employed by the historian fosters the view which we have called historical pluralism.

An objection might be raised to historical pluralism on the grounds that "if we only knew enough" all events would be seen to form one completely interrelated whole. This is the standard objection to all forms of pluralism, and a consideration of it must await our treatment of the problem of the philosophy of history in the next chapter. Here we need only point out that a monism of the type suggested by this rejoinder consists in holding that the historical process *as a whole* is to be conceived monistically. The particular form of historical monism with which we are here most anxious to deal lies, however, not in a complete, but in a partial, monism. This form of monism is specifically historical, rather than metaphysical, and is best represented by aspects of the phenomenological approach to history, and by organismic theories of the historical process.

In the realm of historical inquiry, as elsewhere, phenomenology has been concerned with pointing out the concrete nature and characteristics of objects without attempting to "reduce" them to fit the preconceptions of the observer. This has been an undeniably healthy tendency, and one which was needed in historical, as well as in other, investigations. The phenomenologist, however, has often tended not merely to accept objects at their face value but to deny that these objects are in any sense analyzable. The tendency among phenomenologists to treat every object as representing an ideal essence has had unfortunate consequences in the realm of historical inquiry. For it has too often been assumed that historical entities are simple, directly apprehensible entities which are capable of being termed essences. It has therefore been assumed that the task of the historian has been to portray these essences, to render them apprehensible to the reader in their concrete simplicity.

It cannot be denied that any historical event is in some sense a unity; on this point we ourselves have

278

repeatedly insisted. Likewise, it cannot be denied that a historical event cannot be reduced to atomic units, to a mere set of "associated" facts; on this point, likewise, we have insisted. But the phenomenologist who sees historical description as contemplative in an unanalytic sense falsifies the nature of historical understanding.[1] We have constantly referred to the historian's task as one of descriptive analysis, and it is the analytic side of this characterization which the phenomenologist overlooks. Let us make this clear through an example.

If the historian attempts to deal with the political history of the German Republic, there is before him one event of comparatively long duration. This event, to be sure, has a certain unity, or it would not be an event at all. We do not attempt to deny this unity, reducing it to atomic facts of a non-historical sort; it is an event of a certain level in the historical process. However, it is not an event which is simple in nature, for apart from its concrete subevents it has neither being nor essential character. It cannot be grasped by an intuition which refuses to see it as the concrete result of many other historical subevents; its nature can only be laid bare through following the chain of events which not only condition its existence but determine its nature. This process, which is the process of historical understanding, is that which we have called descriptive analysis.

[1] *Cf.*, M. Weber: *Gesammelte Aufsätze zur Wissenschaftslehre*, p. 244 (in the context of pp. 241 ff.).

It must be admitted, however, that the phenomenologist is not usually concerned with defending the simple and unanalyzable character of events such as the history of the German Republic. Phenomenological consideration of historical events has often tended to limit itself to certain types of events, especially those which can be characterized as epochs. It is with respect to these events, therefore, that our view of descriptive analysis must justify itself.

The phenomenologist points out that in both the history of individuals and the history of society the concept of an epoch is a well-grounded concept, and that the delimitation of epochs rests not upon caprice, but upon something given in the nature of the historical materials.[2] Against this contention no one can raise a word. But the phenomenologist goes further than this in his contention, for he holds that the concrete nature of an epoch is an unanalyzable indwelling quality, an essence which pervades the phenomena belonging to it, but which is not exhausted in the concrete nature of these phenomena. An epoch is, in short, an essence or type to which historical objects conform: it can be apprehended and described, but it is unitary, and cannot be analyzed with reference to the nature of specific historical events. It is with this monistic view of epochs that the doctrine of historical pluralism must take issue, for if this monism is established it undermines the theory of descriptive

[2] This is clear in the excellent discussion of epochs in Schneider: *Wesen und Formen der Epoche,* Ch. I.

analysis upon which historical pluralism ultimately rests.

We have acknowledged as indisputable the fact that historical events may be said to fall into epochs. Yet it is often overlooked that these epochs are not all-embracing in character; every epoch is by nature either political, artistic, economic, or the like.[3] As every historical investigator well knows, the epochs which are attributed to phenomena in one field do not coincide with the epochs attributed to phenomena in some other field. The epoch which is called the epoch of Romanticism in literature, and which some persons have attempted to extend to non-literary fields such as historical writing, can scarcely be called an epoch in the field of medicine and still be held to possess a unitary character. This limitation of an epoch to some definitely designated field of events should show that an epoch is not a unitary psychological phenomenon which embraces all people (or most people, or the "leading" people) during a specific time-span. Furthermore, it should be clear that every epoch is limited in scope not merely to a definite type of historical phenomenon, but to a definite geographical location: the artistic epochs of Western Europe do not coincide in time or nature with the artistic epochs of the Orient. A comparison of the epochs of cultural achievement of Europe with even those of the Near East should have made this

[3] This is explicitly recognized by Schneider (*Wesen und Formen der Epoche*, pp. 142 ff.) but he does not draw the same conclusions from this fact.

abundantly clear. This factor suggests a consideration of prime importance for our understanding of the concept of an epoch. For it suggests that an epoch is defined in terms of some comparatively long-enduring event which takes place within a given locality and concerns a given class of historical phenomena. Thus, the epoch of the Industrial Revolution (whatever its precise termini may be) is an epoch because within one given locality and in one field of historical phenomena, there was a long-enduring event which we may call the rise of the factory system of production. Likewise, the literary epoch known as Romanticism, if it have any meaning at all, rests on the fact that within Europe there occurred the development of a new type of literary accomplishment, or a new interest in the literary expression of certain materials, which was an event of importance in the formation of European literature as a whole. Thus, an epoch is characterized by the emergence of a certain comparatively long-enduring event, and the epoch is itself nothing but this event. This we can understand as soon as we give up the notion that events are atomic units, and recognize that there are many levels of generality among historical (as well as among scientific) events. And, in truth, the very fact that an epoch is considered as a temporal entity, and not merely as an essence, should show that every epoch must be considered as an event.

This analysis of the concept of an epoch, brief as it has been, brings to light the fact that our understanding of an epoch rests upon descriptive analysis, and not upon a direct phenomenological contemplation. For the concrete nature of an event, as we have seen in countless other cases, depends upon analyzing out the subevents which not merely condition its existence, but determine its nature. Every concrete description of an epoch, whether it be that of the Industrial Revolution, or that of literary Romanticism, depends upon tracing the nature of the subevents which entered into it. Romanticism, for example, has no concrete meaning which can be determined without an examination of specific literary works. The phenomenologist has done well to insist that the epoch (the long-enduring event) has a certain unitary nature which can not be found in any one of its subevents (nor in all of these subevents treated in an atomistic fashion), but he has tended to hypostatize this nature by holding that it exists over and above the whole set of events which have actually determined it.[4] Such a procedure can only result in the non-historical attempts which have been made (largely under the influence of phenomenology) to set up non-temporal phenomenal "types" which, because they lie outside of the field of events, furnish us with no positive knowledge concerning the concrete historical phenomena to which they are then applied.[5]

[4] This is in a large measure true of Nicolai Hartmann's theory (*Cf., Das Problem des Geistigen Seins*, Ch. 29).

[5] This is *not* true of Max Weber's methodological concept of the "*Idealtypus*" (*Cf., Gesammelte Aufsätze zur Wissenschaftslehre*, pp. 194 ff.).

We may therefore say in regard to the phenomenological theory of historical understanding, that its
monistic emphasis on the essential unity of specific
events such as epochs, provides no adequate substitute for our own view of descriptive analysis. As a
consequence, it leaves historical pluralism (as we understand it) essentially untouched. Let us now examine the more violently monistic theories of history
which may be called "organismic."

The organismic view of history starts where phenomenological analysis leaves off; for not content
with concrete descriptions of such supposedly unitary
historical events as epochs, it attempts to show that
an epoch or a nation exercises a determining influence over all the events which fall within its scope.
We find the upholders of this view emphasizing the
spirit of an epoch (the Zeitgeist), or the spirit of a
nation (the Volkseele), to such an extent that every
historical event comes to be looked upon as a product
of it. The analysis which we have brought to bear
upon the views of the phenomenologists likewise applies to organismic conceptions of an epoch. The
organismic conception of the national spirit is open
to similar objections. To be sure, the national character is not an event, and thus our argument against
the monistic view of an epoch does not apply without some modification. Yet it should be clear that
without denying the fact that there are "national
characteristics" we can point out that they do not of
themselves explain the historical process. On the con-

trary, they are typical ways of behaving which we learn to distinguish through historical scrutiny; they develop and are changed through the course of events, and thus they provide us with no concrete explanation of the actual processes of history. Even in such cases as those in which an entire populace shows a surprising subservience to externally imposed authority, we cannot, as historians, explain the dominance of the authority by an appeal to some element in the national character of the people. Our task *as historians* lies simply in tracing out the fact that no effective resistance was offered. If it be asked why there was no effective resistance we can trace out the means which were taken to suppress such resistance as was offered, what measures were taken to obtain submission through consent, and the like. In this manner we shall discover how those qualities which characterize a given people at a given time have been formed. This is a legitimate field for historical inquiry. On the other hand, speculation which attempts to account for phenomena in terms of the national character affords us no concrete historical knowledge; [6] to indulge in it (to appropriate a phrase from Spinoza) is to flee to the asylum of ignorance. And this is the more evident since we know of no generalizations concerning the national character of any people which remain applicable through many successive generations. On the contrary, the national

---

[6] It is undeniably true that the problem of "national characteristics" is a legitimate field for psychological investigation.

285

character seems to change almost continuously, when seen in historical perspective. This fact alone should lead us to surmise that the national character is not something that can be appealed to as an explanatory historical principle in concrete cases; it is, rather, something which not only demands concrete explanation, but which demands constant reinterpretation in the light of actual events.

These considerations should in themselves be sufficient to undermine the organismic form of monism, but to them we can add one other point of importance. It is a fundamental, and often noted, fact that organismic views of history break the continuity of the historical process into single self-contained wholes.[7] When one insists that within a given period or within a given nation every event must be seen in the light of the whole, the strands of history which connect one epoch or nation to another are severed. Only teleological views, such as that of Hegel, avoid this error. With them we shall later be dealing. Without a teleological conception each epoch or nation becomes a self-contained entity, and the manifest interpenetration of nations and cultures must be minimized or else entirely overlooked. One can see this most clearly in Spengler's morphological view of history, with its distorted and exceedingly misleading conception of contemporaneity. The conception of epochs which we advanced in opposition to the view of phenomenology avoids this error. For it will be

---

[7] Cf., G. v. Below: *Ueber Historische Periodisierung*, p. 16.

seen that when an epoch is considered merely in relation to the emergence of a new and significant event of considerable duration, the continuity of the historical process remains unbroken. For on this view the epoch, which is itself an event, depends upon sub-events which stretch back in history, and it does not include the relations between events which fall outside of its specific province. When, on the other hand, the organismic interpretation of an epoch is substituted for this view, all events fall within the province of some epoch, and the epoch itself appears to be independent of all that has gone before.

These considerations should be sufficient to defend historical pluralism against the empirical attacks which might be levelled against it by phenomenologists or supporters of organismic monism. It may, however, be well to say a few further words in regard to the pluralistic conception of the historical process.

William Stern points out what we have been attempting to emphasize: that "the total structure of history is to be understood as vertically stratified; not as a single linear connection of occurrences ('universal history'), and also not as a set of independent historical unitary entities standing side by side ('cultural morphology')." [8] This view is essentially pluralistic. The strata of the historical process represent events of different types and different levels of generality; their continuity represents their duration. Yet, like almost every figurative illustration, this schema

[8] *Person und Sache*, v. III (*Wertphilosophie*), p. 284.

fails to do justice to the elements of dynamic inter-dependence which are involved. We might better say that every event, taken with its subevents, forms a stratified figure, in which some of the strata are of longer and some of shorter duration. No figurative representation will then be able to render justice to the pluralistic nature of the historical process as a whole, for each event appears in that process in the context of many different events. It is this essential pluralism, in which entities stand in partial but not complete relation to each other, which makes such an overwhelming impression of both flux and fertility in history. Yet it is this same pluralism which enables the historian to achieve some measure of concrete knowledge. Were all events bound together in a complete system, in which every part depended upon every other, the historian could never commence to achieve understanding, for understanding would rest upon a mastery of the system as a whole. It is this essential unknowability of a completely monistic system that we had occasion to note in our discussion of Croce.[9]

Perhaps enough has now been said with regard to historical pluralism as it arises out of the nature of historical understanding. It will therefore be in place to see what light historical pluralism can throw on a few of the crucial arguments which have arisen in regard to the aims and function of the historian.

An argument arose at the time of Voltaire between

[9] *Cf.*, R. G. Collingwood: *Speculum Mentis*, p. 232.

the defenders of political history and the defenders of cultural history (the history of civilization). This argument has, in various forms, continued almost unabated down to our own times. The most violent portion of the history of the argument is probably to be found shortly before the turn of the present century when Lamprecht threw himself into the center of the discussion. At various times extraneous issues have become intermingled with the argument itself: for example, those introduced by the rationalism of Voltaire, and those introduced by Lamprecht's social-psychological emphasis on "historical laws." And the argument itself has become modified in being forced to take into account the development of specialized histories which lie wholly or partially within the cultural field. (Thus the investigation of cultural history which was considered, at the time of Voltaire and Herder, as a unitary project has since been broken into so many fragments that the scope of each is not less specialized than that which is embraced by the political historian. We now have economic historians, legal historians (who developed early out of contact with political history), historians of literature, of the arts, of dress, of customs, and so on almost indefinitely.) This refraction of cultural history has not, however, done away with the problem, for it is still necessary to ask the general question as to the scope of historical inquiry and the specific question whether political history can ever be overshadowed by any other type of historical writing.

In regard to the general question we have already suggested that the scope of historical inquiry includes all human events considered in their societal context and with their societal implications. Clearly, such a definition includes within the realm of historical knowledge not merely political history, but all forms of cultural history. How then are we to answer the question as to whether political history takes precedence over other forms of historical inquiry?

When we consider the multiform aspects of history, and the interconnections which have been traced between even the most divergent of these aspects, the question as to the precedence of any one aspect turns out to be devoid of all meaning. The political life of any nation or nations belongs to a more general societal framework in which it plays an important, but not an exclusively important, part. On every hand we find phenomena of purely economic origin influencing political events, no less than we find political phenomena influencing the course of economic history; to inquire as to which is the more worthy of attention is to fall into the error of exclusiveness. And this holds true not merely of political and economic history, but also, and to a like degree, of political and all other kinds of cultural history. Each is justified in so far as it investigates societal events with care and objectivity.

This willingness to grant autonomy to every field of cultural history is demanded not only by the actual successes registered by historians in each of these fields, but also on grounds dictated by historical pluralism. For it will readily be seen that once we deny that the events in the historical process form a completely interrelated set, we are free to examine each field of our general societal life without attempting to ascribe unique importance to any one "basic" field. It may be that, in the end, laws of historical development will be discovered, and that these laws will express functional relations between all historical events and the events in some one field of societal life. In such a case we might, perhaps, be able to speak of that field of investigation as the primary one. However, at the present time such a possibility seems exceedingly remote, judging both on the basis of current historical investigations and on the basis of a comparison with the development of the natural sciences. And even if that possibility were actualized, we would still have many diverse fields of historical investigation, even though some one of them could, with right, be termed basic.

This acceptance of the validity of the most diverse historical investigations does not, however, lead to chaos. To accept the validity of historical investigations in many fields strengthens the hand of the historian in any particular field. For example, the political historian of a certain period may derive great benefit from economic histories of the same period, and even from well-conducted investigations in literary history. This is the case whenever an event in one field of inquiry enters as subevent into an event belonging to some other field. Because such interconnections between the fields occur as frequently as they do, the boundaries between the fields tend to disappear as our knowledge increases. They are distinct merely at the outset of an investigation, when the phenomenon to be investigated can be readily classified; by the time descriptive analysis has accomplished its task the investigation will be seen to have spread over many fields. To substantiate this point one need but recall the attempt of Justus Möser to write (in opposition to Voltaire) a specifically political history; by the end of his attempt Möser had covered so many diverse fields that he is now looked upon as one of the earliest and most successful of the cultural historians. Thus it is the material involved which integrates and harmonizes the diverse fields of historical investigation. These fields are equally worthy of investigation, and, from the point of view of one's choice of a subject of inquiry, they may all be spoken of as autonomous. But the fact that historical events of the various types interpenetrate renders worse than useless any attempt to draw sharp and final distinctions between the fields. At the same time, it is this very interpenetration of events which saves historical inquiries from chaos.

In summary of this argument concerning political and cultural history we may say that what we have "discovered" is something long known and sanctioned by practice. We have merely pointed out that all history is cultural, or, to use a less ambiguous term, societal. Political events have, on this basis, as much place in history as have other events. The exclusiveness which sees all history in terms of politics merely because the field of politics can be comparatively sharply defined, breaks down in so far as it must include many non-political facts in its explanations. In the economy of history there is place for all types of investigation, and since societal events do as a matter of fact interpenetrate there is no likelihood that the multiplication of "separate" fields of research will do anything but clarify the knowledge which any particular investigator gains.

However, a second problem in regard to the field of history arises out of the answer just given to the long-standing problem of political and cultural history. This problem lies in the sharp division which is often made between "research historians" and "great" or "synthetic" historians. This division is an unfortunate one, since it has led to many polemics which have divided the ranks of historians themselves. It is all the more unfortunate since, to a large measure, it rests upon a misunderstanding of the nature of historical knowledge.

By the research historian is generally meant not merely the editor of texts, but every historian who chooses for the subject matter of his investigations historical phenomena which are comparatively narrow in scope and short in duration. It is commonly assumed that the historian who deals with the minutiae of the historical process merely "gathers the facts" in a routine manner, and that his more imaginative colleague who deals with large-scale events, such as the fate of empires, has merely to select from the body of amassed fact those items which when brought together and "interpreted" serve to "give a picture" of the great event with which he is concerned. But it need scarcely be repeated after all that has been said concerning historical understanding, that no matter how short or narrow in scope are the events with which the historian deals, he does not merely uncover facts, but places them together in a context; no less than the historian of empires, the so-called research historian "gives a picture" of the event with which he is concerned. As we have repeatedly emphasized, the primary task of historical understanding tolerates no bifurcation between fact-finding and synthesis. Yet it is on the basis of such a bifurcation that the false distinction between history as research and history as synthesis has been raised.

When we seek to understand why a historian enters into the painstaking analysis of historical minutiae, the answer lies within the pluralistic nature of the historical process itself. For when one historian traces the existential conditions upon which a particular event depends, this immediately raises innumerable problems concerning the nature of each of these conditions. Whether these conditions are small-scale political events, or whether they concern the details of conditions of life at a given place or time, they provide a valuable field for historical inquiry. For before such inquiry takes place we have no adequate means of knowing whether these same small-scale events do not also play an important part in other events, where their influence has remained hitherto unnoticed. It is for this reason that the historian, as historian, is justified in taking as his province the small-scale events which are sometimes looked upon as trivial. Furthermore, if the historian aims at co-operating with the theoretical social sciences, the investigation of the minutiae of the historical process becomes of great significance. Without such investigations economic history, ethnology, and other theoretical social sciences would lack much of the important data upon which their generalizations must rest. Thus, it is not merely for the sake of history as history, but also for the sake of the theoretical social sciences, that the work of the so-called "research historian" is carried on.

One of the reasons why the false distinction between the "research historian" and the "interpretative historian" has been utilized in such an invidious manner is to be found in the non-theoretic interests which have often determined the work of the "interpretative historians." One can find, for example in Leo, in Sybel, or in Treitschke, the demand that the historian should be a political educator; on the basis of such an appeal the historian who is concerned with the minutiae of the historical process must assume an inferior position. It is true that the politically oriented historian does not always underestimate the work of the so-called research historian, yet the ethical demands which are raised by the former tend to react to the discredit of the latter. It is for this reason that the element of dispraise has often been introduced into the distinction between the "two" types of historical inquiry.

The problem which is raised by politically oriented historians regarding the rôle of the historian in the political activities of his times allows of no "theoretical" solution. The question has been dealt with by Sybel,[10] and even more feelingly by Max Weber,[11] but it must remain forever an ethical question of a personal order, upon which no one can generalize. The only consideration which is important here is the obligation that the objectivity of every historical investigation must be guarded against distorting factors which always, and at every point, threaten it. This in itself is an ethical obligation.

There is, however, a second factor which has led to the invidious character of the distinction between "research historians" and "synthetic historians." This is to be found in another non-theoretical interest which is sometimes evidenced in historians: the attempt to show the human significance of certain past events by depicting their great formative rôle in history. This attempt is in itself legitimate, and perhaps praiseworthy. Its effect on historical works is

---

[10] *Ueber den Stand der neuern deutschen Geschichtschreibung* (in *Kleine Historische Schriften*, v. I).

[11] *Wissenschaft als Beruf* (in *Gesammelte Aufsätze zur Wissenschaftslehre*).

clear: it leads the historian to portray human events on a large canvas in order that we may discern, in their proper perspective, the full magnitude of certain epoch-making events. Yet such an attempt is not merely a "synthesis" or "interpretation" of facts already known, for, as we have seen, epochs are themselves merely large-scale events. In such historical writing, if it be worthy of the name, the historian depicts the actual interconnections which he finds within the material. Although his choice of a topic for consideration may be determined by valuational factors, he need not sacrifice objectivity in his description. Thus, the so-called synthetic historian does not differ from a historian who is concerned with the minutiae of the historical process: both have open to them the possibility of genuine historical understanding, the difference between them lying solely in the sort of interest which each manifests in historical truth. It is only when the so-called synthetic historian attempts to encompass a survey and evaluation of the historical process *as a whole* that he forfeits the objectivity which is rightfully his. And, as we shall see in our concluding chapter, he does so because he ceases to be a historian: he becomes a philosopher of history.

It has often been contended that each age must write history anew. If Goethe, and others who have put forward this contention, are justified in their assertions, serious doubts must assail the reader concerning the validity of the position which we have adopted. And it is certainly true beyond all possibility of denial that much history has been rewritten in every age. We must attempt to explain this in the light of our own position.

There are several reasons why historical accounts are from time to time radically revised. Not all of these reasons are directly attributable to the influence of the historian's own period; but some of them are clearly so influenced, and others are to a lesser degree. Let us consider each of them.

One. New source materials may be discovered.

Such discoveries most often take the form of an unearthing of new documents. However, at other times they consist in the practical application of new methods of research to documents which were already known but never adequately exploited; for example, the historical knowledge derived from the deciphering of hieroglyphics or the contributions brought to history by the extension of field-work in archaeology. The discovery or utilization of such new source materials may radically alter the views which have been previously held concerning historical events, but no one could argue from this fact that all historical writing is relative to the age in which the historian lives.

Two. The sources constantly undergo critical re-examination.

Under the impact of new materials bringing fresh views regarding historical events, the historian is constantly forced to exercise the analytic function of external criticism. This is particularly important with respect to tracing the interrelation of the sources as new sources come to light. Discoveries in this field can lead to the rejection of a previously accepted source, and consequently to the rejection of a previously accepted historical view. Comparable to this further exercise of external criticism with respect to old sources, we may mention one further factor which leads to a new historical view. This factor lies in the progress of what has been called "hermeneutic" (or *positive* internal criticism). As philological studies advance, old texts open up new meanings to us, and these new meanings may demand that we revise our previous views. Contemporary philosophers should be well aware of this factor, since the reinterpretation of Plato in the last years has depended very largely upon hermeneutic investigations.

Three. New approaches to the historical process constantly appear.

By the term "new approaches to the historical process" we mean to indicate the fact that men have at various times singled out of the historical process events which were either totally disregarded by previous historians or were never consistently explored. Karl Marx's inauguration of a new type of economic history serves as an example of this. In fact, it may more correctly be said that Marx discovered not only one new approach to the historical process, but paved the way for countless others. Such new approaches to the historical process explain a large portion of the revisions which historical knowledge must always undergo. At rare intervals these approaches may cause a radical displacement in previously accepted views; at other times they serve in a merely supplementary manner. Yet even in those cases where they demand an almost wholesale revision of previously accepted views, they cannot be interpreted as overthrowing the historian's ideal of objective knowledge. For it will be seen that they are accepted only because it is held that they are true; previous accounts are then rejected because they failed to uncover those historical factors which the new approach is in a position to recognize. The only conclusion which we can draw from this situation is the sorrowful one which is forced upon us in every field of knowledge: that no single generation has ever fathomed perfect truth.

It must be acknowledged that the discovery of new approaches to the historical process are sometimes (and perhaps always) dependent upon general conditions which characterize the times in which they are made. However, this fact does not serve to uphold Goethe's dictum, for the validity of these new approaches is not limited to the age in which they are discovered: they are utilized until they are no longer held to be true.

It may well be asked how any age can know its own

approaches to history to be truer than the approaches utilized at other periods in historical writing. This question leads us to the fourth factor which explains why historical accounts are rewritten.

Four. The new approaches to history can only be validated through their effect on historical practice and their relation to the theoretical social sciences.

The establishment of new approaches to history gives rise to new types of historical accounts. If these accounts appear to throw light upon the nature of the past, the approaches upon which they were founded come to be formulated in terms of principles of the historical process. They thus become part of the body of the theoretical social sciences, taking their place in a systematic view of the factors inherent in the processes of history. But since such principles are at the outset merely working hypotheses they are likely to be overthrown. As a consequence much historical writing which is based upon a new approach will have to be discarded because the approach cannot be validated through further historical inquiries. Only those new approaches which can be taken up by the theoretical social sciences, and thus serve as guides to further historical practice, will prove to have been justifiable ones. This accounts for the fact that not every revision of history will be acceptable to future generations: many revisions must be discarded or revised anew.

Five. All contemporaneous historical accounts must be rewritten.

The historian who undertakes a descriptive analysis of the flow of events which goes on about him can never envision clearly and in its actual detail the manner in which that series of events will terminate. If his conjecture regarding the series as a whole is substantially correct, then much of his history will not have to be materially altered. If his conjecture turns out to be false, all of his account must be discarded. Thus, we may say that every contemporaneous historical work will in the future be partially or wholly rewritten.

Six. Many developmental accounts must be rewritten.

The historian who sees the events which he is describing as developmental in character stands in a peril similar to that which always overwhelms the contemporaneous historian. A developmental series is characterized not only by unity and temporal sequence, but also by a uniform direction. Taken as a single event, a developmental series is cumulative. If the historian envisages the event with which he is dealing as cumulative in character, and if he stands "too close" to this event, the future may completely unravel that which he believes to be a developmental process. One cannot read much quite recent historical writing which concerns the last few generations without a slight feeling of disgust merely because the historians of the period so often focused their accounts upon the development of "democracy." Such is the danger in a developmental account when the historian does not stand at a sufficient distance from the events which he describes.

Seven. The last factor which leads to the rewriting of history is that which Goethe and others have had chiefly in mind. It relates particularly to cultural history taken in the narrower sense. It is an undeniable fact that much that has passed for cultural history has undergone periodic revisions of the most radical sort. One need but think of the transvaluations which have shaken former critical appreciations of Shakespeare, Gothic architecture, Vergil, "the Greeks," Raphael, or any of countless other personages of periods of art. Every age, we may say, tends to estimate events of the past in terms of itself. Yet what has this to do with history? The examples which we have cited, and which those who hold to this form of relativism continually cite, are not examples of historical writing, but of critical appreciation. Even the changing views of "the Greek Spirit" (of the Greek way-of-life) are *views about* history; they are not historical accounts. What Goethe failed to find in the temple at Paestum tells us nothing—and purports to tell us nothing—of Greece; it is a fact which tells us something of Goethe. Thus it belongs in an account of Goethe, and not in an account of Greek life. Similarly, the contemplation of historical epochs, and the constant reshuffling of the boundaries of these epochs, are not historical accounts if they are merely "phenomenological" descriptions of the essence of an epoch. Such attempts depend upon historical investigations, but in addition demand that we view a specific event as being of great importance. It is in this that the valuational aspect enters into the characterization of an epoch. In so far as such valuations change from age to age, a constant reinterpretation of "the epochs of history" must always result. But, as we cannot too often insist, the mere delimitation of epochs is not historical knowledge, but, rather, presupposes such knowledge. Thus the facts most often appealed to in order to justify the contention that each age must always rewrite past history for itself are not facts of a truly historical character. With this our argument concerning the rewriting of history may be brought to a close.

We have cited many reasons why history must often be rewritten, yet none of these reasons demands that we give up the ideal of objective historical knowledge. If these reasons are sufficient to explain the actual rewriting which we find in the field of history, then our argument for historical objectivity receives a final confirmation within the empirical field which concerns us.

CHAPTER X

The Philosophy of History

THE PRECEDING chapter has illustrated the familiar
fact that one cannot confine one's self to methodological discussions. Every analysis of a field of knowledge terminates in the acceptance of some view regarding the data with which the field is concerned. It
was thus that we were led from a consideration of the
nature of historical understanding to the view which
we have called historical pluralism. In the present
chapter we shall see that the acceptance of historical
pluralism in its turn leads us on into the province of
the philosophy of history.

The term "the philosophy of history" is a vague
one. Taken in its broadest sense it involves every concern which philosophers may have with the knowledge of history. It is not, however, in this broad sense
that we shall at present use the term. In a narrower
sense the philosophy of history refers to the attempts
which have been made by historians, sociologists, and
philosophers to interpret the meaning or significance
of the historical process as a whole. These attempts
are characterized by an appeal to the empirically dis-
cerned facts of history; they represent the search for
an ultimate message which can be found in the his-

torical process as a whole. In this they are distinguished from those "universal histories" which are really compendia of historical knowledge, and make no attempt to reveal a message which the historical process as a whole contains. They are also distinguishable from "pragmatic histories," which find particular lessons applicable to present dilemmas in specific portions of the past. The philosophers of history survey the "trend" of the past, seeking to derive philosophically significant knowledge from such surveys. This type of inquiry into universal history is that which since the time of Herder has been called "the philosophy of history." [1]

It is obvious that the doctrine of historical pluralism which was put forward in the last chapter leads to a discussion of the philosophy of history, for historical pluralism seems to deny the very possibility of the philosophy of history taken in this sense. If there is an ultimate pluralism in history the attempt to decipher the message which is contained in "the historical process as a whole" is futile. And yet we find that philosophers, sociologists, and historians have occupied themselves with attempts to construct philosophies of history. Unless we can demonstrate that all such attempts are by their very nature invalid theoretical constructions, we shall not have given a satisfactory defense of the doctrine of historical plu-

[1] That which is sometimes called the philosophy of history is really general sociology: an attempt to discover the laws or principles of historical development. (Cf., Rickert: *Probleme der Geschichtsphilosophie*, p. 5.)

ralism. Let us therefore examine the basis upon which any philosophy of history must rest.

It will be recalled that in the preceding chapter we offered no concrete objection to the attempts which have been made to establish a *complete* monism with respect to the historical process, apart from pointing out that such a monism would render the historian's enterprise incapable of any measure of fulfillment. We concerned ourselves wholly with historical monisms which were less ambitious in scope. At this point, however, it becomes necessary to examine the grounds on which any complete form of monism might be established.

The root conception out of which all historical monisms have grown is to be found in the principle of teleological development. As we have had previous occasion to note, the conception of a development is applicable only to those series of events in which there is an inherent non-temporal order of a specific type, in which, as we may say, the last element contains the fruition of that which in the first element has its beginning. In a developmental series of events change proceeds not merely in a definitely determined order, but in a definite direction. Where this directional line is broken we say that the development has been cut off. Now such a term as development cannot readily be applied to every series of events in the historical process. It is a matter of empirical fact that historical events often do change their directional lines; the last aspect in a process of historical change often seems to contain something quite different from that which the first aspect began. Thus, in order to validate the conception of development in empirical historical investigations some further element is needed. This element the conception of teleology supplies.

By means of coupling the conception of teleology with that of development, it is possible to hold that every series of historical events is developmental in character. For if the nature of the last element in a series of events determines the nature of the earlier elements, then the direction of the series as a whole is thereby fixed once and for all. The events in the series then take on a more unified character, and the pluralism which seems to be demanded by the nature of historical events tends to disappear. This disappearance soon becomes final. For every series of events can be considered as a part of some other series of events which is larger in scale, and the teleological development which characterizes that series then becomes part of a larger teleological development. Ultimately, then, the whole of the historical process comes to be regarded as a teleological development, and historical monism is adopted.

It is in this fashion that the application of the concept of teleological development to historical events leads to historical monism. It is well to examine what justification can be found for regarding history as a teleological development.

We have already pointed out that there seems to

be no empirical basis for holding that every historical series of events possesses a uniform direction. It
likewise seems impossible to hold that every historical event is teleologically determined. The only empirically verifiable point at which teleology enters into
the nature of historical events is to be found in the
influence of human volition on those events. But
human volition can not account for the whole of the
historical process; it must have materials upon which
to work, and these materials are not manufactured
by it. At every point at which human volition comes
into play in history we find that limits are set to its
influence, and that the nature of any event which it
partially determines is also partially determined by
countless other factors which are not expressly volitional in character. Thus we may say that so far as
empirical evidence is concerned there seems to be
no reason why we should hold that every historical
event is either developmental or teleological in character.

Another attempt to justify the view that historical
events always exemplify a teleological development
is to be found in certain analyses of the nature of
historical understanding. It has often been claimed
that the concept of teleological development is fundamental to the historian's grasp of the past; that only
in viewing events in a teleological light can the
past be rendered intelligible. It is therefore claimed
that history as we know it must represent past events
as teleological developments. To this contention a

twofold reply can be given. In the first place, we have just pointed out that history as we know it does not seem to show that events possess this characteristic. In the second place, on the basis of an examination of actual historical knowledge, as well as on the basis of the arguments advanced by such persons as Rickert and Troeltsch, we have come to the conclusion that historical understanding does not impose itself upon its materials, but rather follows where these lead. The whole of the present analysis of the nature of historical knowledge may thus be taken as an answer to this attempted justification of the concept of teleological development in history.

A third type of defense for teleology in history has also been offered. It has often been claimed that the apparently pluralistic character of historical events is an illusion forced upon us by a short-sighted empiricism. It is suggested that if we take a longer view of historical events, refusing to allow ourselves to become bogged down in trifling details, the historical process as a whole will reveal itself to be teleological and developmental in character. It is by means of this ostensibly empirical method that philosophies of history are constructed.

Their creators who seek to trace the course of the historical process in the large lay claim to an empirically sound method. Undaunted by the repeated failures of sociologists, historians, and philosophers to uncover any acceptable view of the historical process as a whole, these adventurers grasp at every new attempt as containing the possibility of a solution to their problem. It will be our task to show that the problem is essentially insoluble.

In the first place it should be noted that when the philosopher of history draws a distinction between what is true of the historical process in the large, and what is true of small-scale events in that process, he immediately forfeits his right to claim that the process as a whole must be monistically conceived. It must be granted that teleological development may not be equally obvious through the whole range of the historical process, but one should be suspicious of any attempts at historical construction which find teleology only in large-scale events. It would seem far more likely that if the historical process were truly characterized by teleological development, we should find instances of such teleology scattered indiscriminately through the whole scale of historical events. In this respect the historical teleology of an Augustine is far more convincing than the teleological developments which are traced by Hegel.

The philosopher of history who draws a distinction between the discernible teleology of large-scale events and the hidden teleology which is supposedly none the less present in the minutiae of the historical process is very likely to accept a bifurcation between historical research and historical synthesis.[2] For him "synthesis" is the ultimate goal of historical inquiry,

---

[2] *Cf.,* Hegel's classification of "the methods of treating history" in the introduction to his *Philosophy of History*.

since this synthesis uncovers the true teleological development of history. At first glance the most surprising fact to be found in those historical syntheses upon which philosophies of history are based is the exaggerated stress which they place upon problems of periodization. In Comte as in Hegel the question of periodization comes to the forefront and almost dwarfs other historical problems by virtue of the magnitude of its all-encompassing framework. However, when one reflects upon the relation which periodization bears to the problem of teleological development, this emphasis upon the periods of history becomes readily understandable.

In dealing with the problem of periods of history, we have already had occasion to point out that periods are delimited with respect to some comparatively long-enduring event which appears to be of great significance. We found that the periods of history are not to be considered as unitary historical entities which embrace all of the historical phenomena of a given time, but, rather, that they are particular abstractions from the historical process as a whole, and have reference only to certain areas of that process at the time in question. It will be well to apply these findings to the periodization which is to be found in philosophies of history.

If we ask why it is that philosophies of history, which aim to trace teleological development in the historical process, should concentrate their attention upon problems of periodization, we find an answer ready at hand. When we say that a period is delimited by some *long-enduring event of importance* the clue to this answer is already given. For what can so easily define the importance of a long-enduring event as its place in a teleological development? It is a traditional failing of a mind which is not historically oriented to examine the importance of any event merely in terms of its relationship to succeeding events of the same scale. To a degree, it is also characteristic of the non-historic mind to confine this discussion of importance to the relationship which the event in question bears to events which are generically similar to it. Thus, when asked to define the importance of the Protestant Reformation, the layman is likely to confine his answer to its supposed influence on modern European freedom of thought, an event quite similar both in scale and in generic nature to that which he understands by the Reformation. The historian, as we well know, would give no such facile answer. But philosophers of history are not conspicuous for their historical orientation; all too frequently they share the layman's tendency to confine their estimates of historical importance to tracing the relationship which one event bears to other events of the same scale and kind. This leads them to a demarcation of historical periods in terms of teleological development. For it will be seen that if we judge the importance of a historical event by what it has contributed to other events which are fundamentally similar to it, we cannot fail to have before us a pic-

313

ture which gives the illusion of a teleological development. Each period having been demarcated with reference to its contribution to a future period, the historical process as a whole takes on a deceptively monistic appearance.

Now, it might be objected that we have failed to take into account the fact that in some philosophies of history certain periods are held to contribute nothing to the teleological development of the process as a whole, and yet that even these blank periods fall within the purview of the philosophers of history. This, however, fails to touch the crucial point in our argument. If there are any philosophies of history in which a "period" is held to be blank, the principle of periodization is adopted without reference to the period in question. It is only held to be a period because it represents a chronological gap in the teleological development which is in question. Thus, in the prevalent common-sense periodization of history (which, strangely enough, is an intellectualistic one) the so-called Middle Ages (usually referred to as the Dark Ages), represent a chronological gap in a teleological development of "free inquiry." The periodization is undertaken on the basis of the positive character of Greek and Modern thought, and the Middle Ages are seen as contributing nothing to history.

In Hegel's philosophy of history the aspect of teleological development is everywhere evident. It is not only specifically formulated in the Introduction to his *Philosophy of History*, but it is evident in the actual historical studies which he undertook in the fields of philosophy and fine art. In Comte, who with Hegel most clearly represents the tendency of a philosopher of history to proceed by periodization, a similar emphasis on a unitary or teleological development can be discovered. The periods which Comte finds represented in the historical process are periods of relative "enlightenment"; they are periods ascribed to the history of social and moral thought. We see in the transitions from religious to metaphysical, and from metaphysical to scientific thought, a pure line of development. To be sure, Comte's positivism would not allow him to adopt an explicitly teleological view of this development, yet it might be contended [3] that there is a strong teleological ingredient within it. Whether or not this is the case, we can see that Comte's periodization of history rests upon his acceptance of a developmental standpoint which binds the periods he has singled out into an apparently monistic unity.

These illustrations, drawn from widely known attempts at periodization, show the degree to which the conception of a unitary or teleological development enters into those attempts. As a consequence it is not to be wondered at that in their attempts to establish monism on an empirical ground, philosophers of history should focus their attention on those large-

[3] *Cf.*, Comte: *Positive Philosophy*, v. II, p. 265. Also Troeltsch: *Der Historismus und seine Probleme*, pp. 427 ff.

scale events which they designate as periods of history. It remains for us to show by means of concrete argumentation what was already implicit in our treatment of historical periods: that no teleological periodization of history can establish historical monism.

We have already pointed out that every so-called period represents but a segregated portion of the historical process at any given time. Thus teleological periodization of history does not demonstrate that the historical process as a whole is teleological. With this in mind let us examine Comte's view of "the three stages of development."

Comte held that all thought goes through three stages of development; these stages he termed theological, philosophical, and scientific. By means of this law he sought to unify all historical phenomena. Yet such a law, it will readily be seen, can not possibly suffice as a basis for historical monism. For even if Comte were correct in his contention that "the whole social mechanism is ultimately based on opinions," [4] no law which abstracts out of the historical process merely one set of determining factors can ever do justice to that process as a whole. The historical process does not consist merely in thought-factors, no matter what formative significance we may attach to them. Opinions may determine certain aspects of economic, political and artistic forms, but the actual existence of these forms is something over and above the opinions which may have helped to determine their nature.

[4] Quoted by J. B. Bury: *The Idea of Progress*, p. 292.

Thought does not spin social forms out of itself, it operates on those forms which are already given in the historical process to which it itself belongs. Thus, no law of the development of thought can be held to unify all that is included within the historical process. The periodization of history from the standpoint of the development of thought is merely one possible periodization of the historical process. No matter how accurate it may be, and no matter how teleological in character it may appear, it cannot serve to establish historical monism.

Furthermore, we can point out that any periodization of the historical process represents an abstraction from that process not merely with reference to the types of phenomena which it includes, but also with reference to the scope of its survey. As is well known, Comte followed Condorcet in his willful exclusion of non-European elements from the survey of history. Such an exclusion (which is all too common) makes it impossible to argue for a complete monism of the historical process on empirical grounds. And even in philosophies of history such as Hegel's in which non-European elements are introduced, other gaps are always present. These gaps are usually to be found in so-called pre-history, in the omission of contemporary primitive civilizations,[5] and in the failure to include the complete history of any one geographical sector within that survey. In the case of Hegel's phi-

[5] On these points *Cf.*, Hegel: *Philosophy of History*, p. 63 and p. 69.

losophy of history this appears particularly clearly; the teleological development of history finds a place for one era of each nation's history, and all other eras of that history are excluded.[6] Here again we see that the periodization of history is an abstraction from the historical process, and, thus, that a historical synthesis based upon periodization cannot be used to establish historical monism.

A second major objection to the attempt to establish historical monism through the apparently teleological character of historical periods follows closely upon this first objection. For it will be seen that every abstraction from the historical process as a whole, every focusing of attention upon some one aspect of that process, follows from an original value-charged choice. This we have already had occasion to note with reference to the historian's choice of his subject-matter. It applies equally well to the choice made by the philosopher of history with respect to the principle of his periodization. Comte chose, for definite and specifically assignable reasons, to periodize history with respect to social and moral ideas; von Below contends that history should be periodized with reference to political events.[7] This value-charged element in the philosophy of history has been ably indicated by Troeltsch,[8] and it demonstrates the essential subjectivity of every attempt to prove historical

---

[6] Cf., Hegel: *Grundlinien der Philosophie des Rechts*, # 347.
[7] G. v. Below: *Ueber die Periodisierung*, p. 18.
[8] It is almost the *leitmotif* of *Der Historismus und seine Probleme*.

monism through an appeal to the teleological development which can be discovered in the sequence of "the great historical periods."

A third objection can be found in the fact that every philosopher stands in the midst of the historical process itself. It is impossible to hold that history represents a teleological development unless one knows (or believes that one knows) what the end of that process will be. But no empirical survey of the past can demonstrate the future to the philosopher of history. It therefore becomes impossible to ground historical monism upon an empirical appeal to the apparent teleology of past periods of history. In order to establish historical monism upon a teleological view of the periods of history it is therefore necessary to transcend one's temporal standpoint. In this Augustine and the entire Christian philosophy of history again represent a sounder approach to the problem of historical monism. For in Augustine and his followers we find an appeal to the non-temporal realm of God as the basis of historical monism. In addition, the belief that the world was soon coming to an end seemed to justify a complete periodization of history. The necessity of attaining a non-empirical, transcendent point of view before one can regard the historical process as a teleological development has long been noted by analysts of the idea of progress. But what holds of the conception of progress holds equally well of any unitary or teleological view of development. For the conception of progress is just such a view, save that it explicitly embodies the standpoint that this development represents the attainment of increased value. We may therefore say that in so far as historical monism rests upon the conception of teleological development it can only be established through some non-empirical (transcendent) approach. Thus we conclude our third and final argument against historical monism.

II

We have now seen that historical monism cannot be established through a direct empirical approach, nor through analyzing the nature of historical understanding, nor through an appeal to the great synthetic surveys of periods in the history of civilization. With ultimate metaphysical arguments concerning historical monism we cannot here concern ourselves. It is sufficient for us to have shown that philosophies of history in the commonly accepted meaning of the term cannot be constructed upon any empirical basis. And this, in fact, suffices to dispose of the traditional philosophies of history, for if historical monism can only be proved by means of a non-historical (transcendent) approach, the whole theoretical significance of empirical attempts to construct philosophies of history disappears. In that case every philosophy of history becomes a form of apologetics based upon a belief in the omnipotence and omnipresence of the forces of Providence or Progress. With such apologetics the historian, as historian, need not be concerned.

All that remains for us now to consider is a justification of the method of argumentation which the present work has employed. The need for such a justification becomes especially apparent as the result of the stand which we have taken in regard to philosophies of history. It may well be asked whether we have not robbed history of its fullest significance in denying the possibility of theoretically valid philosophies of history.

A philosophic approach to the knowledge of history must assume one of three forms: it must either commence with a general methodological analysis of historical understanding; or it must attempt to place historical understanding within the context of all human experience; or, finally, it must accept the methods of empirical research and seek to derive some ultimate meaning from the historical process as a whole. Of these three approaches to history we have chosen to follow the first.

It should be clear that he who attempts to construct a metaphysics of experience which will include the historian's experience must already accept some view of the concrete nature of that experience. Every person doubtless possesses such a view, but implicit methodology is no less dangerous for philosophy than is implicit metaphysics. One does better to make his theory of methodological analysis explicit before attempting to construct a metaphysics of the historical experience. This lack of explicit analysis explains the fundamental emptiness of the current approach to historical experience as we find it in the writings of many phenomenologists.[9]

Enough has already been said to expose the danger which lies in following the third philosophic approach to history. Attempts to construct philosophies of history assume the ultimate compatibility of their enterprise with empirical historical investigations. But the present methodological analysis has attempted to show that these philosophies of history rely upon a false method of historical "construction," a method not sanctioned by actual historical research. Thus the attempt to construct philosophical interpretations of history which go under the name of "the philosophy of history" can lead only to error. This is not to say that the philosopher cannot find an abundance of material for philosophical speculation in the human past as historical research reveals it; we merely contend that such lessons are not to be gained by the teleological approach which is implicit in monistic philosophies of history. Moreover, the philosopher has no justification for speculating upon the human past as historical research reveals it to him unless he has first determined that such research can lay claim to objectivity.

It is in the light of these contentions that the pres-

[9] I have in mind particularly Heidegger and Jaspers. *Cf.*, Jaspers: *Philosophie*, v. II, pp. 118-148; 393-414, and, for Heidegger, Kaufmann: *Geschichtsphilosophie der Gegenwart*, pp. 118-129. Something of the same approach is also to be found in the Introduction to Hegel's *Philosophy of History*.

ent methodological analysis of historical knowledge must be considered. We have attempted to understand the historian's activity by accepting it on its own grounds. We have not made our analysis subservient to any previously accepted metaphysical views which are not implicit in the historical enterprise itself. If this be considered an "unphilosophic" procedure, we can only answer that philosophy must always proceed upon the basis of data which are given to it. These data, so far as the present work is concerned, are to be found in the historical enterprise itself, and it is only with reference to the conditions and implications of that enterprise that we can ever estimate its claim to be considered as knowledge. Epistemological or metaphysical arguments have no place in such an estimate, for the historian lays no claim to a more ultimate knowledge than can be gained by any other empirical investigator. We therefore leave the consideration of these ultimate philosophical problems to other investigations. So far as the present work is concerned we have sought to show that the historian need not consider his task a hopeless one, that within the bounds of his own province there are no insurmountable obstacles which render his enterprise meaningless.

BIBLIOGRAPHY

BIBLIOGRAPHY

THE following bibliography does not aim to be a complete survey of the material available. Its primary aim is to serve as a bibliography of the volumes which have chiefly been used in the preparation of the present work; its secondary aim is to acquaint the reader with the most important of those works which deal specifically with the problem of the validity of historical knowledge.

For the sake of greater usefulness this bibliography has been arranged according to the following tabular form.

I THE FIELD OF HISTORICAL RESEARCH

1. *Histories of the study of history*

Barnes, Harry Elmer: A History of Historical Writing; Norman (Okla.), 1937.
Below, Georg v.: Die Deutsche Geschichtsschreibung von dem Befreiungskriegen bis zu unserem Tagen; Muenchen/Berlin, 1924.

Berr, Henri, *and others:* History and Historiography (Encyclopedia of the Social Sciences).

Black, J. B.: The Art of History, A Study of Four Great Historians of the 18th Century; London, 1926.

Breysig, Kurt: Die Meister der Entwickelnden Geschichtsforschung; Breslau, 1936.

Bury, J. B.: The Ancient Greek Historians; New York, 1909.

Creuzer, Frederich: Die historiche Kunst der Griechen in ihrer Entstehung und Fortbildung; Leipzig/Darmstadt, 1845.

Fueter, Eduard: Geschichte der neueren Historiographie; Muenchen/Berlin, 1911.

Gooch, G. P.: History and Historians in the 19th Century; London, 1913.

Meinecke, Friedrich: Die Entstehung des Historismus, 2 vol.; Muenchen, 1936.

Ritter, Moritz: Die Entwicklung der Geschichtswissenschaft; Muenchen/Berlin, 1919.

Rocholl, R.: Die Philosophie der Geschichte, v. I; Goettingen, 1878.

Rosa, Gabriele: Storia generale delle storie; Milano/Napoli, 1873.

Schulz, Marie: Die Lehre von der historischen Methode bei den Geschichtschreibern des Mittelalters (6.-13. Jahrhundert); (Abhandlungen zur mittleren und neuren Geschichte, 13); Berlin/Leipzig, 1909.

Shotwell, James T.: An Introduction to the History of History; New York, 1922.

Wach, Joachim: Das Verstehen, v. 3 (Das Verstehen in der Historik von Ranke bis zum Positivismus); Tuebingen, 1933.

(also: Croce, Benedetto: History, Its Theory and Practice; *cited below.)*

2. *Methods of Historical Research*

Bauer, Wilhelm: Einführung in das Studium der Geschichte; Tuebingen, 1928.

Bernheim, Ernst: Lehrbuch der historischen Methode; Leipzig, 1889.

Cohen, Morris R. and Nagel, E.: Introduction to Logic and Scientific Method; New York, 1934.

Droysen, Joh. Gust.: Historik (hrsg. Rudolf Hübner); Muenchen/Berlin, 1937.

Fling, Fred M.: Outline of Historical Method; Lincoln (Neb.), 1899.

Fling, Fred M.: Writing of History; New Haven, 1920.

Freeman, Edward A.: The Methods of Historical Study; London, 1886.

Johnson, Allen: The Historian and Historical Evidence, New York, 1926.

Langlois, Ch. V., and Seignobos, Ch.: Introduction to the Study of History; London, 1925.

Salmon, L. M.: Historical Material; New York, 1933.

Vincent, John M.: Historical Research; New York, 1911.

II THE VALIDITY OF HISTORICAL KNOWLEDGE

1. *Croce, Dilthey, and Mannheim*

Croce, Benedetto: Aesthetic as Science of Expression and General Linguistic (trans. Ainslie); London, 1922. (2. ed.)

Croce, Benedetto: Breviary of Aesthetic; Rice Institute (Book of the Opening of,), v. II, #4.

Croce, Benedetto: Historical Materialism and the Economics of Karl Marx (trans. Meredith); London, (no date).

Croce, Benedetto: History, Its Theory and Practice (trans. Ainslie); New York, 1923.

Croce, Benedetto: Logic as the Science of the Pure Concept (trans. Ainslie); London, 1917.

Croce, Benedetto: Philosophy of the Practical (trans. Ainslie); London, 1913.

Croce, Benedetto: Primi Saggi, v. I, pp. vii-72; Bari, 1919. (The main body of this is also to be found in the Atti della Accademia Pontaniana, 1893, 1894.)

Croce, Benedetto: Problemi di Estetica; Bari, 1910. (pp. 1-30 consist of "the Heidelberg Lecture"; also cf. pp. 467-504.)

Croce, Benedetto: Task of Logic (in Encyclopaedia of the Philosophical Sciences, Editor, A. Ruge, trans. B. E. Meyer); London, 1913.

Croce, Benedetto: Von der Geschichte der Geschichte (a review of Fueter: Geschichte der neueren Historiographie); Internationale Monatschrift für Wissenschaft, Kunst u. Technik, v. VII, pp. 835-856.

Croce, Benedetto: Ueber die sogenannten Werturteile; Logos, v. I, pp. 71ff.

Croce, Benedetto: What Is Living and What Is Dead in the Philosophy of Hegel (trans. Ainslie); London, 1915.

(also: Croce, Benedetto: scattered articles in the journal La Critica. Attention may be called particularly to the following: v. III, pp. 250ff.; v. V, pp. 248ff.; v. VII, pp. 301ff.; v. X, pp. 237ff., and 239; v. XVII, pp. 125ff.; v. XXVIII, pp. 396ff., 401ff.; v. XXXI, pp. 153ff.; v. XXXII, pp. 397f., 472f.)

Dilthey, Wilhelm: Gesammelte Schriften, v. I-IX, XI, XII; Leipzig/Berlin, 1923—.

(also: Dilthey, Wilhelm: Von Deutscher Dichtung und Musik; Leipzig/Berlin, 1933.

(also: Dilthey, Wilhelm: Briefwechsel zwischen W. Dilthey und dem Grafen Paul Yorck v. Wartemburg; Halle, 1923.)

Mannheim, Karl: Der Historismus; Archiv für Sozialwissenschaft u. Sozialpolitik, v. 52, pp. 1ff.

Mannheim, Karl: Ideologie und Utopie; Bonn, 1930.

Mannheim, Karl: Ideologische und Soziologische Interpretation der Geistigen Gebilde; Jahrbuch für Soziologie (hrsg. G. Salomon), v. II; Karlsruhe, 1926.

Mannheim, Karl: Ideology and Utopia (trans. L. Wirth and E. Shils); New York, 1936.
(This work brings together in translation Mannheim's Ideologie und Utopie, and his article on Wissenssoziologie, both cited here. It also includes a new introductory chapter.)

Mannheim, Karl: Das Problem einer Soziologie des Wissens; Archiv für Sozialwissenschaft u. Sozialpolitik, v. 53, pp. 577ff.

Mannheim, Karl: Wissenssoziologie (in Handwörterbuch der Soziologie, hrsg. A. Vierkandt); Stuttgart, 1931.

2. Simmel, Rickert, Scheler, and Troeltsch

Rickert, Heinrich: Der Gegenstand der Erkenntnis; Tuebingen, 1928.

Rickert, Heinrich: Geschichtsphilosophie (in Die Philosophie im Beginn des 20. Jahrhunderts, hrsg. W. Windelband); Heidelberg, 1907.

Rickert, Heinrich: Die Grenzen der Naturwissenschaftliche Begriffsbildung; Tuebingen, 1929. (5. Aufl.)

Rickert, Heinrich: Kulturwissenschaft und Naturwissenschaft; Tuebingen, 1921.

Rickert, Heinrich: Die Probleme der Geschichtsphilosophie; Heidelberg, 1924.

Rickert, Heinrich: Psychologie der Weltanschauungen; Logos, v. IX, pp. 1 ff.

Rickert, Heinrich: Les quatres modes de l'universel en historie, (Revue de synthèse historique, 1901.)

Rickert, Heinrich: System der Philosophie, v. I; Tuebingen, 1921.

Rickert, Heinrich: Vom System der Werte; Logos, v. IV, pp. 295ff.

Scheler, Max Ferdinand: Der Formalismus in der Ethik und die Materiale Wertethik; Halle, 1927. (3. Aufl.)

Scheler, Max Ferdinand: Erkenntnis und Arbeit (included in M. F. Scheler: Die Wissensformen und die Gesellschaft; Leipzig, 1926.)

Scheler, Max Ferdinand: Probleme einer Soziologie des Wissens (included in M. F. Scheler: Die Wissensformen und die Gesellschaft; Leipzig, 1926; also included in Versuche zu einer Soziologie des Wissens, hrsg. M. F. Scheler; Muenchen, 1924. Page references are given with respect to the work as it appears in the former place.)

Simmel, Georg: Die Historische Formung; Logos, v. VII, pp. 113ff.

Simmel, Georg: Die Probleme der Geschichtsphilosophie; Leipzig, 1923. (5. Aufl.)

Simmel, Georg: Vom Wesen des Historischen Verstehens; Berlin, 1918.

Troeltsch, Ernst: Der Historismus and seine Probleme (Gesammelte Werke, v. 3); Tuebingen, 1922.

Troeltsch, Ernst: Der Historismus und seine Ueberwindung, (Fünf Vorträge); Berlin, 1924.

Troeltsch, Ernst: Historiography (in Hastings: Encyclopaedia of Religion and Ethics, 1914).

Troeltsch, Ernst: Die Revolution in der Wissenschaft; Schmollers Jahrbuch, v. 45, pp. 1001ff.

3. *Other works concerned with the validity of historical knowledge*

Barth, Paul: Die Philosophie der Geschichte als Soziologie; Leipzig, 1915.

Beard, Charles A.: That Noble Dream; American Historical Review, v. 41, pp. 74ff.

Beard, Charles A.: Written History as an Act of Faith; American Historical Review, v. 39, pp. 219ff.

Beard, Charles A. and Vagts, Alfred: Currents in Historiography; American Historical Review, v. 42, pp. 460ff.

Becker, Carl L.: Everyman His Own Historian; New York, 1935.

Berr, Henri: La synthèse en histoire; Paris, 1911.

Bradley, F. H.: Presuppositions of a Critical History (in Collected Essays, v. I); Oxford, 1935.

Cornforth, K.: Explanation in History; Aristotelian Society, Supplementary Volume #14.

Ginsburg, M.: Explanation in History; Aristotelian Society, Supplementary Volume #14.

Grotenfelt, Arvid: Die Wertschätzung in der Geschichte; Leipzig, 1903.

Haldane, R. B.: Meaning of Truth in History; London, 1914.

Harnack, Adolph v.: Die Sicherheit und die Grenzen Geschichtlicher Erkenntnis; (Deutsches Museum, Vorträge und Berichte, #17), Muenchen, 1917.

Hashagen, Justus: Ausserwissenschaftliche Einflüsse auf die Geschichtswissenschaft (in Versuche zu einer Soziologie des Wissens, hrsg. M. F. Scheler); Muenchen, 1924.

Hessen, Sergius: Individuelle Kausalität; Berlin, 1909.

Heussi, Karl: Die Krisis des Historismus; Tuebingen, 1932.

Kaufmann, Fritz: Geschichtsphilosophie der Gegenwart; Berlin, 1931.

Klibansky, R. and Paton, H. J. (editors): Philosophy and History, Essays presented to Ernst Cassirer; Oxford, 1936.

Kuhn, Helmut: Das Problem des Standpunkts und die Geschichtliche Erkenntnis; Kant-Studien, v. XXXV, pp. 496ff.

Lessing, Theodor: Geschichte als Sinngebung des Sinnlosen; Leipzig, 1927.

Maier, Heinrich: Das Historische Erkennen; Göttingen, 1914.

Meyer, Eduard: Zur Theorie und Methodik der Geschichte (in Kleine Schriften, v. I); Halle, 1924.

Milanov, Kajic: Die Gesetzesbildung, das Verstehen, und die Anschauliche Abstraktion im Geschichtlichen Erkennen; Berlin (doctoral diss.), 1933.

Oakeley, H. D.: Explanation in History; Aristotelian Society, Supplementary Volume #14.

Parker, Dewitt H.: Metaphysics of Historical Knowledge; University of California Publications in Philosophy, v. II, #5.

Parsons, Talcott: The Structure of Social Action; New York and London, 1937.

Riezler, Kurt: Idee und Interesse in der Politischen Geschichte; Die Dioskuren, Jahrbuch für Geisteswissenschaften, v. 3 (1924), pp. 1ff.

Rothacker, Erich: Logik und Systematik der Geisteswissenschaften (in Handbuch der Philosophie, v. II): 1927.

Schelting, Alexander v.: Max Webers Wissenschaftslehre; Tuebingen, 1934.

Schmeidler, B.: Ueber Begriffsbildung und Werturteile in der Geschichte; Annalen der Naturphilosophie, v. III, pp. 24ff.

Scott, Ernest: History and Historical Problems; Oxford, 1925.

Simkhovitch, V. G.: Approaches to History; Political Science Quarterly, v. 44, pp. 481ff.; v. 45, pp. 481ff.; v. 47, pp. 410ff.; v. 48, pp. 23ff.; v. 49, pp. 44ff.; v. 51, pp. 117ff.

Smith, T. C.: The Writing of American History, 1884-1934; American Historical Review, v. 40, pp. 439ff.

Spranger, Eduard: Die Grundlagen der Geschichtswissenschaft; Berlin (doctoral diss.), 1905.

Spranger, Eduard: Der Sinn der Vorraussetzungslosigkeit in den Geisteswissenschaften; Sitzungsberichte der Berliner Akademie, Phil.-Hist. Kl., 1929, pp. 2ff.

Teggart, F. J.: Processes of History; New Haven, 1918.

Teggart, F. J.: Prologomena to History; Berkeley, 1916.

Teggart, F. J.: Theory of History; New Haven, 1925.

Weber, Max: Gesammelte Aufsätze zur Wissenschaftslehre; Tuebingen, 1922.

Xénopol, A. D.: La théorie de l'histoire (being the second edition of Les principes fondamentaux de l'histoire); Paris, 1908.

III   OTHER MATERIALS CITED

Alexander, Samuel: Space, Time, and Deity; London, 1927.

Aron, Raymond: La sociologie allemande contemporaine; Paris, 1935.

Below, Georg v.: Ueber historische Periodisierung; Berlin, 1925.

Bergson, Henri: La Pensée et le Mouvant; Paris, 1934.

Bradley, F. H.: Essays on Truth and Reality; Oxford, 1914.

Broad, C. D.: Examination of McTaggart's Philosophy, v. I; Cambridge, 1933.

Broad, C. D.: Scientific Thought; New York, 1923.

Bury, J. B.: The Idea of Progress; London, 1924.

Butterfield, H.: The Whig Interpretation of History; London, 1931.

Carritt, E. F.: The Theory of Beauty; London, [1931].

Cohen, Morris R.: Reason and Nature; New York, 1931.

Collingwood, R. G.: Speculum Mentis; Oxford, 1924.

Comte, Auguste: Positive Philosophy (trans. H. Martineau); London, 1896.

Ducasse, Curt J.: Causation and the Types of Necessity; University of Washington, Publ. in Social Sciences, v. I, n. 2; Seattle, 1924.

Eaton, Ralph M.: General Logic; New York, 1931.

Eddington, Arthur S.: Nature of the Physical World; Cambridge, 1929.

Ewing, A. C.: Idealism, A Critical Survey; London, 1934.

Frank, Philipp: Das Kausalgesetz und seine Grenzen; Wien, 1932.

Frischeisen-Köhler, Max: Wirklichkeit und Wissenschaft; Leipzig/Berlin, 1912.

Hartmann, Nicolai: Das Problem des geistigen Seins; Berlin/Leipzig, 1933.

Heim, Gustav: Ursache und Bedingung; Leipzig, 1913.

Hegel, G. W. F.: Grundlinien der Philosophie des Rechts (in Die Philosophischen Bibliothek, # 124a); Leipzig, 1930.

Hegel, G. W. F.: Philosophy of History (Sibree trans.; in "World's Greatest Literature Series"); New York/London, 1900.

Husserl, Edmund: Logische Untersuchungen; Halle a. S., 1900-1901.

Jaspers, Karl: Philosophie; Berlin, 1932.

Johnson, W. E.: Logic; Cambridge, 1921-1924.

Joseph, H. W. B.: An Introduction to Logic; Oxford, 1916.

McTaggart, J. McT. E.: The Nature of Existence; Cambridge, 1921-1927.

McTaggart, J. McT. E.: Philosophical Studies; London, 1934.

Quigley, H. and Clark, R. T.: Republican Germany; New York, 1928.

Russell, Bertrand: On the Notion of Cause; Proceedings of the Aristotelian Society, N. S., v. XIII, pp. 1ff.

Saw, R. L.: An Aspect of Causal Connexion; Proceedings of the Aristotelian Society, N. S., v. XXXV, pp. 95ff.

Schneider, Wilhelm: Wesen und Formen der Epoche; Muenchen (doctoral diss.), 1926.

Stebbing, L. M.: A Modern Introduction to Logic; New York, 1930.

Stern, William: Person und Sache, v. III (Wertphilosophie); Leipzig, 1924.

Sybel, H. v.: Kleine Historische Schriften, v. I: Muenchen, 1869.

Windelband, Wilhelm: Geschichte und Naturwissenschaft; Strassburg, 1904. (Also in W. Windelband: Präludien, Tuebingen, 1907.)

INDEX